The Inland Northwest

A Modern History of a Dynamic Region

Spokane and Inland Washington • Coeur d'Alene and the Idaho Panhandle

By Kay F. Reinartz

Published by

Heritage Media Corp.

Heritage Building

1954 Kellogg Avenue, Carlsbad, California 92008

www.heritagemedia.com

ISBN: 1-886483-75-2

Library of Congress Control Number: 2002116342

Kay F. Reinartz *Author*

Charles E. Parks *CEO/Publisher*

Lori M. Parks *Editorial Director*

Stephen Hung *Executive Vice President*

Randall Peterson *CFO*

Administration	**Editorial**
Kelly Corcoran *Human Resources Manager*	Betsy Baxter Blondin *Editor-in-Chief*
Lisa Barone	Betsy Lelja *Softcover Managing Editor*
Melissa Coffey	Mary Campbell
Juan Diaz	John Woodward
Cyndie Miller	**Staff Writers:**
Stephanie Stogiera	Julie Gengo
Vicki Verne	Gregory Lucas
	Victor Menaldo

Design	
Gina Mancini *Art Director*	**Production**
Robert Galmarini	Deborah Sherwood *IT/Production Manager*
Chris Hamilton	Dave Hermstad
Marianne Mackey	Arturo Ramirez
Charles Silvia	

Profile Writers

Mitchell R. Compton Jr.

Jay Davis

Addy Hatch

Linda Hagen Miller

Anne M. Tucker

Printed in cooperation with the

Northwest Museum of Arts & Culture

www.northwestmuseum.org

Printed by Heritage Media Corp. in the United States of America

First Edition

Dedication

"To my husband Richard for sharing a life"

Contents

Preface

When thinking of the Pacific Northwest, most people focus on the Puget Sound and coastal areas and overlook the fact that a significant portion of the Pacific Northwest lies inland. Historians have also tended to overlook the history of the inland region in favor of the coast. This might have been valid in the 19th and early 20th centuries. However, from World War II on, the inland and coastal Pacific Northwest have been increasingly intertwined with the inland region providing significant support to the coast, ranging from hydroelectric power, aluminum production for the airplane industry, and food to feed the ever-expanding population. In addition, the Inland Northwest could be said to have far exceeded its destiny, as determined by its geography and arid climate, in the second half of the 20th century.

While there are many excellent books dealing with specific inland areas, e.g. the Palouse and Spokane, and there are numerous community history books, there have been few works dealing with the inland area as a distinct region. This book, the first history dealing with the second half of the 20th century, is a modest attempt to describe and interpret the main historical themes of that dynamic period. From the time of the construction of Grand Coulee Dam to the end of the century, Inland Washington evolved from a "quiet hinterland" to a dynamic region with an increasingly diversified economy. At the beginning of the 21st century, the region continues to be in transition with many issues yet to be resolved, the greatest of which is the dependence of the new economy on water — water for irrigation farming, for hydroelectric power (for industry), for the burgeoning recreation/tourism industry, for cheap commercial transportation and for the traditional salmon runs.

This history book has evolved from research undertaken for the major exhibit, "Hometowns: Heart of the Inland Northwest," developed for the grand opening of the newly enlarged Northwest Museum of Arts & Culture (MAC) formerly known as the Cheney Cowles Museum. The historical themes and selected details presented in this history book follow the story of the Inland Northwest told in the MAC exhibit.

While this history is the story of the key factors and influences that shaped the region's recent history, it is first and foremost the history of people who lived through the period. A major goal of both the exhibit and this history book has been to bring forth the "voice of the people." It is impossible to include here all of the subtle influences and factors that shaped specific districts within the great inland region. Many of those selected for inclusion in this history have been chosen based on how they affected human lives.

The "Hometowns: Heart of the Inland Northwest" exhibit and this book were created through the effort of hundreds of people who make their homes in the Inland Northwest. The contributors range from business and municipal leaders to county historical society members, museum directors (paid and volunteer), newspaper editors, government agency staff, loggers, farm laborers and factory workers, irrigation and dry land farmers, homemakers, ministers, teachers and community volunteers.

A key factor in the success of the Hometowns Project has been "the Partners." The Partners are about 45 people, mostly affiliated with local historical societies and museums across the Inland Northwest, who met at the old Cheney Cowles Museum between the winter of 1998 and the spring of 2000 to hammer out the themes included in the exhibit and this history book. The MAC staff, Marsha Rooney, Larry Schoonover and Karen DeSeve, and Alice Parman and Craig Kerger from Formations, the company selected to design and construct the exhibit, and the historian met repeatedly with the Partners and listened carefully to what they had to say about the things that had shaped their region over the past half century. The themes found in the exhibit and this book are the result of those intense, but most enjoyable, discussion sessions. The work phase followed and the Partners helped with each step — writing and collecting stories themselves, and referring the historian to others for interviews and oral histories. They also helped Marsha Rooney, MAC Curator of History, gather exhibit artifacts and photographs. With renewed energy and commitment some of the Partners tackled the laborious task of reading drafts of book chapters correcting names and historical details.

The Partners' creativity in responding to the vision of the "hometowns" theme made a major impact on the exhibit and book alike. The unflagging interest and active support of this dedicated group of people energized the museum staff and the historian through the intense months of putting together the final works. Sticklers for accuracy, many searched out obscure facts to assure historical accuracy. Undoubtedly, there are still historical errors in the history book and an apology is extended to those affected by these errors.

This book is the first history of the period 1950 to 2000. In addition to extensive interviews and oral histories, historical information was drawn from government reports, newspapers, journal articles and unpublished works. The section on "The Legacy of Harnessed Rivers" draws on a number of recently published books as well as newspaper articles and interviews.

To acknowledge and thank all of those who contributed to the book would fill several pages, thus the following list is restricted to those Partners who participated in the work sessions at the museum, contributed to the research and, most importantly, dedicated many hours to carefully reading the book manuscript for errors or missing information. These "lovers of history" include Lorinda Travis, Loon Lake; Joseph Barrecca, Kettle Falls; Madilane Perry, Republic; Florence E. Stout, Odessa; Evelyn Reed, Newport; Rowena McIntosh, Kettle Falls; Nancy Ellis, Davenport; Carol Kelly, Lind; Belva Fieder and Mary Lou Curran, Pomeroy; and Garfield County Museum members who reviewed the manuscript: John and Betty Capwell, Jenny O'Dell, Quest Kaetts, Betty Waldher, Barbara McCellahan and Margaret Wolf; and John Amonson, Wallace, Idaho. Others who reviewed the manuscript for content and accuracy and provided corrections are Jim Pope, Wenatchee; Keith Williams, Wenatchee Valley Museum; Tracy Warner, Wentachee World; Jane Foreman, TRIDEC, Tri-Cities; Wayne Rimple, city of Moses Lake; Jim Kuntz, Port of Walla Walla; Dan Peterson, Seattle (grew up in Grand Coulee); and Elvin L. Kulp, Washington State University Cooperative Extension, Ephrata. From MAC, Marsha Rooney, Larry Schoonover, Karin DeSeve and Lynn Pankonin. Invaluable research and technical assistance were provided by Paula and Steve McCann, Rebecca Anderson, Jody Braun, Heather Gianni and Leah Pelto. Special thanks to my husband, Richard Frith, who provided support in innumerable ways ranging from making dinner to reading numerous drafts, critical editing, and providing energy and enthusiasm throughout the project.

Kay F. Reinartz

Introduction

By Kay F. Reinartz

Part I.
A Region in Transition

Across the United States the 20th century was a time of great change. The second half of the 20th century brought such profound changes to the Inland Northwest that by the 1960s parts of the region would be unrecognizable to someone who last visited before 1935. From the 19th well into the 20th century the Inland Northwest was generally viewed as the hinterland — remote and populated with rugged miners, loggers, and tough, determined dry land farm families. The only significant city was Spokane, the historic capital of the Inland Empire of mining, railroad and lumber barons. Today's inland region is no longer the empire of that early era and is now known as the Inland Northwest.

At the time of writing this brief history, the geographic area that comprised the Inland Northwest was the subject of considerable debate. In its broadest definition the region includes central and eastern Washington, northern Idaho, south central British Columbia and northeastern Oregon. Generally, it is recognized as a region bound by common economic and climatic factors. The unique climate is called "maritime-modified continental" because of the moderating influence inland of the Pacific Ocean. This history is limited to the Washington and northern Idaho portions of the Inland Northwest region.

The Inland Northwest, 1950-2000

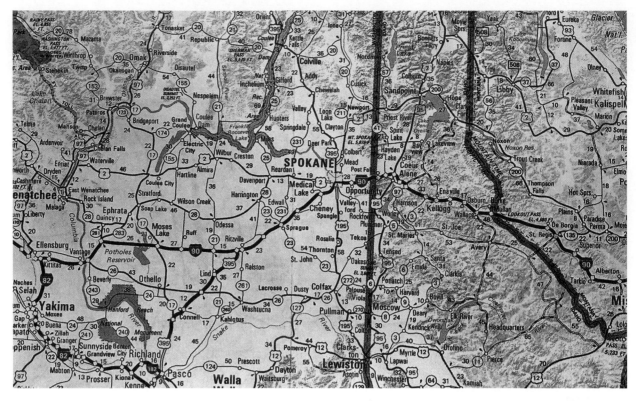

The transition from the old, basically 19th-century economy to the new economy built on water power, large-scale irrigation agriculture, large-acreage dry land farming, and growing industrialization has put the region under considerable strain. The new water-based economy was built on damming the region's many rivers, thereby controlling the water for human purposes. By the 1980s the collective effect of harnessing the rivers was apparent. On a regional level government agencies, farmers, hydroelectric interests, fishermen, Native Americans, the water transportation industry, and environmental concerns struggled to reconcile water needs. On a national level the water use issue placed the Inland Northwest in the center of the stage in a tense drama focused on an array of economic and environmental issues that would bring into sharp focus the purpose of the Endangered Species Act and Pacific salmon species.

The seeds of change, including the vision of large-scale irrigated agriculture, were present in the minds and dreams of inland residents in the early years of the 20th century. However, few envisioned the final scope or social and cultural upheaval that would accompany realization of this vision. By century's end the Inland Northwest was running on a substantially altered economic basis, which gave great prosperity to those lucky enough to have found a place in the new economy. Others, lacking the financial or personal resources to compete or living in the wrong place when the plans were executed, were left out. For some it has been a fast and exciting ride with rewards of prosperity and leisure time. For others it has been a melancholy time of loss — loss of a traditional way of life, loss of community, loss of a sense of place, commitment and, ultimately, belonging. This book focuses on how the regional historical themes and events affected the lives of those who lived through the era. Every effort made to have the people share their experiences in their own words.

In the early decades of the 20th century, 35 percent of Washingtonians lived in the inland region. After 1950 the proportion of the population living east of the Cascades gradually decreased as the population of the Puget Sound cities rapidly rose. By 1990 only 21 percent of the state's total population was living inland. While the inland area had a smaller proportion of the state's population, in real numbers the population steadily grew from 1942 forward.

Impacts of World War II

In retrospect it is clear that World War II served as a powerful catalyst in breaking down the region's isolation. Attracted by high-paying wartime jobs, the population of Washington State nearly doubled between 1940 and 1947. It ranked sixth in the nation for absolute population increase and fourth in percentage of increase during the war years. In the 1940s the inland population expanded by 37 percent. The wartime migrants to Washington were largely mobile younger people and after the war many stayed to make permanent homes in an area that was booming. While postwar pay rates declined, they still averaged three times higher than in 1939. Even with the increased cost of living of the late 1940s, the average person in Washington had 160 percent more real disposable income than before the war.

After the war ended, a series of massive federally funded public works projects in inland Washington contributed mightily to the transformation of the region. The Yakima Irrigation Project, begun in the 1910s with Bureau of Reclamation funding, and the Columbia Basin Irrigation Project, also a Bureau of Reclamation project, both came "on line" in the 1940s and 1950s, converting essentially desert land into lush farmland. A 30-year dam construction spree, principally by the Army Corps of Engineers, converted all the major rivers in the inland region from free-flowing natural waterways to "working rivers" with provision for commercial shipping. The postwar road-building boom reduced rural isolation and supported the centralization of goods and services in a handful of larger cities. The so-called modern way of life, with its plethora of electronic devices that came in the latter part of the 20th century — television, satellite dishes, computers and the internet —put the farmer on an equal footing with the urban dweller for the first time in history.

Hometown Changes

Traditionally, small rural towns populated the inland region. The dynamic economy of the irrigation projects spurred the growth of cities and suburban communities. Spokane continued to be the economic, business and cultural leader for the inland region, although other cities transformed into significant business and industrial centers in their own right, especially cities within the Columbia Basin and the Yakima irrigation projects. In 2000 three out of five people were living in one of the region's nine cities of over 15,000: Spokane, Pullman, Walla Walla, Yakima, Moses Lake, Wenatchee, Richland, Pasco and Kennewick. The rest of the population was scattered across the region on farms and in about 140 incorporated and unincorporated communities. More than half of them live in communities ranging from 30 to 1,000 people.

As the old economies disappeared, the towns they supported were hit hard. Towns in the traditional mining and lumbering districts were decimated with population losses of 50 to 80 percent commonplace. At least 15 towns have been destroyed and a dozen new towns established because of the hydroelectric and irrigation projects. However, small towns seem to have a staying power in the region, in many cases because, as this history shows, those who live there refuse to let their town die. The people are strong and determined to keep their special places. In many cases the communities have taken the initiative to launch a new economic base "to keep things going." The hearts of the people are in their hometowns and losing them would be an unwelcome experience.

The Cascade Curtain

Since the 19th century, many Washingtonians have been convinced that because of the dramatic geologic, climate and economic differences that distinguish the eastern and western parts of their state, two separate states should exist. Retired Secretary of State Ralph Munro once famously remarked that there are two Washingtons. "There is the Space Needle State, which includes everything visible from the observation deck of Seattle's landmark. Then there is the Goat Rock State, which includes everything else visible from the promontory near Mount Rainier. There are indeed two Washingtons: one urban and suburban, its economy based on technology, manufacturing and exports; and one rural, its economy based almost entirely on natural resources. The two Washingtons are separated by the Cascade Range, which functions as a Cascade Curtain."

As the 20th century wore on, the economic, political and cultural differences between the regions became increasingly apparent. Some would prefer to discard the idea as little more than Seattle's urban snobbery and the Inland's provincial paranoia. However, there is substantial evidence that the Cascade Curtain is a reality and it has had serious detrimental impacts on the Inland Northwest most evident in the realm of politics and state government.

For example, in 1995, Wenatchee's celebrated Republican legislative leader Dale Foreman announced his candidacy for governor of Washington State. "The Cascade Curtain is about to fall," he told a cheering hometown crowd. In the primary election Foreman carried nearly every county east of the Cascades but fell to Poulsbo's Ellen Craswell, who was not as well known or as well financed as Foreman, but received more than half her votes from four populous Puget Sound counties. The Cascade Curtain did not fall. The curtain, the not-so-mythical cultural, economic and political divide between east and west, was as high or higher than it was eight years earlier. In 1987 Sid Morrison, moderate Republican State Representative from the Yakima Valley, was considering running for the U.S. Senate. As a preliminary move, Morrison commissioned a voter attitude poll, which concluded that 44 percent of the state's population would not vote for a candidate from Eastern Washington. Survey participants revealed that geographical prejudice dominated many people's political preferences ranking "where the candidate was from" above party affiliation and ideology, i.e. liberal, conservative or moderate. Morrison concluded he had no chance of winning.

It was not always like this. Politics once blurred the divide. Washington's Congressional Senators Magnuson and Jackson did not operate on the geographic-prejudice principle. They often championed Eastern Washington economic development and were the power behind numerous large and small instances of federal support for inland economic development. At the end of the 20th century, statewide candidates frequently campaigned on their ability to slow development and stifle new projects.

As Tracy Warner, editor for the *Wenatchee World*, observed in 2001, "Eastern Washington's beginnings are recent, a fact that still shapes its attitudes. Many still gauge success by human effort, to build something that spurs growth and sustains future generations — a dam, a farm, a factory, a mine. We are only a generation removed from the people who first turned the soil here. The people who poured the concrete for Grand Coulee Dam are still here to tell the tale, and we see the results of their effort all around us and are glad. Most of us do not think it is a bad thing."

To inland Washingtonians the vigorous attack on the aluminum industry in 2000 by western Washington powers carried great symbolism. The industry represented the effort to use the Inland Northwest's natural resources, hydroelectricity in this case, to create something where recently there was nothing. Nothing, at least, in terms of human enterprise and sustenance.

By the 1990s, highly charged conflicts arising from the great differences in eastern and western Washington interests, needs and attitudes were everywhere. In 2000 the Seattle City Council passed a resolution endorsing the breaching of four federal dams on the Snake River to save salmon. Council members were deluged with messages from the outraged eastern parts of the state, and they were condemned openly by city councils from Wenatchee to Clarkston. The Seattlites seemed genuinely stunned by the reaction and sent out numerous conciliatory messages and letters to newspapers. What the Seattle City Council did not understand is that they had resolved to undo more that just a few remote power stations for an environmental cause. In the eyes of the inland residents, they wished to tear down the work of a generation that had built a new world through hydroelectric power, commerce, irrigation and river transportation. In the words of Tracy Warner, "Seattle had looked east and said: You are a mistake."

Heritage Media Collection

There is more to the curtain than economics, but economics makes it strong and higher. The Corporation for Enterprise Development, a nonprofit consultant group, recently ranked states by the disparity between their urban and rural economies. Washington finished fourth. Only California, Georgia and Texas had greater gaps between urban and rural prosperity. And the gap is growing. In the 1970s the annual personal incomes of Eastern Washington counties were 24 percent of the state's total. In 1998 they were 17 percent.

Inland State Sen. Bob Morton, (R-Orient), drew attention when he introduced a resolution to the State Legislature in 2001 calling for a study contrasting the "lifestyles, cultures and economies" of western and eastern Washington, with the eventual goal being a division into two states. That's a pipe dream, but the frustration that creates it is real. When the Olympian asked Morton if the Cascade Curtain is still rising, he replied, "Absolutely. My patience has worn out. We've tried working together. I came here to do that. I've tried and tried. And it keeps getting worse and worse."

Part II:
A Land Formed by Fire and Water

The Inland Northwest is a region unique in North America, indeed the world, for its geologic formation. Unraveling the mystery of these geologic forces is a fascinating aspect of the Inland Northwest 20th century story. A quick review of those forces also provides insight into how the contemporary inland economy is a direct result of powerful geologic forces that took place millions of years earlier.

On a journey inland through the Cascade Mountain passes, one literally travels from one Pacific island to another. Approximately one million years ago a large "island," the Okanogan micro-continent, floated in from the Pacific and docked onto the western coast of the North American continent, located where Spokane is today. The highlands of northeastern Washington and western Idaho were created by folded sedimentary rocks and a chain of volcanoes that formed along the crest of the newly attached Okanogan micro-continent. The north central section

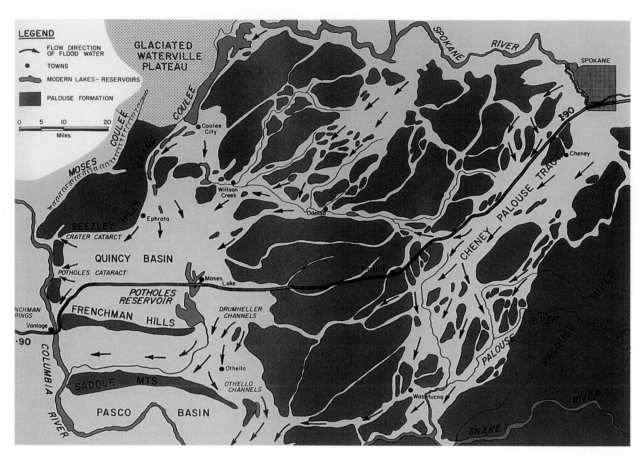

of the region consists of granite domes, Kettle Dome and Okanogan Dome, built by magma from these volcanoes. About 50 million years after the Okanogan, another micro-continent floated in from the Pacific and docked onto the first. The numerous active volcanoes on this micro-continent continued erupting after docking and formed the Cascade Mountain Range.

About 10 to 15 million years ago, volcanic activity shifted to central and southeastern Washington. A gigantic volcano, called the Grande Ronde by geologists, formed the Columbia Plateau when it repeatedly flooded the region with enormous lava flows that formed great pools of molten basalt often more than 100 feet thick and covering thousands of square miles. The flows buckled steeply into large folds along its western edge. These ridges are now known as the Frenchman Hills, Saddle Mountains, Yakima Ridge and the Rattlesnake Hills. When these eruptions ceased, volcanic activity shifted back to the Snake River plain of Idaho and the Cascade Range region where very large volcanoes formed what geologists now call the high Cascades.

The Ice Age Floods

The second major factor shaping the topography of the region was a series of catastrophic floods resulting from the waters of Glacial Lake Missoula pouring into Washington about 12,000 years ago. The glacial lake, up to 2,000 feet deep, repeatedly filled and drained when its waters broke through a natural ice dam, and it shook the earth for hundreds of miles around as it poured across the Idaho Panhandle and into Washington. Imagine a 2,000-foot high wall of ice water with 500 cubic miles of water behind it heading with a thundering roar, with velocities reaching 45 mph, for Spokane and points southwest.

Called the Spokane Flood, the racing floodwaters created the spectacular features of the region including the Columbia River Gorge, the Channeled Scablands, the Palouse hills (dunes) and the region's dramatic coulees. It is estimated that it took about 40 to 80 years for Lake Missoula to refill to flooding point. Geologists have concluded there were between 10 to 40 Spokane Floods. Each flood lasted about two weeks during which time the entire contents of Glacial Lake

Missoula, estimated at 10 times the combined flow of all of the world's rivers, scoured the Columbia Plateau. The Spokane Floods hold the geologic record as the most catastrophic floods known to have occurred anywhere on the planet.

The name "coulee" came from the French explorers who erroneously interpreted the channels as dry canyons cut by ancient rivers. One of the most ancient coulees in Washington is Moses Coulee in north central Washington. This coulee contains sets of giant current ripples 30 feet high that measure hundreds of feet from crest to crest. Giant gravel bars rise over 300 feet above the floor of the coulee. Grand Coulee, younger than Moses Coulee, was formed during the last ice age. Lower Grand Coulee is, in fact, the deep gorge left by Dry Falls as the spectacular 400-foot-high, three-mile-wide waterfall retreated upstream. Frenchman Coulee formed as water drained from Grand Coulee and the Quincy Basin toward the Columbia River during repeated floods. Roads running through the coulees and the Scablands offer hunting and fishing, but not many people actually live there. Farmers use the Scablands mainly for rangeland and grow wheat where there is enough soil.

Dry Falls is a dramtic remnant of the Spokane Floods, which scoured the Columbia Plateau almost 12,000 years ago. *Spokesman Review Photo Archives*

A souvenir pennant from Dry Falls State Park. *Northwest Museum of Arts & Culture*

Formed by Fire in 1980: Mount St. Helens Eruption

The fire, lava and ash of volcanoes have been major factors in forming the Inland Northwest from the dawn of its history. Once again the region was subject to cataclysmic volcanic forces when Mount St. Helens erupted at 8:32 a.m. Sunday morning, May 18, 1980. The first event was an earthquake of 4.9 Richter magnitude, which set off a large landslide on the north side of the mountain. A cloud of dark ash rose from the north flank and quickly spread laterally to the north. A few minutes later there was an explosive lateral blast directed northward through the slide block that blew out the side of the volcano, and this was followed by a summit eruption of ash and steam. The summit plume rose to approximately 50,000 feet in altitude and began drifting eastward across the Cascades inland. Throughout the day the volcano spewed ash and steamed. Around 4:30 p.m. intensified activity pushed the ash column to approximately 63,000 feet in altitude.

The first cloud of volcanic fallout reached the Yakima Valley around 10 a.m. on the 18th. The bright sunlight sky darkened to twilight, intense bolts of lightning sliced the sky while the earth shook from continuous rolling thunder. Everywhere there was the acrid smell of sulphur. In a short time the lightening and thunder subsided and it became pitch black and totally silent except for the sound of the steady raining of gray volcanic ash.

Carol Kelly shares her memories of what happened in her hometown of Lind, Adams County, the day the mountain blew.

"Through a freak accident of geography, Lind received one of the heaviest loads of volcanic ash in the

state. It was noon, May 18, 1980. I will never forget that day or the many days and weeks that followed. It was unbelievably still and quiet at noon, and in talking to a neighbor, we both commented on the stillness. It was bright and sunny, but there was not a whisper of a breeze or sounds except for the hum of a lawn mower in a nearby yard. All at once, we noticed that the sky was beginning to fill with gray, billowing clouds. They were floating in, almost as if in slow motion, from the west. In the next hour the town was slowly covered with an unfamiliar and strange matter... remotely resembling flakes of snow. In what seemed like a very short period of time, the entire town was enclosed in darkness. The skies were turning an eerie black and it did not pass for the next 16 hours. The feelings of disbelief and apprehension that spread throughout the community and the eerie, frightening feeling of being smothered in the blackness was beyond what any of us could have ever imagined. Going to bed that night was difficult for everyone. We all secretly prayed that in the morning we would be able to see the familiar daylight. Upon awakening we were shocked to see that the entire town was totally covered in 4-6 inches of gray ash — and still no hint

of blue sky. It reminded me of what I had imagined the earth would resemble after an atomic blast."

An estimated 200,000,000 cubic yards of volcanic ash rained down on the countryside, towns and cities alike. Forty-nine percent of Washington State was affected, chiefly counties in central and eastern Washington. Among the hardest hit counties were Yakima, Grant, Franklin, Benton, Adams and Spokane. The ash fallout varied in the region with Yakima receiving one to two inches. Moses Lake, Ritzville and other central Washington towns received up to four inches. Spokane, 255 miles away from Mount St. Helens, was covered with from one-half to one inch of light ash.

The Inland Northwest the week after the volcano erupted was the scene of the greatest clean-up effort ever undertaken in the Pacific Northwest. Across the region, in towns and cities alike, people responded to the ash fall as Florence Stout describes her hometown of Odessa. "After the ash stopped falling, the townspeople did not stand around wringing their hands, but every able bodied person was busy cleaning up the ash fallout, while at the same time housing and feeding stranded travelers."

Large cities were not outdone by the small towns in rallying to the cause. In Yakima a committee of three was formed, the mayor, county executive and county sheriff, to plan and oversee the cleanup of the Yakima district. Yakima Mayor Betty Edmondson declared Ash Week and asked everyone to help with the Herculean task of cleaning up the city. The citizens turned out 100 percent. Everything closed — schools, businesses, and offices — equipment was found, and Yakima was cleaned roof by roof, street by street, all the way through town. A giant vacuum cleaner was procured for vacuuming the ash from the roofs of commercial buildings. While the depth of the ash was not great, cleaning it up was not easy since the ash was extremely dense and heavy. Dump truckloads of ash were hauled to dump sites, such as a gully on 40th Avenue that eventually filled and became Chesterly Park. There were at least 40 dump sites around the city and each of them had lines of pickup trucks, wheelbarrows, and even children's red Radio wagons waiting to dump ash. Experts estimated that Yakima received more than 600,000 tons of ash. Nearly 16,000 tons were cleared from the airport runways alone. The city was completely cleaned up in 10 days after which time people went back to "life as usual."

The aftermath of the eruption brought surprises and good fortunes as well as setbacks. Soil in many parts of the Inland Northwest is naturally rich and phenomenally productive when supplied with irrigation water. Geologists have attributed this to the volcanic origin of the soil, most famous of which is the yellow loess of the Palouse. Mount St. Helens ash covered the land and crops in some of the key agricultural areas in the region, Big Bend, the Yakima Valley, and the Columbia Basin Project. At the time of the eruption, soil experts and farmers were intensely apprehensive as to the effect of the ash on the crops. Almost everyone agreed that there would be damage, or worse, a total crop failure that season and perhaps for years to come. In fact, the ash had a very positive effect on plants. Ash-washed plants remained erect and healthy looking. In a few weeks it was obvious that flowers, vegetables and field crops were experiencing phenomenal growth. Farmers reported having a greater yield of high-quality vegetables than ever before.

In the dry land farming districts, the wheat crop was the biggest in many years. A few specific plants, most notably tomatoes in the Yakima Valley, suffered damage and were below normal in their yield. Other crops sustained external damage from the ash that interfered with the harvest or made them unfit for market. Among the most important of these problems was the coating of ash that defied removal from fuzzy-skinned fruits, such as peaches and apricots. Alfalfa and other hay crops ready for harvest were knocked down flat and became a total loss.

All across central and eastern Washington, the Mount St. Helens eruption and ash-fall cleanup is remembered with great pride because people instantly, without question or hesitation, closed ranks to stand together and help one another and their community until everything was done. Through the disaster they learned they were still cohesive communities that care — and can work well together.

Heritage Media Collection

Among the greatest 19th-century

mining bonanzas in the American West was the discovery of silver in the Wallace-Kellogg district in the Idaho Panhandle, which proved to be one of the richest-known deposits in the world. While mineral wealth on the scale of Idaho's Silver Valley was never found in inland Washington, mining was also the first great pull of population into the region. Logging grew in importance at the turn of the 20th century. By mid-century, mining and lumbering were still major factors in the inland region; however, by the 1970s the economic significance of these industries was greatly diminished. The demise of mining and lumbering brought great hardship for workers, families and communities in the mining and lumbering districts. At the end of the 20th century some of the communities were well on the way to disappearing while others were making progress in forging a new economic base.

In the 1960s agriculture rapidly moved into the No. 1 place in the inland regional economy. Dry-land farming, the traditional farming method of the arid inland region, continued to be practiced in the great wheat-growing districts. However, improved farming methods and crop varieties greatly increased yields and brought unprecedented prosperity. The new factor in the agricultural economic equation was the conversion of vast tracts of dry desert land into lush farm fields. Irrigation farming made possible by the harnessing of the region's great rivers in the Columbia Basin and Yakima projects soon had farmers regularly reporting record-breaking yields.

Chapter One

The Inland Cornucopia: Old and New Economies

Part I: Mining and Lumbering
The Idaho Panhandle: The Coeur d'Alene Mining District

"This area has mined a billion ounces of silver in less than 100 years — more than any other place in the world. Many geologists believe that there is still as much metal left in the ground as there has been mined."

John Amonson, Silver Valley miner 1964-1986

Over the past century the Idaho Panhandle mining district has been the No. 1 silver-producing district in the world with a total output of more than 192 million ounces of silver. The district has also produced 1.3 million tons of zinc and 3.5 million tons of lead, as well as other minerals. Northern Idaho's silver mines boomed into the 1970s. As late as 1981 Idaho was still producing 37 percent of the nation's silver.

A number of market and local factors that came together in the 1970s and 1980s contributed to the closing of the mines in northern Idaho. In the late 1970s Americans, frightened by a galloping inflation rate that reached 18 percent, bought gold and silver as a hedge against the eroding dollar. As the rate of inflation dropped, the price of silver also plummeted. Mining activity in northern Idaho temporarily dropped to a minimal level of activity with the shutdown of the Bunker Hill Mine & Smelter, Kellogg, in 1981. As Idaho's second-largest employer, the closure of Bunker Hill had substantial regional impact. The closure of the Lucky Friday and Sunshine mines in 1986 in reaction to depressed metals prices put another 700 miners out of work. Twenty thousand people, a quarter of whom worked directly in mining, had lived in the 50-mile-long Silver Valley. In four years there were only 400 working in mining and the bustling community of Kellogg lost almost half of its population. For the miners it was like the Great Depression of the 1930s.

In September 1988, after $9 million in refinancing, the Bunker Hill mine was reopened and once again producing. The long-range plans included reopening the Crescent silver mine and having a third mine up and running within five years. In 1995 mining activity in the Idaho Panhandle took off again when the Silver Valley Resources Corp. took over the Galena and Coeur mines. With 200 miners at work, the operation produced

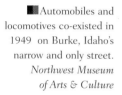 Automobiles and locomotives co-existed in 1949 on Burke, Idaho's narrow and only street. *Northwest Museum of Arts & Culture*

3.5 million of ounces silver a year. The new mining operations are environmentally sensitive and innovated new methods to protect the environment. The technological changes in mining that came in the final decades of the 20th century, like those in the lumber industry, permanently eliminated hundreds of jobs, and mining as a solid economic base for the region disappeared.

While the loss of the silver mining industry hurt the companies and workers, it was a boon for the environment and human health. For decades, smelter-polluted air hung above Silver Valley, which resulted in the highest levels of sulfur dioxide gas ever recorded in the United States. Falling as acid rain, the smelter effluents denuded the surrounding hillsides of vegetation. Kellogg school children were found to have abnormally high levels of lead in their blood. In the mid-1980s an Environmental Protection Agency (EPA) investigation found that the entire valley was highly contaminated, and it was listed as a hazardous waste site to be cleaned up by a federal program.

Tourism Comes to the Silver Valley

"When the Bunker Hill Mine went down in '81 the Silver Valley went from mining to a tourist-based economy. We had no choice."
Diane Van Broeke, Wallace, Idaho 1999

While tourism is a far cry from hard rock mining, the people of Kellogg found common ground for the new venture in the story of their founding. It seems that Noah Kellogg was gold prospecting in the valley when his newly acquired donkey ran off. Kellogg found his runaway on the mountainside next to a large outcropping of lead ore. Kellogg's motto has always been: "The town said to have been discovered by a jackass and inhabited by its descendants." Those who remained after the mine closings pride themselves on being strong and stubborn. Since the 1980s they have proven their resilience through their hard work to transform their hometown from a mining community into an attractive vacation destination with skiing being the winter draw and the mountain scenery and sunny warm weather providing summer enjoyment.

Public art is playing an important role in defining the new town. Visitors come to see the artwork of native artist David Dose. Constructed of "found materials," scrap metal and junk, the 11 sculptures take many forms including a dragon, elk and miners. A year-round schedule of festivals and activities attracts people.

One of the most unique activities offered in the Silver Valley is the Wallace Mine Tour, which allows tourists to experience the underground world of mining. In 1982 the idea of a mine tour was discussed as a way of attracting tourists. After considerable community debate and objections by some local mining companies, it was agreed to develop a mine tour at the Sierra Silver Mine. The community liked the idea. They worked as volunteers in developing the tour and are active as tour guides. Kellogg High School students volunteered to help in getting the tour up and running. The tour begins at the Wallace Mining Museum. Retired miners serve as guides and take the tourists on the trolley down into the working mine where mining techniques are explained, mining equipment is demonstrated and safety procedures are explained and demonstrated. Visitors see the techniques used to mine silver, lead and zinc. The tour has been very successful, with people coming to Wallace from across the nation to experience touring a deep shaft mine. The community is proud of its rich mining history, and the tour is the perfect way to share it with pride. The tour continues to be popular with local residents.

City leaders drew up a plan that included revamping the uptown shopping district into an Alpine Village, a la Leavenworth, Washington. A 16-foot-tall timber arch marks the entrance to the village, and storefronts are now decorated with timber and plaster and Bavarian-style murals. New streets and sidewalks were built. In 1996 the town added a free trolley service to take tourists from the gondola base to the shopping areas. The town centerpiece and big draw for many visitors is the Silver Mountain Gondola, the largest gondola system in the Western Hemisphere, which transports passengers 3.5 miles from the town center to the Silver Mountain ski area high on the nearby mountainside. Funding came from many sources, government and private, as the townspeople forged ahead with their "donkey determination" to accomplish their goals.

Mining in Inland Washington: The Republic Mining District

As 19th-century mining areas in inland Washington became depleted in the early decades of the 20th century, mining operations were launched in the Sanpoil and Metaline districts in Ferry and Pend Oreille counties. At mid-century, mining activities in Washington were the most vigorous in Ferry County, although mining continued on a reduced scale in the Metaline, Okanogan and Wenatchee areas. In addition

to gold and silver, mining included platinum, copper, lead, cobalt, iron, tungsten and molybdenum. By 1990 Republic was the only gold mining area in the entire inland region with a century of continuous operation. The main influences on mining activity in this period were the limited supply of quality ore; a fluctuating, but generally depressed metals market; the consolidation of the mines into the hands of large international corporations; and new environmental protection legislation, which focused attention on environmental damage issues. Mining did not come to an abrupt end but waxed and waned for decades.

After a major downturn in the 1960s, mining enjoyed a brief revival in the 1970s in response to strong market price and new extraction methods that made it possible to retrieve minerals from low content ore previously considered waste. Some mine operations began using cyanide leaching to separate the gold and silver from the ore because it was less expensive. The water and soil pollution that accompanied this process prompted environmental protectionists to challenge mining companies, such as Echo Bay when it proposed using open pit and cyanide wash methods in the early 1980s. The company responded by scrapping the leaching plan and building a large processing mill near Curlew using classic deep-shaft hard rock mining techniques.

After a brief jump in the gold and silver markets in the late 1970s, brought on by high inflation rates, the market became mediocre once again. The low market value, rising labor costs and labor unrest in the early 1980s prompted mining companies to close their mines rather than operate with a slim profit or at a loss. Local ownership ended as mines merged with out-of-state and international corporations or closed down altogether. Many people in the Republic mining district were depressed when local ownership of the Republic mines ended with the merging of the once powerful Day Mines with the Hecla Mining Company, a local company that had become international. Hecla paid $105 million for the Day mining stock. At the time of the merger Day, a local mining company, held over 92 properties in the Republic area, as well as the Hercules and Tamarack mines in Coeur d'Alene.

MINERS OUT ON STRIKE

In the spring of 1987 the Republic mining district was shaken by labor unrest. The miners contended that underground safety was being compromised to meet unrealistic new production quotas. The company told the miners that they were required to meet a 30-percent boost in tons of ore mined, which constituted an increase from the current 268 tons to 350 tons per day. Furthermore, seven-day workweeks became mandatory. The miners talked of going to the steelworkers union for help, but held back feeling that the steel union was too big to be interested in them. Finally there were safety issues. Loose rock and debris created in the mining process underground was not cleaned up regularly, as is considered necessary for safety. Daily, veteran contract miners were "tramping out," i.e. quitting. Spokane's *The Spokesman-Review* focused the public's attention on the miners' situation with a series of stories. Referring to the conditions in the Knob Hill mine, Dennis Hilderbrandt told a reporter, "this used to be the best little mine in the west. Now it's just a cesspool that keeps getting deeper." He tramped out after being told to dynamite a new round of ore from a tunnel that he believed needed to be cleared of loose and potentially dangerous overhead rock. Apparently the newspaper exposé helped the miners and the Knob Hill mine soon returned to a five-day production week and the mines were cleared of debris regularly.

These times were very difficult for the miners as mines operated sporadically. For example, the "old girl" of the Republic mines, Knob Hill, which employed from 100-150 men, closed three times before it was bought out by Hecla. Many of the miners were younger men with families who had come over to work the Republic mines from Kellogg and Wallace, Idaho, where they had mined lead and zinc until those mines closed. There was a short, intense period of exploration for new veins in the late 1980s. Republic Mayor Bert Chadick observed at the time, "there are an awful lot of geologists wandering around in the woods." The activity brought renewed hope for economically depressed Republic. However, the miners were insecure about the future and kept asking, "Can I buy a house? Will the ore last long enough to pay for it?" A few new veins were found, but they produced only for a short time.

Throughout the 1990s the revitalized mining region was wracked with conflicts between the mining companies and environmental protection groups. While some companies agreed to use environmentally safe mining methods, others were regularly dumping wastewater from the cyanide processing of ore. Tests revealed toxic levels of chemicals in streams and soil that were causing wholesale killing of fish, birds and other wildlife.

Finding New Livelihoods

Inland communities that grew up around mining were hard hit by the ending of the traditional economy. Some people moved on, but others, determined to keep their hometown alive, stayed and are struggling with the difficulties that accompany the transition to a new community economy.

Republic, population 954, saw its mining economy disintegrate in the 1970s and 1980s. When the Knob Hill Mine was about to close for the third time, the

■ Every detail of this 100-million-year-old fossil gingko leaf is visible in this fine specimen from the preserved sediments of an ancient lake bottom in the town of Republic. *Stonerose Interpretive Center*

community's leaders got together, determined to develop economic alternatives to mining. After much discussion it was agreed that they had wonderful scenery and a wide array of activities appealing to the outdoors person — hiking, camping, birding, fishing and hunting — and they should work on attracting tourists. They took their inspiration from Winthrop and Leavenworth, two north central Washington towns that gave their Main Street a radical face lift for the sake of entertaining visitors, and have enjoyed a goodly number of tourist dollars as a result.

In the 1980s Republic's Main Street was transformed to "rustic Victorian," as some of the locals call the new look. Madilane Perry describes Republic's facelift as "a take-off on Winthrop's take-off on Hollywood's impression of the Wild West." And many would agree with her. A few business owners have refused to participate in the facelift and have simply restored their vintage buildings to their original appearance. The community remains divided on the success of the facelift. Many believe the town should be restored to its authentic appearance. At the time of the revamping, Republic's Main Street was lined with the old storefronts from the era when the businesses served the needs of miners, farmers, loggers and their families.

Ironically, the Wild West veneer of Main Street has taken a back seat to the Stonerose Fossil Center in attracting visitors. Located on a hillside near Main Street in the center of Republic, the fossil beds, the site of an ancient lake bottom, consist of plant, fish and insect fossils. The Stonerose Fossil Center is named for a remarkable fossil of a rose discovered at the site. At this scientifically important site, from the time of its discovery, paleontologists from the Burke Museum in Seattle have been involved with the work. The Stonerose Fossil Center, a part of the Republic Historical Center, was established to both protect and preserve the site and oversee public participation in fossil bed digging. The center has a fossil exhibit and an instructional center. Everyone who wants to dig at the fossil site must register at the center, go through a training session and obtain a dig permit. In 1999 over 8,000 people visited the

Stonerose Center, many of whom came just to go through the training and then dig for fossils.

The Metaline Mining District

In the Metaline Mining District in the Pend Oreille Valley, mining operations dropped off sharply in the 1960s and 1970s. When "old girl" Pend Oreille Mine, which had produced iron, zinc and lead for nearly 80 years, closed in the early 1980s, the region was thrown into an economic depression.

The depression was intensified by the closing of the old Lehigh Cement Company, which had originally established Metaline Falls as a company town. Farge Inc., which had purchased Lehigh, closed the plant in the early 1990s. The final blow came when the last operating sawmill closed, thereby eliminating the last significant employer in the district. With little prospect of finding employment, many people packed up and left. Others, many of whom were descendants of the first miners, were determined to stay and find new livelihoods.

In the 1980s and 1990s several dynamic programs were launched through local initiatives, and they were showing positive results by 2000. In 1991 a group of people calling themselves the North County Theatre Group bought the 1912 Metaline School, which had been designed by the famous Spokane architect Kirtland Cutter, and renamed it The Cutter Theatre. Under the leadership of Eva Gayle Six, retired Selkirk High School English teacher, The Cutter Theatre was restored. Considering the heavy financial hardship the community had been suffering for many years, it was a bold and creative move. Government grants, private donations and a steady stream of volunteers, mostly locals, began flowing in.

Metaline Falls found a new sense of community and pride, and residents of north Pend Oreille County began to develop a stronger sense of their regional identity. Since the restoration, the theatre has become the focal point of both the community and the North Pend Oreille region. The theatre draws performers and audiences from across the Inland Northwest, as well as tourists, and the town is gaining a reputation as an art community. In 1998 Metaline Falls was listed in the guidebook *One Hundred Best Small Art Towns in America*.

Encouraged by the success of The Cutter Theatre project, around 1998 Metaline Falls community leaders decided to band together with the handful of nearby towns under 500 — Metaline, Ione and Tiger — and develop their stretch of SR 31 as a Heritage Corridor. The heritage program is a Washington Department of Transportation (WSDOT) program geared toward both conservation and interpretation of local heritage and tourism. Under the energetic and creative leadership of Metaline Falls artist Connie Wilson, the citizens rallied around the concept of the North Pend Oreille Scenic Byway. The group obtained county, state and federal funds to support their enterprise. The region has stunning natural beauty, mountains, a wild scenic river, all varieties of outdoor sports and recreational activities, but it lacked traveler amenities. These issues, as well as how to preserve and interpret local heritage, are taken up at regularly held local meetings that often have 50 to 100 people in attendance. Accomplishments by 2000 included producing a visitors guide and the opening of the North Pend Oreille Visitor Information Center in the historic Tiger Store. In 2000 Connie Wilson summarized the vision behind the Pend Oreille Scenic Byway: "We do not want to become Disney World. People who come to visit our area... will have a genuine natural experience. We have lost all of our traditional employers and we know that we will never have them again. Ultimately we want to protect a way of life for the people who have lived here for generations and have lost their livelihoods."

By 2000 the Republic district and the Hecla Mining Company's Republic activity were limited to the K2 Mine. The Cannon Mine at Wenatchee had closed, and exploration for precious metals had ended except in the Republic and Chiwaukum districts. Cominco Mining found a new deposit of quality ore in the Metaline district and was back in operation at the end of the 1990s. Many believe that great riches still remain below the surface. However, efficient, low-cost methods of extracting the metal from the ore that do not poison and pollute the natural environment are needed for mining activity to go forward.

The Lumber Industry

Following mining, the great forests of the Northwest were a major factor in initially attracting people to the region. From the time the first logs were milled at Spokane Falls in 1872, the Inland Northwest forests supported a lumber industry that reached its peak in the early 20th century. The majority of the Washington mills were located in Stevens, Ferry, Spokane and Okanogan counties, where the forests grow thick and tall on the mountainsides, and in the valleys of the Okanogan, Kettle and Selkirk mountain ranges. In the southeast Asotin County region, the forests cover the slopes of the Blue Mountains south into Oregon. The Idaho Panhandle National Forest is the center of the northern Idaho lumber industry.

The main species found in the inland forests are ponderosa pine, Douglas fir, western larch, paper birch, western red cedar, western hemlock, lodgepole pine and western white pine. Western white pine is perhaps the most distinctive tree species in the inland region. Called the "king of timber," it is the largest in size and is tall, straight, fine-grained, fire adapted and quickly revegetates a site. Unfortunately, the western white

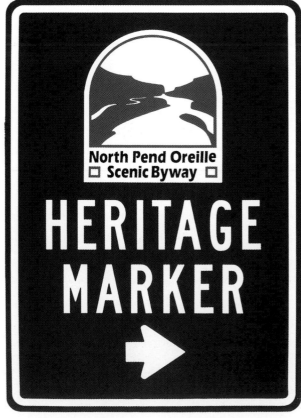

■The North Pend Oreille Scenic Byway encourages visitors to explore the beautiful scenery of northeastern Washington. Efforts to boost tourism have bolstered the economic base of many towns whose principal industries of mining or logging have declined.
North Pend Oreille Scenic Byway

pine is prone to blister rust disease, brought in from Europe, which has devastated much of the remaining pine forest in Idaho.

St. Maries is located in the heart of the Idaho Panhandle lumber region and encompasses 2 million acres of forest. Lumber industry activities in the St. Maries area include wood product processing plants, a large plywood mill, a wood chip plant and saw mills manufacturing cedar shakes, pickets, fence posts, lathe and poles. Millions of board feet of lumber pass through town each year via the St. Joe River, the railroad and truck transport.

A giant statue of Paul Bunyan, team mascot of the local Lumberjacks, welcomes visitors to St. Maries, Idaho. *Photo by Linda Strong*

Lumber production in eastern Washington was at the same level as the entire state until the end of World War II. The postwar building boom sustained a high national demand for wood products well into the 1960s. In the 1950s there were about 4,800 men employed in the mills while the wood markets were good. Between 1946 and 1969 eastern Washington's softwood lumber production increased 83 percent as compared to 66 percent for western Washington. From 1946 to 1953 the number of mills operating in eastern Washington remained the same, except for a flurry of temporary closures at the start of the Korean War when the young mill hands joined the military.

Technological Advances
Close Small Mills

The closing of small mills that were not able to meet the competition of the new, more sophisticated milling process hit many small rural towns in which the local sawmill was a major employer. The postwar advances in milling technology and wood products decimated the small local mills. In 10 years, 1953-1963, four out of five small mills closed. New high-volume equipment such as planers, drying kilns, barkers and chippers made it possible to produce finished lumber more quickly as well as turn a profit utilizing what was

formerly discarded as waste products. Although the lumber industry expanded in the 1950s, the number of active mills dropped from 296 to 77 by 1963. The small mills could not afford the huge investment in the new specialized equipment. The trend toward small mill operations being either bought out or squeezed out accelerated in the 1970s and 1980s. By 2000 inland lumber manufacturing was concentrated in relatively few hands.

The traditional sawmills ranged from two-man operations capable of producing 4,000 board feet in an eight-hour workday, to big mills employing more than 500 people, capable of producing over 200,000 board

Sawdust "teepee" burners were a common sight throughout the lumber towns of the Inland Norhwest. *Roberta Vaagen Collection*

feet in a single shift. These typically ran two eight-hour shifts, while the small ones had a single shift.

Herb Slusser tells about his work in a Newport mill in the 1970s. As the planer foreman he had one of the most important jobs in the mill — keeping the saws and knives sharp and mill machinery in working order. He had 20 men working under him — oilers and feeders.

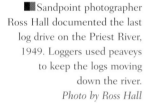

A peavey has been used to free logs from jams since its invention in 1857. *Northwest Museum of Arts & Culture*

"Our regular workday at the mill started at 6:30 a.m. I always worked nine hours or more, sometimes 12 or 14. All day I saw to the sharpening of the saws and knives used in mill processing the lumber. My day didn't stop when the whistle blew and the others left. I had to stay because I was responsible for seeing that the dull knives and blades were changed for freshly sharpened ones. I was paid overtime, time and a half, for every hour over eight. I was a planer foreman, but everyone called me the 'set-up man' since I set up the saws. In the sharpening process we used a knife grinder and saw grinder. Ripsaws had to be hand filed. I have only three fingers on each hand. I lost two in 1962. Then one day in 1974 I was working under a saw adjusting the saw blade when someone accidentally turned the saw on and I lost two more fingers. I decided to retire then."

In the second half of the century, an increasingly large part of the wood products industry was just that — wood products. In addition to construction lumber and millwork, pulp, paper and engineered wood products were an increasing part of the market. Engineered products are based on gluing and laminating and include laminated veneer lumber, glued laminated beams and fiberboard. The pulp and paper industry expanded during the second half of the 20th century, with processing mills operating at Spokane, Wallulla, Wenatchee and Yakima.

Many of the new engineered wood products were developed in the Wood Materials and Engineering Laboratory at Washington State University, Pullman.

Sandpoint photographer Ross Hall documented the last log drive on the Priest River, 1949. Loggers used peaveys to keep the logs moving down the river. *Photo by Ross Hall*

The large companies established their own research and development (R & D) programs dedicated to achieving maximum production and payback from every tree they purchased. The growing emphasis on engineered wood products worked to eliminate the remaining small to mid-size mill operations. They simply could not afford the research, equipment and marketing to make such products.

In the 1980s several factors came together to plunge the Northwest lumber industry into an unprecedented low: competition from Canadian imports, a housing construction slump caused by high interest rates, the revival of logging in the faster-growing southeastern U.S. pine forests, and a shifting market. The industry revived in the late 1980s; however, high-tech innovations, computers and lasers had caught up with the lumber industry and fewer workers were needed.

At the end of the 20th century little accessible old-growth forest remained. Much of the second-growth forest was poorly managed in the past and will take a long time to recover. Current logging practices on federal and state lands, as well as on timber company lands, are much better regulated than previously. The new philosophy is to manage the forest to assure a sustainable timber harvest in the future. However, it is too late for vast logged-off areas, which will take decades or even centuries to recover. One example is Umatilla National Forest in the Blue Mountains where poor logging practices and poor management caused forests to become overstocked with the "wrong" species for lumber needs, resulting in much lower production as well as susceptibility to fires, disease and insects.

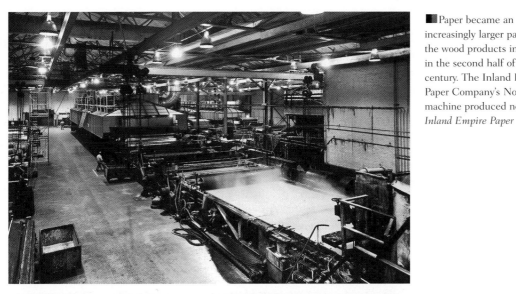

Paper became an increasingly larger part of the wood products industry in the second half of the 20th century. The Inland Empire Paper Company's No. 2 paper machine produced newsprint. *Inland Empire Paper Company*

Plywood and wood veneer products were in demand after World War II, with the postwar building boom and the need for less expensive building materials. *Potlatch Corporation*

The story of the decline of the lumber industry in the later 20th century in the Idaho Panhandle parallels that of eastern Washington. By century's end nearly all the private timber company holdings and most of the federal lands had been cut at least once and there were 10,000 miles of logging roads in the Panhandle National Forest. An era had clearly ended. Sawmills closed for good in Potlatch, Coeur d'Alene and other communities. At century's end tourism was slowly developing in the former lumber areas.

Forestry experts predict that the eastern Washington and Idaho Panhandle timber industry will continue to shrink until it becomes small enough to be sustainable. The forests on the east side of the Cascades produce perhaps only 20 percent of the

board feet/acre of the lands west of the Cascades. Because of the dry climate it takes two to five times longer to produce new stands of harvestable timber, 80 to 100 years on the east side compared to 20 to 40 years on the west side.

In the 1970s lumber jobs began disappearing because of over-harvesting, poor management practices in previous decades, increased mechanization and environmental restrictions. Many small communities in the forest regions traditionally depended heavily on the lumber industry for their livelihood. From the 1980s on they experienced intensifying economic depression with the loss of well-paid jobs in the woods and mills and little prospect of new employment locally. Many people left the small sawmill communities where their families had lived and made their livelihoods off the woods for generations. Those who remained in their hometowns in 2000 faced an ongoing struggle to make a living.

Part II: Land of the Combine and Irrigation Sprinkler
Agriculture Leads

Driving across the Inland Northwest the landscape unfolds like a series of beautiful paintings. There are the rolling hills of the Palouse that continue east into Idaho. Planted to wheat for more than a century, the district is emerald green in springtime and undulating gold at harvest time. In the lush irrigation districts the painting is a checkerboard of intense green and black. Big Bend, the heartland of wheat country, is a sea of waving wheat stretching on as far as the eye can see. The road turns and suddenly, unexpectedly the eye beholds dramatic outcrops of black basalt in the channels and coulees carved by the Ice Age floods. In some areas there remains vast expanses of native sage and bunch grass range-land that has never been cultivated.

At the end of the 20th century, of the original three industries — mining, logging and farming — only

■Springtime in the rolling Palouse landscape is a sea of ever-changing colors of green. "Quilted Hills," *Photo by John Clement*

farming was still a significant economic factor. While the inland region comprised only one-third of the geographic area of Washington and had only 21 percent of the population, it contained 94 percent of all cultivated farmland. In Idaho 22 percent of the state's population lives in the Panhandle.

In 2000 dry-land farming was still the most prevalent form of agriculture. However, between 1950 and the end of the century, irrigation farming developed on a scale found only in Colorado and areas in California. Approximately one acre out of every three acres under cultivation was being irrigated. The outstanding yields produced in the irrigated agriculture districts is reflected in the fact that in 1999, 53.9 percent of the total agricultural revenue for the entire state was from the produce of five counties in the Yakima Valley and Columbia Basin irrigation projects. Both dry land and irrigation farming are practiced in the Idaho Panhandle.

Geographers have divided the Washington region into five agricultural districts. The Walla Walla district in the southeast is the oldest and led the way in commercial farming and production for international markets. With higher annual precipitation it was the most productive and diversified in 1950 but lost ground to the irrigation projects in the 1960s. The two great wheat-growing districts are the Big Bend and the Palouse. The Big Bend, named for the Big Bend of the Columbia River, encompasses the Inland Northwest's most extensive dry land agricultural region. The Yakima irrigation district, alongside the Yakima River, is a cornucopia of fruits and table crops. The North Central Wenatchee apple fruit district spills out of the Cascades.

"Palouse Farm," a 1948 wood engraving by Spokane artist Jane Baldwin *Northwest Museum of Arts & Culture*

Rural farms dot the Inland Northwest landscape. *Deanne Jackson*

Apples bruise easily and are inspected and packed by hand, a tedious and backbreaking job. *Yakima Valley Museum*

In the latter decades of the 20th century, inland Washington consistently ranked No. 1 nationally in its production of apples, wheat, hops, sweet cherries, dry peas, spearmint and peppermint oil, and lentils.

In addition, it has ranked second nationally in the growing of potatoes, pears, grapes, apricots, green peas, asparagus, sweet corn (for processing), plums and prunes. The level of prosperity enjoyed by farmers in Whitman, Grant and Yakima counties places them in the top 50 out of 3,072 counties in the United States. Yakima County ranks number 10 nationally, the highest of all non-California counties in the nation.

Larger Farms, Fewer Farms

Across the United States the national trend since the 1960s has been the consolidation of farmland into larger farms. This has also happened in the Inland Northwest, but not at the scale of many other regions, such as the Midwest. Washington's farm census information shows that for the past 40 years around 74 percent of Washington's farms consist of 180 acres or less. The average farm in the 1990s was 68 acres on the western side of the Cascades. In contrast, the average inland farm was 727 acres.

In the 1950s, farming continued as it had for decades. However, in the 1960s everything began to rapidly change as factories that had produced heavy equipment for the war effort put out new, improved heavy farm machinery. Where the farmer had previously hired custom operators — e.g. a threshing machine or combine to harvest the crop — now each farmer bought his or her own machines and many

others. To make farming cost effective, huge acreages were necessary to justify the farmer's investment in this expensive new machinery: large tractors, trucks, 12-row cultivators and combines. Farmers, often with college degrees in agriculture and business, became savvy about marketing their products and handled the business end of their work, such as sales and shipping, directly rather than relying exclusively on railroad agents or farmer's co-ops, as was the earlier practice. By the 1990s many farmers had professional computerized home offices where they could check market prices on a daily basis as well as keep up on such things as weather conditions and potential crop dangers posted on the agricultural bulletin boards.

The actual farm size within the Inland region varies. About one-third of the farms are over 1,000 acres. The Palouse wheat district illustrates how farm size has changed. In the Palouse the average farm in 1940 was 532 acres; in 1969, 913 acres; and in 1982, 1,143 acres. By the end of the 1980s two out of three family farms that had existed at the turn of the 20th century were gone, their land bought and combined with other land by large-scale farmers. The population figures by county illustrate the loss of population in the Palouse region as farms were consolidated into larger single-owner holdings. Yakima County is a notable exception to the "larger and fewer" pattern. With 3,651 farms in the 1990s it ranked No. 1 in the state in terms of the most farms. The average Yakima Valley farm consists of 40 intensively cultivated acres, with crops such as hops, mint, tomatoes or fruit trees.

In spite of economic pressures, the inland farms in the 1990s continued to be family enterprises. The

■Women are no strangers to farm work. Wheat harvest on the Palouse, 1942
Spokesman-Review Photo Archives

Women Farmers

Tony Benzel of Ritzville, in the heart of the Big Bend Wheat Country, tells of the life of the farm women working with and beside their husbands for the family livelihood.

"On smaller ranches it is not unusual for the women to get up early, prepare lunch, go out and drive a wheat truck all morning, hauling the grain to the elevator. Then it's back to the house, put lunch on the table, throw the dishes into the dishwasher and head back out to the field. Lunch is a big meal and always includes roast meat or meatloaf, potatoes, vegetables, salad, and pie or cake and ice cream — everything homemade, of course. The same routine applies to dinner. It is common to feed six to 10 hungry people at every meal. It is a strenuous and exhausting time. When we are harvesting several miles from the house, the women or older girls who drive take the food out to the field. Lunch would be casseroles, sandwiches and fruit. It has to be nutritious and filling."

■ Harvest time is a tapestry of tawny golds and browns in sharp contrast to the deep blue skies of the Palouse.
Photo by John Clement

U.S. Department of Agriculture found that in 1997, 89.6 percent of Washington farms were family businesses. Nine percent were family partnerships and less than 1 percent were operated by large corporations. Toward the end of the 20th century more farmers than ever before were raising crops on a contract basis. For example, a farmer may contract with McDonald's for its tomato crop. In the 1990s onions were in high demand in the Japanese market and farmers were contracting for their entire onion crop.

> "Wheat, wheat and more wheat. It's what keeps the economy going."
> *Nancy Ellis, Davenport, Lincoln County, Washington*

The Inland Northwest is among the top wheat producing regions of the United States. Since 1950 there has been a real effort by farmers to diversify their crops; however, wheat continues to be the key crop. In the Big Bend region more than 1 million acres are put into wheat each season. While the rich yellow

■ Early Palouse farms were small family businesses, often situated in idyllic locations, as depicted in the lithograph, "Tekoa Farm," by Robert Engard.
Northwest Museum of Arts & Culture

inland crops exported. Over 94 percent of the food exports go to four major regions: Asia, Canada, Mexico and South America.

Wheat country is a land of neat attractive small towns, generally under 1,000 population, with a strong sense of tradition and community. The centerpiece of the town has always been the grain elevators by the railroad tracks, which tower like cathedral steeples over the surrounding wheat fields. Many families have lived in the region since pioneer days. The people know who they are and have a real sense of place within their community and the region. There is a strong sense of loyalty, and community spirit is strong.

loess soil of the Palouse yields between 100-150 bushels per acre as compared to 40-125 in the Big Bend, the harvest in the Big Bend exceeds that of the Palouse by 30 percent. Whitman (Palouse), Lincoln and Adams (Big Bend) counties rank among the counties in the nation with the greatest yield. With 400,000 acres put into wheat annually in the Walla Walla district and a yield of up to 100 bushels per acre it also ranks as one of the major wheat producing areas of the nation. As if this were not enough wheat, from the 1950s to the 1990s wheat ranked among the top three crops produced in the irrigated Columbia Basin Project.

Inland agricultural products have been exported throughout the 20th century. Only 25 percent of Washington's farm products are sold within the state. Since the 1980s the U.S. market for many crops has been poor and export has been encouraged for new markets. Soft winter wheat and apples are the top

Inland Northwest Centennial Farms

As a part of the statewide observance of Washington's State Centennial in 1989, every farm that had been in the same family for 100 years or more was identified and honored as a "Washington Centennial Farm." The Inland Northwest was home to 70 percent, 274, of the total Centennial Farms, 392. Six of the top seven counties in the state with the greatest number of old farms were located in the Inland Northwest. The farms distinguished as Centennial Farms were all found in the Wheatland counties. Whitman County, the heart of the Palouse, ranked in first place with 78 farms, 40 percent more 100-year-old farms than the next ranking county. The other counties with a noteworthy number of 100-year-old farms were: Walla Walla, 47 farms; Spokane, 38 farms; Lincoln, 34 farms; Columbia, 20 farms; and Garfield, 15 farms. Source: *Washington's Centennial Farms: Yesterday and Today.* Olympia, WA: Washington State Department of Agriculture, 1989, pp. 260-267.

Nuestro Viaje al Norte:
The Latino Demographic Presence in the Inland Northwest
Carlos S. Maldonado, Ph.D.

The Chicano/Latino demographic presence in the Northwest has deep roots and is premised on the notion of *Nuestro Viaje al Norte* (Our Journey North). *Nuestro Viaje al Norte* has taken place at various historical points beginning with the Spanish exploration to the Northwest in the 1770s. The most significant *Viaje*, however, has taken place since the mid-20th century.

Following the historical tradition of the *Viaje al Norte*, with its roots in the 19th century, Latinos made their way into the Inland Northwest during the 1920s and 1930s. During the World War II years, workers were actively recruited from Mexico for farm work through the *Bracero* program. An estimated 16,000 men participated in the program between 1943-47. During this time, Latinos from other areas of the United States moved to the inland Washington region, especially from the Southwest and *El Valle*, the Texas Rio Grande Valley.

The development of labor-intensive agriculture in the Yakima Valley in the 1940s and the Columbia Basin Project in the 1950s stimulated the movement of Chicanos/Latinos to the inland region. After the war, the movement of Chicanos/Latinos transitioned into *Nuestro Hogar del Norte*, "Our Northern Home," as families settled in the region. While maintaining family ties to the Southwest and Mexico, Latinos developed communities in the inland towns, establishing their own church communities, businesses, community organizations and cultural celebrations. They gradually became part of the larger community as they secured non-agricultural work and their children attended public schools.

The last 30 years has witnessed significant growth of Latinos in Washington. Today, Latinos constitute the largest ethnic minority group in Washington, estimated to number 356,500 in 2000. Seventy-three percent of these are of Mexican descent. Much of the demographic growth among Latinos is attributed to immigration and a high birth rate.

Latinos are an active part of Washington's labor force. According to 2000 state figures, they constitute about 4.9 percent of the state's labor force. Washington's Latinos maintain a high participation rate in the labor force. They are active in all employment sectors in Washington. The top ranking occupation categories among Latinos include technical, sales, and administrative support occupations. Farm, forestry, and fishing related occupations fall in second place.

Latinos who are engaged in agricultural related employment face numerous issues relating to employment, housing, health, wages and immigration concerns. The United Farm Workers of America has historically worked to organize and advocate on behalf of farm workers. The UFW has pursued efforts to secure legislation granting amnesty for undocumented farm workers and organizing against *Bracero* type guest worker legislation. In 1999 the Teamsters, a newcomer to agricultural related workers organizing, recently staged a successful organizing effort at Stemilt Growers in Wenatchee, Washington. The union, however, was unsuccessful in its organizing effort at the Fruit and Produce Company in Yakima.

Latino demographics in Washington will continue to grow. The youthfulness of the Latino community as reflected in the median age of 22.6, positions Latinos to be much more visible in the state and its labor force. State policy leaders will certainly have to address the issues that these growing Latino demographics demand.

Part I:

The Great Depression and the New Deal

"With the possible exception of the Great Wall of China or the Panama Canal, few structures on Earth have had such an effect on the course of human events as has Grand Coulee Dam, the concrete monolith that divides the upper and lower portions of the Columbia River."

Earl Roberge, Columbia, Great River of the West, 1985

The Great Columbia Desert

Early explorers and settlers making their way into Eastern Washington in the 19th century compared the center of the hot, dry and desolate Columbia River Basin to the Sahara and Arabian deserts. It became widely known as the Great Columbia Desert and was deemed to have little value. When it was used at all it was the domain of cattlemen and roving herds of range sheep. It was after 1900 when all the land in the surrounding districts with higher annual rainfall, the Palouse, Walla Walla and Big Bend, was taken up, that the farming frontier pushed down into the central basin.

The higher than average rainfall in the basin between 1900-1910 convinced the new-comers that it was suitable for dry land wheat farming. After a few seasons of reasonable yields, the realities of farming in the central Columbia Basin became all too clear to the farmers. Each year they struggled with erratic weather patterns, severe wind erosion and

Chapter Two

Depression, Democrats, Defense and Dams

the invasive cheat grass. Despite great effort they experienced marginal harvest yields in good years and total crop failure during the frequent droughts. By 1924 the wheat acreage in Grant County, destined to become the largest section of the Columbian Basin Irrigation Project, was less than half of that of 1910. A brutal drought beginning in 1928 and continuing the next season turned the district into a dust bowl and the light sandy soil formed dunes. Doris Angell recalls on the pages of her story of farming in the basin, *Pioneers to Power,* "To add to the discomfort were the frequent dust storms. One could see them coming down the coulee for miles. All doors and windows would be closed, although the temperatures were 114 degrees in the shade. The houses were suffocating! ... The streets were inches thick with dust in summer and mud in winter."

For those who had held on for more than a decade, the final blow came with the Great Depression, which brought rock-bottom wheat prices and no possibility of bank loans to "keep going" until things got better. Basin farm families packed up and headed over to the coast or Spokane, leaving their farms to blow away. In less than 12 months more than half of the farmers had left. Their abandoned farmsteads remain as weather-beaten monuments to early-20th-century agrarian dreams dashed by the vicissitudes of the weather and economy.

The idea of irrigation farming was already in the air. Some of the determined farmers who remained in the Quincy area were German immigrants. Florence Stout recalls her parents mentioning that they often heard their German neighbors say in the 1920s, "Wenn das wasser kommt zum Quincy," meaning, "when the water comes to Quincy everything will be alright."

■The Columbia Basin was once the desolate domain of sheep ranchers and cattlemen on horseback. *Northwest Museum of Arts & Culture*

■Vanessa Helder's rendering, "Jackhammer Crew," shows Grand Coulee Dam under construction, c. 1940. *Northwest Museum of Arts & Culture*

Not in their wildest dreams would the destitute basin farmers have predicted that by the end of the century the region would become one of the richest agricultural areas in the Pacific Northwest, if not the nation. A new era was ushered in by President Franklin D. Roosevelt's decision to build Grand Coulee Dam as a New Deal project. The New Deal made a two-fold promise: to put the economically destitute basin farmers to work and bring irrigation water to support farming of the arid land.

When the Grand Coulee Dam project was launched it was not a new idea. Columbia Basin irrigation schemes reached back to the early 1890s. At the close of World War I the promoters of two equally ambitious opposing plans went public with their schemes. Ephrata attorney Billy Clapp and the outspoken editor of the *Wentachee World*, Rufus Woods, championed a dam on the Columbia at the Grand Coulee, the work of the Spokane Floods. Irrigation water for the Columbia Basin would be pumped from the dam's reservoir. Opposition came from a Spokane-area group whose plan was to divert water from the Pend Oreille River at Albeni Falls on the Washington-Idaho border. The water would be brought

to the Columbia Basin via a 130-mile-long gravity waterway system of canals and natural drainage routes, and stored in a reservoir near Ritzville. Through the 1920s and 30s the opposing forces engaged in a true donnybrook on the front pages of the local newspapers with each side hiring experts to prove their claims and denounce their opponents. Each side agreed only on one point — their project would irrigate between 2 to 2.5 million acres of Columbia Basin desert land.

Federal authorities heard from both sides as they were defining the New Deal project for the Columbia Basin. The north central Washington forces won out, and in July 1933, $63 million in National Recovery Act (NRA) funds were allocated to construct the Grand Coulee Dam. The great reservoir that formed behind Grand Coulee Dam's thick concrete walls was named Lake Roosevelt. Many say that Grand Coulee is the ultimate monument to the Democratic president who worked to put the country back on its feet through the New Deal. Roosevelt's promise of jobs was fulfilled. In 1934 construction was in full swing with 8,000 men at work constructing the all-concrete, 550-foot-high, 5,225-foot-long Grand Coulee Dam. Construction boomtowns sprung up named for the work in progress — Engineers Town, Contractors Town, Mason City and

Government Town. After the dam was completed some towns were dismantled and others just faded away. Four that survived are Coulee Dam, Electric City, Elmer City and Grand Coulee, known as Mason City during the construction years.

Personal and Community Costs of the Great Dam

While the Grand Coulee Dam certainly was one of the "mightiest things ever built by man," as song-writer Woody Guthrie wrote in the 1930s, it was to

bring great agriculture and prosperity as well as loss and suffering to people and fish in the next half century. An immediate source of human and community loss was the backed-up water of Grand Coulee Dam's reservoir. Lake Roosevelt is 150 miles long, 100-350 feet deep and reaches within 35 miles of Spokane on the east end. The dammed-up waters destroyed 10 communities, the Colville Tribes ancestral burial ground and 400-500 farms. Columbia River waters eventually drowned the towns of Peach, Keller, Lincoln, Gerome, Gifford, Daisy, Kettle Falls, Marcus, Boyds and Inchelium — the latter, a Colville Nation community that had been on the banks of the great river for untold generations. In addition, Fort Colvile, the historic site of the original Hudson's Bay Company post named for Andrew Colvile, was lost below the waters of Lake Roosevelt.

■ The generating capacity of Grand Coulee Dam has increased several times since it opened, from 978,000 kilowatts in 1940 to 6,890 million kilowatts today. *Northwest Museum of Arts & Culture*

■ Inchelium, home to the Colville Indians for generations, was one of many communities, fishing grounds, and ancestral burial grounds drowned by the rising waters of the Columbia River. *Stevens County Historical Society*

OLD INCHELIUM, WA HITS THE RIVER
'CREEK WHICH ENTERS THE COLUMBIA'

Everyone had to move. Chet Widner, who grew up in the town of Peach, recalls that it seemed that the government generally paid a fair price. "My father received $10,000 for the house and eight acres of orchard land. The government wouldn't pay for anything above the waterline. You didn't fight it. It was just part of the world that was going on." The *Wenatchee World* reported that approximately 5,000 buildings were removed from 400-500 farms that were soon inundated by the rising waters. The government assisted property owners in moving their buildings.

In addition to moving farms, whole communities were relocated. Some created new town sites on higher ground, some merged with nearby towns located above flood level, and others simply disappeared forever. The federal work crews helped relocate the towns by rebuilding roads and bridges and moving buildings or constructing new buildings. Construction materials were obtained locally whenever possible. The sawmills at Kettle Falls, Lincoln and Coulee City cut 30 million board-feet from logs floated down river to their mills.

The people of Kettle Falls pulled up stakes and moved to the smaller nearby incorporated community of Meyers Falls. Once settled in, the Kettle Falls émigrés voted to change the name of the town to Kettle Falls. While they have all continued to live side-by-side for two generations since this happened, memories are long and the original Meyers Falls people have never really forgiven Kettle Falls for taking them off the map. Rowena McIntosh reflected in 1999 on the events of the past 50 years for her town. "The flooding of the town in 1940 and moving it to the town site of Meyers Falls and renaming the town Kettle Falls was the most pivotal thing ever to happen in our community. However, since the 1950s and the closing of several sawmills, our biggest struggle continuing to this day is trying to give the town a more tourist orientation."

Small-town people often have an attachment to their community that those living in large cities may find hard to understand. Among the many things lost by those whose hometowns now lie at the bottom of Lake Roosevelt are a loss of place, a way of life, the birthplace and graveyards of their forebears — loss of continuity with the past — and for many a part of their own identity.

The residents of the pretty orchard community of Peach and their descendants have lived with these losses for over a half a century. They have found it a comfort to keep their memories alive by banding together once a year. For more than 60 years and three generations the Peach Picnic has been held on the second Saturday of June. Steve Timmons was a child when Peach was destroyed by the Grand Coulee Dam project. Still he has clear memories of that happy childhood place. In 1999 he told *The Spokesman-Review* "Peach was located along Hawk Creek, between Seven Bays and Lincoln, about 30 miles from Davenport... And so Peach vanished from the maps. Residents moved on and started over. But they never forgot where they came from." The descendents of the original residents that had to move from Peach have a strong attachment to the now almost mythic town. As the years go by more and more of those who faithfully attend the Peach Picnic never actually saw the town themselves, but feel attached to it through their parents' and grandparents' stories and caring. They come to the Peach Picnic and participate in the old timers' dreaming.

Part II
Defense: World War II

"The Second World War inaugurated the modern era of Pacific Northwest history."
Carlos A. Schwantes, The Pacific Northwest, 1996

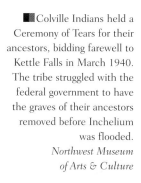

The Colville People, as a group, undoubtedly lost the most to the backed-up waters of the Columbia behind Grand Coulee Dam. The Indians struggled with the federal government from 1934 to 1938 to have the graves of their ancestors removed before Inchelium was flooded. This was only partially accomplished when the gates of the dam were closed. The day the waters of the Columbia rose over Kettle Falls the Indians gathered on higher ground and held a Ceremony of Tears. To this day they occasionally gather to give respect to their ancestors in their watery graves.

In 1951 the tribes filed a claim against the federal government for lost salmon fishing rights at Kettle Falls, the flooding of numerous home sites, root digging areas, the traditional burial site on the banks of the Columbia, and, most significantly, the destruction of their way of life. In 1975 the tribes presented the government with claims of $100 million and 185 megawatts of power annually to compensate for the damages done to them through the construction of Grand Coulee and Chief Joseph dams. They presented their case in a 28-minute color film, *The Price We Paid*. Joe Kohler, Colville Tribal Councilman, testifying in 1975 before the federal Task Force on Tribal Claims, regarding the loss of place and way of life for the Colville People caused by the construction of Grand Coulee Dam said: "Families and communities were close together geographically and in extreme close communication in times of sorrow and festivity... [How a person] stored and preserved salmon and other foods, and his function in the salmon ceremonies — these were matters of importance and status. Suddenly, within a period of four years, all of this is wiped out."

Talks between tribal leaders and a federal task force continued into the mid-1990s when, unexpectedly the federal officials offered and the Colville Confederated Tribes accepted a settlement for damages of a lump sum of $53 million and a minimum of $15.25 million annually thereafter. The yearly payments represented the tribe's share of the power revenues generated at Grand Coulee Dam.

America's entrance into World War II in September 1941, three months after Grand Coulee Dam was completed, quickly shifted the value of the new dam to electricity. Aluminum production takes enormous amounts of electricity, just what Grand Coulee was producing. Immediately after America entered the war, aluminum companies were offered low-cost electrical power if they would operate in the Northwest. By the end of 1942 there were new plants in Spokane, Trentwood, Vancouver and Longview working 24 hours a day, seven days a week. In 1943, 60 percent of the kilowatts produced by the waters of the Columbia pouring through the dam's turbines were supporting the aluminum plants. It is estimated that the aluminum for one out of every three airplanes built for the war came from power

produced by Grand Coulee Dam. In addition to fueling the aluminum plants, Grand Coulee provided electrical energy for a magnesium plant building incendiary bombs and powered Henry Kaiser's Columbia River shipyards.

After the outbreak of the war the greater Pacific Northwest region quickly became a focal point for national defense work. There was large-scale airplane manufacturing and shipbuilding on Puget Sound. Inland activities were focused more on military training facilities and hospitals — and producing plutonium. During the war years the inland region as a whole experienced a 37-percent population increase. In fact, the population expanded only in specific locations where there was war work. For example, by 1943 two out of every three residents in the Tri-Cities/Yakima area were newcomers. Most of the newcomers worked at the Hanford Engineering Project, which employed up to 45,000 people keeping the work going 24 hours a day, seven days a week. Spokane's population grew from 122,000 in 1940 to 161,721 in 1950. The rest of

"*Stay on Your Job!*

Stick to the mining camps where you are now at work—you are as important to the battle as the pursuit pilot or the man behind the bomb-sight."

DONALD M. NELSON
CHAIRMAN WAR PRODUCTION BOARD
(*Radio Address June 13, 1942*)

Buy War Bonds . Invest in Victory!

(Top far left) Kaiser Aluminum & Chemical Corp. depended on electricity from Grand Coulee Dam for aluminum production during World War II. *Northwest Museum of Arts & Culture*

Kaiser Aluminum & Chemical Corp. featured the "Al Luminium" character at the 1954 Inland Empire Industrial Exposition. *Spokesman-Review Photo Archives*

(Bottom far left) Kaiser Aluminum & Chemical Corp. employs thousands of workers and depends upon the inexpensive electricity in the Northwest to keep its production mills operative. *Northwest Museum of Arts & Culture*

War Production Board poster encouraged miners to aid the war effort by "staying on the job." *Northwest Museum of Arts & Culture*

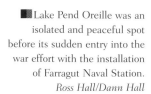

Lake Pend Oreille was an isolated and peaceful spot before its sudden entry into the war effort with the installation of Farragut Naval Station.
Ross Hall/Dann Hall

Farragut Naval Station became Idaho's second-largest city when it was built in 1942 to house and train thousands of naval recruits.
Bonner County Historical Society/Verna Mae Davis

the region continued farming — raising wheat and other food to feed the nation.

Air bases were hurriedly constructed in several inland locations: including Geiger airbase, Spokane, where 100 buildings were put up in 29 days, and Army Air Field, Walla Walla. An Army hospital was built in Spokane and McCaw General Hospital was built at Walla Walla. Constructing the wartime facilities created thousands of jobs overnight. For instance, 263 buildings were constructed in less than a year at Fairchild Air Force Base in Spokane by a work crew of over 20,000. An Air Force base was built at Moses Lake and airstrips near Ephrata and Okanogan. The U.S. Army developed a firing range on 263 acres of sagebrush land west of Yakima. Those living nearby were destined to hear the reports of artillery 24 hours a day as tens of thousands of soldiers went through an intense

training course before being shipped overseas. Since the war the Yakima Firing Range continues to be used as a training center. Chewelah was selected as the site for a huge plant producing magnesite, critical for producing high-grade steel.

In Idaho, Camp Farragut, the second-largest naval training center in the United States, was built at Lake Pend Oreille, not far from Coeur d'Alene, Idaho.

Farragut had facilities for 45,000. Recruits were generally trained in batches of 30,000 at a time in six self-contained training camps. The camp was built in a few weeks by 28,000 workers. For the duration of the war Farragut was the second-largest city in Idaho. After the end of the war the Camp Farragut facility became Farragut College and Technical Institute. The college eventually closed down, and forests and fields have reclaimed most of the area that is now Farragut State Park. Evelyn Reed of Newport, Washington, just across the border, remembers, "When Camp Farragut Naval Station was being built, and after the war when it was being decommissioned, our town was very involved. Local people helped with both and many of our present day homes are recycled buildings from the old navel base."

Towns and cities where major facilities went in often felt like a cyclone had hit them when trucks and trainloads of construction workers and military personal literally poured into town. For example, the construction of Larson Field near Moses Lake (pop. 400) nearly overwhelmed the town as well as the nearby communities of Ephrata (pop. 600) and Soap Lake (pop. 668) with sudden demands for housing and goods.

The war years were not without their humor, and local folks are still chuckling over the time Air Force trainees out on a nocturnal practice bombing mission mistook the twinkling lights of the town of Warden for their practice target and dropped two rounds of sandbag "bombs" as part of a practice run. An alert citizen quickly threw the electrical master switch, which plunged the town into blackness, hence eliminating it as a target. A few minutes later the Grant County Sheriff called the Ephrata Air Force Base commander announcing, "I think Warden is about to surrender." The Moses Lake Air Base closed down after the war only to be reactivated in the 1950s as a Strategic Air Command location to protect Grand Coulee Dam and the Hanford Atomic Works during the Cold War years.

Hanford

While all this activity was moving full-speed ahead, in the shadows was another great war project that would depend upon Grand Coulee Dam's kilowatts. In September 1943 a "mystery load" appeared on the power grid in southeastern Washington that consumed more electricity than all of the region's towns, farms and public utilities combined. Only a few knew that the enormous electrical energy draw was supporting the construction of the world's first nuclear reactor at Hanford. The Hanford site had been selected for this dangerous project because it was a remote location with convenient access to huge amounts of electrical energy and cold water. The newly completed Grand Coulee Dam generators furnished the power to build and operate the nuclear reactors, and the mighty Columbia the water for cooling the nuclear reactors.

The next order of business was clearing the site. Implementing the War Powers Act the federal government confiscated 640 square miles of land, destroying the old Columbia River towns of White Bluff and Hanford and taking over the town of Richland. About 2,000 people were directly affected as every property owner in this highly rural ranching and orchard agriculture area was given 30 days to move out. The farms and villages were leveled and the debris trucked away. Judge Loyd Wiehl, then in college, retells how the abrupt eviction affected his parents:

"In 1943, when my parents received their letter from the government telling them they had to move, they were 60 years old, and ranching along the

"B" reactor, the first full-scale nuclear reactor, produced weapon-grade plutonium from 1944 to 1968. *Columbia River Exhibition of History, Science and Technology*

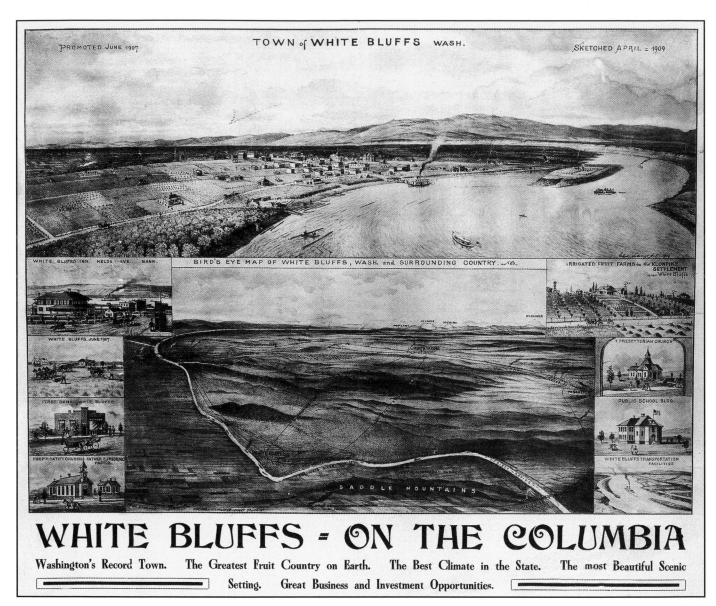

The towns of White Bluff and Hanford, along with 640 square miles of ranch and orchard lands along the Columbia River, were confiscated by the U.S. government under the War Powers Act to create the Hanford Atomic Works, a secret research facility for plutonium production.

Northwest Museum of Arts & Culture

Columbia and running the White Bluff Ferry, like the family had for generations. Using the War Powers Act, the government told them they had to be out of the house where they had lived for 40 years in one month, and paid them the value of the land assigned by the tax appraisal. It was not fair market value for my parents' 15,000 acres of ranch land.

"My parents were shocked and broken hearted. My father practically lived on that river. His forbears had homesteaded the land under the Land Grant Act. My mother's family were 19th-century pioneers in White Bluff across the river. My father tried to get the government to lease the land — and return its use to them after the war. Nothing doing! In 30 days they packed and disposed of generations of keepsakes and memories. First they moved to a place on the Yakima River and then to my brother's at

ABC Homes
The Houses that Hanford Built

A to Z House Plans

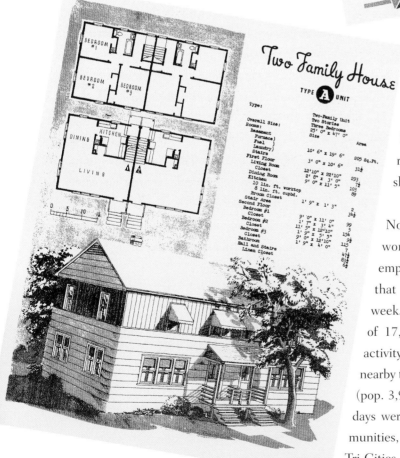

Two Family House
TYPE **A** UNIT

Cle Elum. Every time he (my father) talked about it he broke down. My father said, 'this is killing me'. He died just a few years after his place was taken away from him, around age 65. My mother lived into her 90s. Every time I took her over to our ranch site, the buildings were all destroyed, she sat looking at the land and wept."

Workers poured into the Inland Northwest from the all over the country to work at Hanford Engineering, which employed up to 45,000 people working shifts that continued around the clock seven days a week. Richland, a village of 247, became a city of 17,000 in less than a month. The frenzied activity and large population spilled over into the nearby towns of Kennewick (pop. 1,918) and Pasco (pop. 3,913). By the end of the war the small town days were gone forever for all three of these communities, which became widely known simply as the Tri-Cities. By the end of the century the Tri-Cities was the fastest-growing place in the Inland Northwest.

■ (Above)
Quick, inexpensive housing was required for nearly 45,000 workers in Richland for the top-secret Hanford Project. *Columbia River Exhibition of History, Science & Technology*

■ Officially, house plans for Richland workers were labeled by letter, such as Type A and Type Z, but workers called them "alphabet houses." *Columbia River Exhibition of History, Science & Technology*

OH — ARE YA HOME? I FORGOT MY KEY.

Regardless of the personal loss and lingering pain the Hanford Project cost the local residents, many felt a patriotic satisfaction in helping with the war for America. Annette Heriford relates the local pride when they learned of the connection between the Hanford Project and the end of the war.

"I was over in Selah listening to Gabriel Heater on the radio when I heard about the dropping of the atomic bomb. The next day the Hanford Project newspaper announced that the atomic bomb had been developed with the plutonium from the Hanford 'mystery project.' We were happy that the war had ended and we were very proud that we had helped end the war. We had given up our homes, our hometowns, our farms and our lives for the Hanford Project to be possible. Of course we felt proud."

The Aftermath of World War II

"What's going to happen when the fighting stops? Can the Northwest go back to fish, fruit and sawmills, or have these changes come to stay?"
Fredrick Simpich, National Geographic Magazine, 1942

The war was over in 1945 but the effects were felt on a personal and regional level for decades to come. For starters there was the unfinished work at Grand Coulee Dam and the entire Columbia Basin Project, put on hold by the war. A new era was beginning for the Inland Northwest that would end the image of the region as a remote hinterland once and for all and transform the region into a major economic force within the greater region for the first time in history.

The single most significant consequence of World War II that changed the course of thousands of people's personal lives was the G.I. Bill, which made higher education and veteran's housing loans available to all veterans. Madilane Perry of Republic recalls these impacts on her family.

"I doubt if any later war had the far-reaching effects of World War II. It produced a population 'bulge' eligible for the G.I. Bill and VA loan services that influenced my generation profoundly. My personal memories don't extend back to living in 'Victory Heights' in Spokane or going to my dad's graduation from Law School under the G.I. Bill. But I remember helping to build the house I'm sitting in now which was financed by a VA loan to my mother. The house in which my father's second family was raised was also financed by a VA loan...."

Bob Kissler of Odessa, observes that the G.I. Bill had an ongoing impact in the region as veterans of Korea, Vietnam and other international police actions in the late 20th century also went to college on the G.I. Bill. Kissler notes, "When younger men [from our area] returned from the wars many went to college and upon receiving degrees in other career fields, moved to bigger cities. Those who studied agriculture are more up-to-date and use the new equipment before others. Many farm now using the latest computer type equipment."

Evolution of Dam Construction Communities

In the decades after the war the new Grand Coulee Dam construction towns gradually became more like the surrounding communities, but with the great dam somehow always a shadow in the background. The boomtown days long gone, the communities have become pleasant hometowns for families and retirees. Rodney Bisell of Grand Coulee shared his

Harnessing the Power of the Waters of the Mighty Columbia

The Columbia River is the largest river on the North American continent flowing into the Pacific Ocean and fourth-largest in the United States. The Columbia's watershed drains 298,000 square miles, an area larger than France and England combined. From its headwaters at Columbia Lake in British Columbia, a glacial trench between the Rocky Mountains and the Selkirk Range, the river drops nearly 2,500 feet over its 1,170-mile course to the Pacific. Most of the drop occurs in the middle 900 miles, located in central Washington State.

It has been estimated that potential power that can be generated by weight and flow of rivers in the United States is approximately 150 million horsepower. The mighty Columbia alone contains 50 million horsepower or one-third of the entire U.S. potential.

The original hydroelectric generating system for Grand Coulee Dam placed a powerhouse on both the left and right sides of the spillway on the downstream face of the dam. Each powerhouse contained nine generators each producing 108,000 kilowatts. When the region experienced its first power shortage in the early 1950s, the Bonneville Power Administration, the federal marketing agency for the power produced in the Inland Northwest, decided that the capacity of the dam should be increased. This was accomplished by increasing the power of the existing turbines and building a third powerhouse with increased capacity.

Between 1960 and 1980 each of the original 18 turbines was rewound, thereby increasing its capacity to 125,000 kilowatts, for a total capacity of 2.25 million kilowatts. In the late 1960s work began on Power House No. 3, which was constructed on the downstream face of the dam. Powerhouse No. 3 was built with six generators three producing 600,000 kilowatts and three producing 805,000 kilowatts for a total of 4.215 million kilowatts. The final generator went on line in May 1980. The flow of water through each of the six generating units is equal to the flow in the Colorado River above Lake Powell.

Thus, by the end of 1980 Grand Coulee Dam had reached its maximum generating capacity of 6,890 million kilowatts. Each day the 23 turbines generate an average of 12,000 megawatts of electricity — a dozen times more than Seattle uses on an average day. The Grand Coulee Dam hydro-electric plant ranks as the largest producer of electricity in the United States and third in the world.

■ Vanessa Helder, "Coulee Dam, Looking West," c. 1940
Northwest Museum of Arts & Culture

■ Grand Coulee Dam is the largest producer of electricity in the United States.
Northwest Museum of Arts & Culture

■ Willie Wiredhand logo celebrates 50 years of America's rural electric cooperatives.
Washington Rural Electric Cooperative Association

thoughts in 1999 on life in a hometown that has always been closely tied to the great dam.

"I have lived in Grand Coulee all my life. I worked on the third powerhouse in the 1970s as a part of the drill crew. The town had 30 percent more people then. I felt darn good about working for the Coulee Dam Company.... you couldn't beat the dependability of the job. A drawback with the town is the government owns most of the land here and we don't have a tax base to buy fire equipment, trucks and other things a town needs. One good thing about the town is you [work and live] in one place. I think it is an ideal place to live, less crime."

Hanford: The Cold War, WPPSS and Beyond

After the war the Atomic Energy Commission replaced the Army Corps of Engineers as the Hanford government administration. General Electric replaced Dupont as the site contractor. During the Cold War, 1947-1955, five additional nuclear reactors were built to make a total of eight. Two chemical processing plants and several underground storage tanks were added to the two original reactors. Except for a facility to recover heat for the area buildings, the reactors produced no usable electric power.

Spurred by power shortages resulting from a dry winter and low snowpack followed by a summer of drought in 1972-73, Bonneville Power Administration (BPA) turned to nuclear power as an alternative to hydroelectric power. Sen. Henry Jackson defused private-power opposition to producing nuclear power at Hanford by promising the Public Utilities Districts (PUDs) half the power produced, risk-free, in exchange for participating in the nuclear power project. The public utilities formed a consortium named Washington Public Power Supply System project (WPPSS, pronounced "whoops") and agreed to work with BPA's plan. Between 1972 and 1975 commitments were made to build five new nuclear reactors at Hanford designed to produce electrical energy, and work began. When the Pacific Northwest was hit with another drought in 1975-76, worse than that of three years earlier, BPA issued such dire predictions of future power shortages that the PUDs agreed to build two additional nuclear reactors on the Olympic Peninsula.

There were problems from the beginning. By 1978 only the first two reactors were actually under construction. The entire project was behind schedule and the cost overruns were mounting. Sen. Warren Magnuson, who fully supported the WPPSS project, said optimistically, "it could well become in the years ahead, what the Columbia River system has been for the past 30 years." Magnuson wasn't the only one pro-WPPSS. The Tri-Cities welcomed the WPPSS project and were pleased with the good-paying jobs it created. The construction work pulled in workers and the area prospered.

Complications developed between the Internal Revenue Service and Bonneville Power, and BPA turned full risk for the construction costs over to WPPSS, i.e. the PUDs. From that point on the project became a total fiasco. By 1981 the original cost estimates for five plants had soared from $5 to $24 billion. The failure of the project to move forward had become public knowledge and was the focus of considerable coverage by the media. When asked why the reactors were not completed after five years of work, one Bonneville official was quoted in the newspaper as admitting, "No one anticipated how hard it would be to build those turkeys." In fact, only three new reactors were completed and, in nominal dollars, they eventually cost more than the entire Columbia River Power System — dams, transmission lines and substations. Abandoning construction of the final two reactors ended in the greatest bond default in American history. Northwest power customers experienced a six-fold increase in their power rates between 1979 and 1983 as BPA passed on to its customers BPA's share of the cost of WPPSS. In 2000 the cost of the WPPSS project had still not been paid off.

The Public is Disillusioned with Nuclear Energy

Northwesterners' interest in nuclear energy as an alternate to hydro was further diminished during this period by the serious reactor accident at Three-Mile Island, Pennsylvania. In the summer of 1979 Northwest residents were shocked to learn that the Three-Mile Island nuclear waste was slated to be hauled to Hanford for disposal in the central Washington desert. The rumor was circulated that the boxcars of nuclear waste were already on their way to Washington, and the entire state was up in arms. The story was untrue but the public was frightened. People seriously questioned the safety of producing nuclear power and the current methods of disposing of highly toxic nuclear waste, which had been proven to be deadly to the environment including plant, animal and human life. Strenuous public objection and fast work by Washington's congressional team headed off the move to use the state as a nuclear waste dumping ground.

The immediate Tri-Cities residents did not share the general antagonism felt by people throughout the Pacific Northwest. The local newspapers reflect the fact that many Tri-Cities citizens were pleased with the initial selection of Hanford as the nuclear waste dump. They were alarmed and angry when Hanford was dropped as a potential waste disposal site. All they saw was another economic downturn.

In 1986-87 forces came together that would shut down nuclear energy production at Hanford for the rest of the century. Early in 1986 the Department of Energy released 40 years of Hanford environmental records to the public. Copies were passed around and carefully read. Many people were stunned and horrified by what they learned regarding nuclear contamination of the Hanford site, the surrounding area and the Columbia River. In April a major accident occurred at the Chernobyl nuclear reactor site in the Soviet Union, with extensive injury to people and the environment. The entire incident was thoroughly reported in the American media and the public was alarmed.

Public knowledge and fear of the deadly dangers of nuclear waste were growing rapidly. Widespread concern and intense opposition among residents of the Pacific Northwest, especially those living in the Inland Northwest, was shared by some of the state's political leaders, and things moved fast. Washingtonians resoundingly voted down the dumpsite in a 1986 special state referendum. In December 1986 the multipurpose N-reactor, which had come on line in 1966 and did produce electricity, was shut down and put on "cold standby."

Hanford was still on the list of three potential sites to be used as a national high-level nuclear waste repository. In 1987 hard work by environmentalists, anti-nuclear activists and Washington's representatives in Congress got Hanford off the "dump list." By the end of the 1980s all but one reactor was shut down permanently and research at Hanford shifted to the problems of nuclear waste management and basic nuclear energy. In the 1990s the Department of Energy Hanford Atomic Reserve was the main center for research on nuclear energy and disposal of nuclear waste in the United States. The silent atomic reactor silos can be seen off to the east as one drives SR 240 out of Richland.

Part III:
The Columbia Basin Project: Kilowatts in the Wire and Water in the Ditch

Nat Washington, who grew up in Ephrata, remembers central Washington before the dams.

"We had an agricultural depression beginning in the 1920s. People started to move away. With an average rainfall of about 10 inches, little more than sagebrush grew reliably in the region. Water first from the Columbia River and later its tributaries, has changed the face of the region as much as the Ice Age floods."

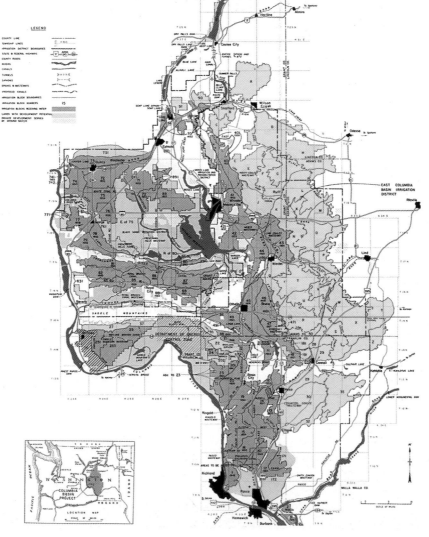

Map of Columbia Basin Project, Bureau of Reclamation
John Alwin, Between the Mountains

At the end of World War II, the Army Corps of Engineers set to work completing the Grand Coulee Dam power generation system. Designed for 18 generators, only six operated throughout the war. Between 1950 and 1980 expansion of the dam's hydroelectric power generating system, including building an additional powerhouse, brought it to its maximum capacity of 6,890 million kilowatts compared to 648,000 during the war years. Initially the question was, "what will we do with all of this cheap electricity?" Power companies energetically promoted electrical consumption among their customers, for example, the all-electric home. No one could imagine that in a few short decades the question would be transformed to "Where can we secure more electricity to meet the region's demands?" But that was still in the future.

The Eisenhower administration decided in the 1950s that future irrigation dams should not be built by the federal government, but by local initiative. Irrigation Districts were formed as a part of the local Public Utility Districts (PUD) to build and oversee management of the dams. The idea was to keep the power under local control. The arrangement allows the local PUD to set the power rates and select its customers. Under this program Chelan County built Rocky Reach Dam and bought and expanded Rock Island Dam, built in 1933. In the 1950s Grant County built Priest Rapids and Wanapum dams.

Regional Progress Orchestrated by Determined Leaders

In the 1950s and 60s the New Deal idea of the value of Grand Coulee Dam expanded from the original goals of reclamation of the Great Columbia Desert and hydro-electric power to include water transportation and recreational facilities. The selection of the Columbia Basin for the first major multipurpose river dam project in the nation after the war was no accident. Like the government's decision to build the Grand Coulee Dam in the 1930s, the Inland Northwest region was chosen as a result of the persistent efforts of a determined cadre of promoters working behind the scenes. For most of the 20th century a mix of professional and business interests bent the ear of elected officials and commercial interests alike. In the 1920s the Columbia Basin Irrigation League was formed to promote reclamation of the basin with Pend Oreille River water. In the 21st century the Columbia Basin Development League continues the behind-the-scene work lobbying in the legislature in both Olympia and "the other Washington."

From the 1950s through the 1970s the Columbia Basin Project had the consistent, enthusiastic support of senior senators Henry Jackson and Warren G. Magnusen. During their extensive tenures in Congress (nearly 40 years each), both of these senators from Washington became nationally prominent, powerful and influential with the Bureau of Reclamation and other agencies operating in the Inland Northwest. Moreover, two postwar factors came into play, a stepped-up need for electrical energy, required by the 1950s-60s

After World War II ended, wartime needs for electrical power decreased. Irrigation of the Columbia Basin with waters from Grand Coulee Dam again became an important objective. *Carlos Maldonado/EWU Chicano Education Program*

manufacturing boom and the modern electric appliance-based home, and a rapidly expanding market for food products spurred by the Baby Boom.

The Desert Blooms

On May 7, 1951, the first Columbia River water was pumped into Banks Lake with much fanfare, and on August 10, 1951, 18 years after the first shovel of dirt was turned to begin dam construction, water

Irrigation water from the Columbia River flows into Franklin County, 1948. *Franklin County Historical Society*

furrow flooding and a variety of spraying techniques, and crops replaced the sagebrush.

The Columbia Basin Project ushered in a second pioneering period in central Washington. The project was promoted to war veterans as a good chance to get started. Between 1940-1950 the population of Grant County almost doubled. But in the next decade the basin area population declined. People were discouraged with trying to eke out a livelihood on one or two of the government-defined 80-acre units. Others who had bought land in the authorized reclamation area anticipating the bumper crops irrigation would bring were broke and tired of waiting for the canals to be built to their area. Bill Preston, owner of Preston Cellars, Pasco, observed in 1999, "the size of [basin] farms has changed a lot since the 1950s when less then 100 acres was a typical farm. Now a family farm is 360 acres, plus. It has to be to justify the expensive machinery."

Gradually the canals were built and by 1977 the 1.1 million-acre basin plan was half completed. Each day nearly 54 billion gallons of water from the Columbia River were withdrawn or diverted to irrigate 5.5 million acres of land in the basin district. Project planners anticipated that between 350,000-400,000 people would live in the basin area when the project was completed. However, the basin population was only 63,700, many of whom worked in non-agriculture activities. Many towns and villages in Grant County, where most of the irrigated land is located, had been steadily declining in population since the 1920s. They were rejuvenated and the overall population grew by threefold in the second half of the 20th century. As the farms became larger in size, the actual farming population shrank. However, the urban population

flowed from Banks Lake into the main canal. Marion Higley remembers when she and her husband with their four small children took up farming in the basin in Block 15, 23 miles north of Pasco in 1961.

"We were young and it seemed to be the only chance to have our own farm. We tried peppermint and spearmint, but it got a disease, and we tried sugar beets and corn for a while too. We grow asparagus and alfalfa hay now. We sell our asparagus to Green Giant or Seneca Foods. It's canned in Dayton. We sell our hay to a man in Basin City. Our four kids have not continued with farming. My husband does not encourage them to farm — it's hard work and it holds you down. I kind of wish they were on the farm, though."

Seven years after the canal gates opened, between 50,000 and 65,000 acres of land were irrigated through steadily expanded. The greatly accelerated increase in the population in the 1990s is attributed to the diversification of the economy rather than irrigation farming per se.

Fruits of the Earth

The land watered by the Columbia Basin irrigation system ranks among the most productive in the Northwest, as well as the entire country. Grant County ranks in the top 35 counties nationally for average farm earnings and in the entire Pacific Northwest ranks second only to Yakima County. The basin has excellent growing conditions — light, rich, sandy volcanic soil, up to 210 frost-free days, abundant sunshine and warm to hot temperatures in the growing season. The application of 40 to 60 inches of water at the right times every season produces a bumper crop.

Basin crop production substantially changed from 1950 to 2000. Until late in the 20th century, potatoes, wheat and alfalfa hay were the key crops. Other crops came and went as focal point crops. For example, dry beans were the highest-valued crop in the 1950s and sugar beets in the 1960s. In the mid-1980s 56 different crops were raised, with five major crops being potatoes, wheat, alfalfa hay, feed-grain corn and sweet corn. By the mid-1980s the trend was away from small grain and hay to high-income crops such as hops, mint, carrots, asparagus, grapes, apples and cherries. By 2000 apples ranked No. 1, followed by potatoes and wheat. Cattle raising has been a major non-crop dollar producer for basin and Yakima Valley farmers. A large proportion of the cattle are feeder-lot finished before being sent to market.

■ Processing asparagus in Dayton

Expanding the Basin Project and Private Irrigation Efforts

While most of Grant County was prospering from irrigated farming, the East High district, which forms a large swath in the southeastern part of the basin area and includes much of Benton and Franklin counties, did not enjoy the benefits of irrigation water in the 1880s. More than 226,000 acres of land continued to be farmed with dry land farming techniques. However, by using fertilizers and other improved 20th-century dry farming methods the land produced acceptable yields of wheat. Only 7 percent of Franklin County farmland was irrigated and farmers kept asking when they were going to get online with irrigation.

The equipment was in place at Grand Coulee Dam to carry enough water to irrigate over 1 million acres and the Bureau of Reclamation was determined to complete the basin plan. For this section of the basin to be irrigated the East Low Canal would have to be extended to carry water south from Banks Lake. In the mid-1980s canal construction was scheduled to begin in 1990. When the plan to expand

■ Asparagus baskets hooked onto the harvester's belt, keeping his hands free to cut the spears. *Green Giant Golden Ambassadors*

■ Once displaced by corn sweeteners, sugar beets are making a comeback to Washington agriculture. *U.S. Dept of Interior, Ephrata*

the basin's irrigated acreage became known, fierce opposition broke out and the plan was scaled back to 87,000 acres. The key issues revolved around the environmental impacts, especially to fish, of drawing off the additional irrigation water from the river and the question of crop surpluses. It was known that basin farmers were having difficulty finding markets for the food they were already producing. Many asked, "Was there an actual need for expanding production?" The issue of the heavy subsidization of the irrigated farming also came to the fore.

Hydroelectric power generation at Grand Coulee Dam always paid for itself and helped subsidize basin irrigation, which has yet to pay its way. From the beginning the Columbia Basin project existed because of heavy subsidies. The electric ratepayer absorbs much of the cost of basin irrigation. Early 20th-century promoters, like Rufus Woods and Billy Clapp, always maintained that irrigation water should be virtually free to basin farmers. Based on the federal government's agreement in the 1950s that electrical power revenues

would be used to cover a portion of the irrigation costs, many inland people have maintained for decades that all reclamation costs should be covered by the government regardless of how high they go.

In the 1980s there was an attempt to transfer management of the basin irrigation system away from government and into private hands. This move was a part of President Ronald Reagan's grand national privatization program. By 1989 private ventures were providing irrigation water, mostly from the Snake River and deep wells, for about 65,000 acres in the dry eastern part of Franklin County. For a while it looked as if the private approach was working. In the late 1980s more than 200,000 acres in Benton, Franklin and Walla Walla counties were receiving irrigation water from private projects. Irrigation water was drawn from the Ice Harbor and McNary reservoirs and deep wells. An additional 68,000 acres were privately irrigated in the Yakima Valley, which is not a part of the basin project, drawing on the Yakima River and deep wells. In the 1980s there was a "green belt" just south of the basin project on both sides of SR 395. The irrigation water was drawn from 100-to-300-foot deep wells. However, in a few years the water table was noticeably dropping in the areas using deep well water for irrigation.

The private irrigation development boom ended as quickly as it had started. *Tri-City Herald* reporter Bob Woehler observed, "The costs of water, electricity to pump the water and land all have risen at a greater rate than the price a farmer gets for his crops." Moreover, the easy-to-reach and cheaper-to-develop irrigated land was available in the nearby Yakima and Columbia irrigation projects.

Vineyards Come to the Inland Northwest

Inland farmers sporadically experimented with viticulture from the 1930s to the 60s. In the late 1960s St. Michelle Winery released several wines, none of which convinced anyone that Inland Washington was wine country. In the 1970s agronomists at the Prosser Agriculture Experimental Station seriously experimented with grapes, searching for varieties that worked well in the Columbia Basin. Between 1976 and 1993 the number of wineries grew from a half dozen pioneers to 80 wineries, each producing a variety of wines. By 2000 there were 160 wineries and Washington was second only to California as the nation's top wine producer. Ninety-eight percent of Washington's wine is produced in the Inland Northwest in four federally recognized viticultural appellations (regions): Columbia Valley, including the Tri-Cities north into the Columbia Basin; Yakima Valley; Walla Walla; and Red Mountain, which lies within the Yakima Valley. Each appellation produces a distinctively different wine. Inland environmental factors create wines that are tarter and crisper, more like European wines than Californian.

Grape harvest in the Columbia Basin. Distinctive wines make Washington State second only to California as the nation's top wine producer. Wine production has grown from a half dozen producers in 1975 to 160 wineries today. *John Marshall*

By 2000 wine grapes were Inland's fourth-most-important fruit crop, behind apples, cherries and pears. Commenting on the appeals of wine Premium Wines, one of the pioneer wineries, something different. Their goal is to be can be held a long period of time without there are a couple of large wine producers, make about 60 percent of the Inland's My wife, Joan, and I have been in the wines are being made by family sell you can enjoy it by drinking it!"

production to the farmer, Bill Preston, of Preston said in 1999, "Farmers are always looking for able to control the market. Wine is a product that loss, unlike fresh produce." He observed "while Chateau Ste. Michelle and Columbia Crest, that wine, wine making is really a family business. business since the 1970s. All of the specialty enterprises. Grapes are a crop that if it doesn't

Basin farmers understand that grapes are basically a desert plant and love hot sunny weather, which makes the inland region ideal. In 1999 there were 25,000 acres of grapes being grown each season. In the beginning white wine dominated. In 1993 twice as much white wine was produced as red. As a preference for red wine has grown, wine makers have changed to reds, which accounted for 56 percent of the production in 2000. The main wine varieties produced in the region are: Grenache, Gewurztraminer, Chardonnay, Chenin Blanc, Lemberger, Merlot, Riesling, Pinot Noir, Semillon and Syrah.

The hot sunny climate of the Columbia Basin is an ideal ecosystem for growing grapes and producing high-quality wines. *Washington Wine Commission*

Forty Years of Private Irrigation Farming

Paul Hirai was in school in Yakima when World War II came, and he was sent to an internment camp with his family. After the war he eventually made his way back to the Inland Northwest. He moved to Moses Lake in 1960 and began farming land in Block 42. He left the basin project and farmed in the dry area with his own irrigation system. In 1999 he reflected back on more than 40 years of private irrigation farming.

"I wanted a lot of land and the only way to get a big acreage was to develop land that wasn't [in the basin project]. I got almost 2,000 acres in the Othello-Connell area. I grew potatoes, onions, wheat, beans, garden seeds (carrots and beans) and dry corn. We sometimes had problems with the well. The water table would keep going down. We were lucky for the most part, but we had some close calls when the pumps would only suck air. But the water always came back. We have pumped with the same equipment since 1968. The biggest changes in farming are in the equipment — it is larger and more efficient. Now one person can farm twice as much land as earlier. Everyone has gone to bigger farms. The biggest handicap is the sanctions on many potential export countries."

By the 1990s a total of 1.2 million acres of cropland in the Inland Northwest were cultivated in the irrigation projects and private developments. The Columbia Basin Project system included 300 miles of main canals and 2,000 miles of secondary canals. The Yakima Irrigation Project irrigation system had 416 miles of main canals and 1,698 miles of secondary canals. While land reclamation made it possible to grow crops in dry sagebrush country, the farms were not immune to fluctuating markets. Sugar beets are an example of an irrigation crop that has ebbed and flowed in value. Beets were a good cash crop into the mid-1970s, then the bottom fell out of the market when corn sweeteners replaced beet sugar in the soft drink industry. Twenty years later sugar beets were once again in high demand.

Part IV:
The Legacy of Harnessed Rivers

The early success of the Grand Coulee Dam project motivated the federal government to undertake a grand plan to convert multiple rivers in the Inland Region and beyond into "working rivers." Between 1934 and 1975, 14 major and approximately 100 smaller dams were built on the river system including the Columbia's great tributary rivers: Kootenai, Pend Oreille, Spokane, Okanogan, Wenatchee, Walla Walla, Yakima, Snake, Lewis, Cowlitz, John Day, Deschutes and Willamette. By the end of the 1990s the network included more than 250 smaller dams and holding basins. The once free-flowing waters of these rivers and their tributaries were impounded in reservoirs and used for hydroelectric power and irrigation agriculture. The large dams, approximately 18 miles apart, converted the rivers from free-flowing waterways into a series of pools. The Army Corps of Engineers or the regional Public Utility District (PUD) built most of the dams. The completion of this great plan represents an incredible technological achievement, probably a civil engineering wonder of the world, which has, in turn, produced incredible problems for which there is no simple solution.

The key players in the conflict over the river waters were on the scene right at the beginning in the 1930s and include: power company interests, irrigation farming interests, river transportation, fishermen — sport and commercial — Native Americans and environmentalists. Beginning with the construction of Grand Coulee and Bonneville dams, an autocratic self-perpetuating tri-part bureaucracy was put into place composed of the Bureau of Reclamation, the Army Corps of Engineers and the Bonneville Power Administration (BPA). The Corps builds the dams, BPA markets the power and moves it around the

Harnessing the Rivers of the Inland Northwest

Major River Dams

Bonneville Dam — 1933-38

Grand Coulee Dam — 1933-1941

The Dalles Dam — 1957

John Day Dam — 1958

McNary Dam - 1047 — 1953

Priest Rapids — 1959

Wanapum Dam — 1965

Rock Island Dam — 1950

Rocky Reach Dam — 1933, 1961

Wells Dam — 1950

Chief Joseph Dam — 1961

Ice Harbor Dam Snake — 1962
(units 1-3); 1976 (units 4-6)

Hells Canyon Dam — 1967

Lower Monumental Dam — 1969

Little Goose Dam — 1970

Lower Granite Dam — 1975

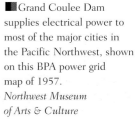
Lower Granite Dam on the Snake River — more than 100 dams have been built on the Columbia River and its tributaries.
Spokesman-Review Photo Archives

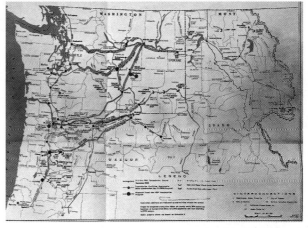
Grand Coulee Dam supplies electrical power to most of the major cities in the Pacific Northwest, shown on this BPA power grid map of 1957.
Northwest Museum of Arts & Culture

Competition over water for electrical power, recreation, fish habitat, transportation and irrigation has become more intense. Demands have increased, and droughts threaten the long-term water supply.
Northwest Museum of Arts & Culture

regional grid, and the Bureau of Reclamation administers distribution of the irrigation water. Collectively, since the 1950s these agencies have viewed their mission as squeezing every possible kilowatt and irrigated acre out of the river system.

The hydroelectric and irrigation requirements have overburdened the rivers, devastating fish, polluting waterways and creating enormous legal battles over the limited supply of water. By the 1980s low water levels were sparking a regular donnybrook with all the interests participating full tilt. Irrigation districts from Wenatchee to the Yakima Valley vied for water allocations. Fish agencies and electrical power managers debate over the size of the "water budget," a release of water in the spring that allows juvenile salmon to move over the dams en route to the Pacific. Irrigation farmers with "junior" water rights squared-off with "senior" water rights neighbors. The Native Americans and commercial and recreational fishermen fought over the few fish remaining in the rivers. Local Chamber of Commerce and tourism offices regularly petition their Congressional representatives to

assure that the reservoirs like Roosevelt Lake, behind Grand Coulee Dam, are full for important events like the annual Kettle Falls Regatta.

The problem has only intensified as the Pacific Northwest region population has rapidly grown in the 1980s and 90s. The economics are an intricate mix of hydroelectric power, irrigation, navigation, wildlife, conservation, recreation, agricultural surpluses and Native American rights. These issues are intertwined with economics and politics on the local, state, national and international levels. The harnessing of the rivers has been a major factor in shaping the course of history of the Inland Northwest in the second half of the 20th century. At century's end no viable solution had been found that met the needs of all interest groups.

"The coming of so many automobiles

and good roads have made it so easy for people to do their shopping in Spokane that many of our stores and our movie theater had to close their doors. The townspeople's sense of community has been affected by the television set and the two-income family much more than by the changes in Main Street."

Nancy Ellis, Davenport, Washington, 1999

Part I:
Hometowns in the Heartland

From the time when American settlers from the older parts of the country established their homesteads, the Inland Northwest has been a region of small communities. They are found along the highways and byways, tucked away among the wheat fields and at the numerous crossroads in the lush irrigated projects. In the early 20th century the region was a place of stable small towns where a significant number of people made their livelihoods from the land that had been settled by their forebears. Dependent upon the train for shipping their grain to market and delivery of supplies, the majority of the communities were established along the railroad tracks between 1901 and 1911. In parts of the Palouse the towns are exactly 12 miles apart — the distance between train flag stops. The people who lived in these towns had a real sense of who they were and "their place." It is ironic that the transportation mode that replaced the railroad — the automobile — has been a key factor in the diminishment of the small town as an important community and cultural center.

Chapter Three

Hometowns in
the Inland Northwest

population shifts from the countryside to the growing urban centers. The decennial census from 1940 forward verifies this trend, which continued unabated to the end of the century.

The Inland Northwest losing rural population to the cities was a part of a national trend that started in the 1920s. By 1960 people living on farms made up only 11 percent of the nation's population. In 2000 less than 2 percent of Americans lived on farms. There are unique features in the inland's population patterns as a result of the federal

Up to World War II the majority of people in the inland region continued to live on farms and in rural towns. The home-front war activities and the great irrigation projects of the second half of the century would significantly change the region and stimulate and Public Utility District dam building. Indeed, much of the expansion of the urban centers of Richland, Kennewick, Pasco, Moses Lake and Yakima is a direct response to the success and prosperity created by the irrigation projects.

When the Grand Coulee Dam, Columbia Basin Project and the numerous other dams on the Columbia and Snake rivers and their tributaries were planned and executed, there was little thought of the deep social upheaval they would cause for the region's existing communities and people. In addition to the easily recognizable repercussions, such as destroying old and founding new towns, there are untold layers of impacts, many of which were subtle but far-reaching. The complex changes brought by the conversion of vast areas of dry land to irrigated farming will probably never be fully understood. At century's end people across the Inland Northwest had to work at keeping their towns alive. Each community, its traditional institutions and the people were struggling with coming to terms with their pursuit of a timeless form of livelihood, tilling the land, and the requirements, challenges, comforts and distractions of the electronic era.

In spite of the great technical, social and cultural changes, the small rural inland community continues to exist, in some cases just surviving and in others moving forward with vitality. In year 2000 two out of five people in the Washington Inland Northwest were living in hometowns of fewer than 5,000. More than half of the towns had fewer than 1,000 residents. In fact, 38 percent had fewer than 500 residents. In the 1990s there were between 126 and 160 small communities in the region. The exact number varies depending upon whether only incorporated communities or all communities are included.

■Rural homes depended on radio for news of the outside world before the advent of television in the 1950s. *Garfield County Historical Society*

At mid-20th century, the inland rural towns were thriving as market and service centers for the farms scattered over the surrounding countryside. An array of businesses catering to the needs, comforts and dreams of the farmers and their wives lined Main Street. In the 1950s the towns prospered along with the farmers and the variety of businesses on Main Street expanded. Cultural and social life was also centered on the hometown. The children were bused into town for school; the family came in for Sunday, and often mid-week church services; and women and men made evening trips into town for social and community activities centered around their lodges and clubs.

■The Gifford Ferry still makes daily runs across the Columbia River from Inchelium to Gifford. *Rowena McIntosh*

Growing Up In Lincoln County in the 1950s

Lila Krueger shares a childhood memory of her life as a country girl growing up on a farm near Davenport.

"My family didn't have a lot of money, but we always had wholesome homegrown food, well made home-sewn clothes and plenty of love. I loved living in the country, but it was the bi-weekly trips into Davenport that we looked forward to. My dad relaxed after a week of hard work while my mom, my two sisters and I headed into town. We bought groceries, loaded up on books at the library, took care of any legal business and ran other necessary errands. But the highlight of the day was our stop at the Mitten Café.

"I loved that restaurant! It was somewhat dark inside and always seemed cool on a hot summer day. Sometimes, if there was enough money, we would get to eat lunch out. I usually ordered a hamburger and fries: a thick patty of real beef, plenty of trimmings, and a generous helping of hot, crisp french fries. Yummy!

The Mitten Café in Davenport served many a blue plate special on dishes like these.
Lincoln County Historical Society

Davenport, Washington, Main Street
Richard Dreger

"But the times when we couldn't buy lunch were also special. We had a milkshake! I would sit on the high red stool at the counter waiting impatiently while the waitress made the delicious treat. She scooped up the rich vanilla ice cream, added the chocolate syrup and blended it in the milkshake machine. It was such a thrill to have that big metal milkshake "cup" and a lovely tall glass placed in front of me. Then you got to fill your own glass. You had to pour carefully because the thick milkshake plopped out in big ripples and often ran over the sides of the glass. Three flavors were available chocolate, strawberry and vanilla. Each color looked so pretty in that fluted glass!

"We would linger over that milkshake, sipping slowly, making it last. The glass held two servings with a little left over, and we would empty that last couple of swallows into the glass, letting every last bit drip slowly out of the metal cup. Delicious!"

Main Street, Where People Meet

The 1960s and 1970s brought changes that were to substantially alter the face of the inland town's Main Street as well as the quality of community life that had been the norm for over a century. An array of factors contributed to the changes. Among the most powerful were increased focus on personal leisure activities, better roads, television, smaller family size, the two-income family and diversified home-oriented discount chain stores, e.g. Target or Wal-Mart. The influence of television increased in the 1980s with the innovation of the satellite dish, which greatly expanded the number of channels available to rural homes. New technology also affected shopping patterns. By century's end 24-hour shopping was readily available via television shopping channels, toll-free catalogs and the Internet. There is less need to drive down to Main Street, Pomeroy, Ritzville, the Tri-Cities or Spokane. With a basic computer and telephone line people living in the most remote place in the region are only a mouse click away from the World Wide Web and its thousands of other merchandise sites.

Main Street, Odessa, Lincoln County, "Now and Then" 1950 scene and 1990s scene

Odessa, a community founded by German-Russian immigrants in the 1890s, is located in southern Lincoln County in the heart of the Big Bend wheat land. In the summer of 1999 longtime residents Mildred and John Deife, Jacque Eide, and Leigh and Janice Murchie talked about their hometown, Odessa, and agreed that although Main Street was not the same place that it had been in 1950, it continued to be a thriving place with new businesses replacing the old ones. Over the 50 years only two buildings have been torn down, but new ones have been built and there are only two empty storefronts. Most people feel that Odessa's Main Street continues to meet the community's basic needs quite satisfactorily, and there is no need to drive to Spokane or Moses Lake, 45 to 75 miles away, except for special things. In the interest of showing the changes in retail shops available in their hometown the group drew up the following list.

Shop	Number in 1950	Number in 1999
Auto dealer	5	0
Bakery	1	0
Barber shop	2	1
Beauty shop	5	3
Clothing store	2	0
Drug store	2	1
Furniture store	1	0
Gas station	7	2
Grocery store	3	1
Hardware store	2	1
Jewelry store	1	0
Movie theater	1	0
Restaurant	4	2
Tavern	2	1
Total shops	**38**	**12**

Colfax Main Street in 1956
Bill Walter/Joan Hubbard

Main Street in a small town is much more than a collection of places to shop. It is a major factor in the social life of the community. Florence Stout of Odessa provides a vivid picture of Odessa's Main Street in the mid-1950s, when the population was 1,127 and the small town was still the center of community life.

"Main Street in Odessa is barely two blocks long. In the 1950s it was where everyone gathered on Saturday, because no matter where one stood he or she would eventually see everyone who had come to town.... At harvest time all of the stores stayed open on Saturday night, so the men could get the parts they needed for repairing the combine or other machinery and the women could stock up on groceries for the coming week. When these important errands were finished it was time to visit. The sidewalks would be so filled with people that you had to walk out in the street to get around the conversation groups in order to go further down the block. If a person stayed inside a shop she or he might miss seeing a friend or relative. Many important issues were discussed and decisions made at a Saturday Main Street gathering. Whether it was a school matter, church matter or a town issue, one could be sure it would be discussed many times on

Odessa's Main Street today. Russian immigrants settled here in the 1890s.
Florence Stout

Barber shops and beauty salons are still the best places in town to hear all the news of the day.
Spokesman-Review
Photo Archives

Gone are the days when a banana split at the corner soda fountain cost 35 cents.
Northwest Museum
of Arts & Culture

SPECIAL
★

Banana Split	.35
Caramel Sundae	.20
Marshmallow Sundae	.20
Butterscotch Sundae	.20
Pineapple Crush Sundae	.20
Fresh Strawberry Sundae	.20
Fresh Banana Sundae	.20
Chocolate Sundae	.20

improvements in equipment let the farmer complete the harvest in a shorter time. Not feeling so pressed for time, he can allow himself time off on the weekend. He will most likely load up the RV or pick-up truck with the boat or jet skiis, get the family and head for the reservoir. Or he might just drive the car to Spokane where he and his family can relax."

In every inland hometown there was at least one or more special gathering places where farmers and towns people alike dropped in knowing they would see friends. The Sommerville Club House in Pomeroy was such a gathering place for men from before the war. Facing Main Street, the bar was in front and the card tables and pool tables in the back. Mounted horns and the stuffed heads of game animals covered most of the wall space. Mary Lou Curren remembers that wives knew where to call if they needed to locate a husband who was late to supper. The Sommerville Club House was a well-run place and respectable enough that women and young people

the street corner. Often decisions were made [on Saturday night] before the regular meeting was held."

After reflecting back on Main Street in harvest time, Florence Stout decided to take a look at Main Street one Saturday evening in August of 1999. At this time Odessa's population was 957. She reports:

"I drove down Main Street in Odessa and it was deserted except for two cars. I saw no people. Today

often ventured in for milkshakes, which were the best in town.

Evelyn Reed, lifetime resident of Newport, Pend Oreille County, observes that her town's Main Street has evolved but not died. The streets and sidewalks have been updated, property is generally well cared for and visitors' comments are very positive. A quick comparison of Newport's Main Street in 1950 (population 1,385) and 2000 (population 1,921) reflects the town's "keeping up" with cultural trends while retaining a pleasant continuity with the past.

The anchor store on Main Street is Owen's Deli, a third-generation business that has been in the same location for about 50 years. Starting out as a basic grocery store in the 1950s, it has expanded twice, doubling its

floor space each time. Changes include a deli, latte coffee service, modern catering service kitchen, meeting space for up to 40, and an old fashioned ice cream parlor serving homemade sandwiches and a special lunch menu. Take out or eat in, Owen's Deli maintains a brisk business on Main Street. Other convenience grocery stores designed for quick pick-up needs have moved to the town's outskirts where there is room for parking lots.

In the 1970s the locally owned Dime Store closed. This is where many a child shopped long and hard struggling to get Christmas presents for everyone in the family for one or two dollars. Since the 1980s a large video store has occupied the building the Dime Store shared with a small grocery store. Small gift and hobby shops, which seem to frequently change both names and owners, occupy other storefronts that were earlier the location of jewelry stores, drug stores, barbershops and restaurants. Main Street's two hotels have been replaced with two motels. One old hotel building is now shops and apartments, and the other has been replaced by a new office building. The two general clothing stores, which sold everything from the rugged denim and canvas clothing needed by the loggers and miners to wedding dresses, have been replaced by a casual women's wear and a children's store. Out on the highway, with a big parking lot, the Ben Franklin Store sells a full line of men's clothing from sturdy workmen's clothes to leisure wear. Although there were several restaurants on Main Street, most of the eateries are located out along the highway where they can pick up the road-trade along with the locals.

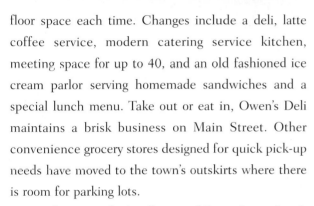

A Main Street Memory

Over in Ritzville, population 1,736, Main Street has not fared as well as some places. The story of Rummers Clothing Store, Main Street's anchor store for more than half a century, is representative of the great losses many communities experienced as market and service centers. For more than 50 years Rummers Clothing, a three-generation store, offered everything from bib overalls to prom gowns. In 1941 Al Rummer

bought a corner building occupied by a general merchandise and grocery store and converted it into a clothing and notions store. Commenting on those days, Ray Rummer, second-generation owner, says, 'There was a lot of business then. Farmers, townspeople and farm workers all depended on our store, and a few others, in the tiny downtown for their clothes... After the war came the days when salesmen from Seattle and Spokane would drop by, eager to supply Rummers with the latest goods... In its heyday, six employees were needed to handle all the customers."

From his store, Ray Rummer watched Main Street gradually change between the early 1960s through the 1980s. First Penneys closed and a smaller store, under local ownership, occupied the old Penney's building for several years. However, insufficient business forced it to close and a title company moved in. The steady decline of Main Street was dramatically played out with the slow demise of the Ritzville Trading Company. Over a period of several

years the store gradually closed, one department at a time, until there was nothing left. A small grocery store occupied the store briefly, but couldn't make a go of it. The building changed hands two more times in quick succession. The last owner moved the building off Main Street to a new location with ample parking. With sadness, not bitterness, Ray Rummer acknowledges the role played by the big discount houses in ruining his family's Main Street business. He says, "Rapid loss of business and volume occurred when the I-90 freeway was completed [1965], making it too easy to reach the Moses Lake, Tri-Cities and the Spokane markets. The final blow came in the 1990s when Wal-Mart and other large operations such as Kmart arrived in Moses Lake, only 45 minutes away."

In the 1980s, Gale Rummer, the third-generation owner, was working alone in the store determined to keep it open. But conditions on Main Street worsened as more and more Ritzville stores folded. Gale Rummer said in an interview in 1998, when her store closed for good, "It's hard to compete with chain stores, volume discounters and the entertainment value of the malls. Also people's shopping habits have changed. The more businesses that fold, the less reason people have to shop here. There's not as much to choose from. I hate to end it. It is a loss of a way of life for the family, but it's also a loss for the town." Michael Nitzche, Ritzville Chamber of Commerce executive director, sadly observed, "Rummers is a kind of landmark. But we all knew this day was going to come. When we're 41 miles from Moses Lake, 60 miles from Spokane and 90 miles from the Tri-Cities it's hard for a small town like us to fend for ourselves."

In spite of the destructive impacts on Main Street businesses, some community gathering places survive where people know they can drop in and find familiar faces and folks with the time to "shoot the breeze." There is one community landmark business on Ritzville's Main Street that was still going strong. The Circle T Restaurant is really a community social institution in its own right. The restaurant has been a gathering place for Ritzville and north central Washington travelers since 1953. A family business, it was started by friends Joe Jaeger and Joe Thomas. Joe Jaeger's daughter, Judy, and her husband, Bob Gross, were operating it in 1999. People who know about the Circle T and its outstanding food make a real effort to get to the restaurant. It is commonplace for people on the Seattle-Missoula flight with sufficient time between planes to walk the few blocks from the airport to the Circle T, to drop in for a home-cooked breakfast or lunch. People living in Ritzville or any of the surrounding communities planning a meeting with a friend or

Henry's Tavern, Republic

During the 1970s and 1980s in Republic, the center of the historic Ferry County mining district, Henry's Tavern (later renamed the Sanpoil Saloon) was a favorite gathering place for a glass or two of brew and some "jawing." Parties were also held at Henry's. Madilane Perry recalls a party from the early 1980s held for a Forest Service co-worker who was retiring early to take up subsistence farming in the district. In the interest of assisting the retiree get set up with livestock for his farm, Madilane and her boyfriend bought a "nice little weaner pig" as their gift. The piglet was brought to the party at Henry's Tavern in a foot locker. Madilane relates that "as people came into Henry's they would ask 'Whatcha got in the box?' Upon being told that it was a weaner pig each person would have to have a look at him." At about the sixth opening of the box the pig made a break for the door, and the whole tavern full of people, about two pitchers into the evening, broke up. People madly grabbed for the piglet as it dashed under their legs. People and chairs went flying every which way, as did people, who crashed into each other in a furious attempt to tackle that pig. Twenty years later people were still chuckling about the night the weaner pig got loose in Henry's Tavern.

business associate just say, "I'll meet you at the Circle T." Menu selections have remained pretty much the same for almost 50 years. A Blimp Hamburger — a grilled hamburger with mushroom sauce — potatoes and salad and toasted French bread was $2.25 in 1976 and $5.25 in 1999. In 1960 a steak dinner — extra large steak — was $3.75 and included bread, salad, potatoes and beverage; the 1999 price $13.95, sans beverage.

Caring for the Community

Well into the second half of the 20th century, community organizations played a major role in maintaining community commitment, building personal friendships, and strengthening a "sense of place" and belonging. Small-town organizations have different appeals and meet a wide range of human needs for those living in rural areas. Significant among these are the need to affiliate and have the security of belonging to a respected established group, and the desire for ritual. Organizations provide an outlet for the human desire to be of service and to support one's church, school or community as a whole. Most importantly, organizations fulfill the basic human desire for socializing and talking with others with whom one has a lot in common. In 1950 television was still in the future and people just liked to "get out and see people" as a break from rural isolation.

By the late 1900s one of the most important roles of the community organization was maintaining community spirit and identity and taking care of many of the problems and needs that are commonly handled by government agencies in large cities. Across the region churches have banded together to take care of outreach to the needy and indigent. Social service clubs perform a wide variety of care-taking functions from sponsoring annual community clean-up days to overseeing the Fourth of July parade. Garden clubs often maintain the community's parks, and women's organizations put on community dinners as well as perform numerous other services. Most organizations regularly mount fund-raising activities to pay for their projects. Formerly the church hall, as the largest room in

town, was the gathering place for communitywide events. By century's end large community gatherings were held in new public buildings including the high school, swimming pool and community/senior citizen centers. Many of these community buildings were built with funding from Federal Block Grant Program and Recreational Facilities programs of the 1960s and 1970s.

A quick look at changes in community organizations in Pomeroy since 1950 provides insight into the changing social patterns and cultural values of the inland hometowns. In the Palouse, where farms are large and towns scarce, Pomeroy, population 1,517 in 2000, is the largest and only incorporated town of the three communities in Garfield County. In the 1950s the town had about 50 adult organizations. By the end of the century only a handful remained.

In 1999 a group of lifetime Pomeroy residents who volunteered at the Garfield County Museum drew up the following historical overview of what had happened to Pomeroy's numerous lodges and clubs in half a century. In 1950 Pomeroy had 10 lodges, most of which had their own lodge hall. The Knights of Pythias and Pythian Sisters disbanded in the 1960s and their hall was sold. The Pomeroy Masonic Lodge combined with the Clarkston Lodge in the 1980s and Eastern Star disbanded. The Masonic Lodge at Clarkston, 29 miles from Pomeroy, had also diminished in size. By combining the two lodges they were able to maintain at least one lodge hall. The fine old Pomeroy Masonic Lodge Hall was occupied by a book-publishing firm in 1999. The Odd Fellows and Rebeccas have shrunk to a small group of dedicated seniors, but they have kept up their lodge hall. In contrast, the Knights of Columbus, unable to maintain their lodge hall, demolished the building in the 1970s; however, the group is still active and meets regularly in at the Catholic School. The Foresters sold their hall in the early 1970s, and for several decades it served as the Pomeroy newspaper office. By the end of the 1990s it was an automotive repair shop.

The collection of community organizations at the end of the 1990s was small by comparison to 1950.

Pomeroy Main Street
Northwest Museum of Arts & Culture

The Grange

A key rural organization from the 19th century was the Grange, founded in the 1870s to promote the interests and needs of farmers as well as meet the social needs of rural communities. For over a century it played a very important role in farming communities, with activities ranging from serving as the farmer's lobby in the state legislature to facilitating formation of farmers' co-ops. Granges built and maintained their own halls, often located at crossroads in the countryside, which served the organization as well as provided a place for other community gatherings including singing schools in the early days, as well as weddings, dances and community meetings. The Granges continue to be prominent participants in regional agricultural fairs, where they continue the tradition of presenting artistic displays of the produce of the farm. In 1950 Pomeroy had six Granges, each with its own handsome Grange Hall that the organization built and maintained. By 2000 there were only two left and they were struggling to keep going.

■ The Grange, founded in the 1870s, plays an important role in the political and social activities of rural communities.
Garfield County Historical Society

■ Kettle Falls selects a new Grouch annually as a fund-raiser for the local Chamber of Commerce. The Grouch acts as the town's ambassador for the year.
Deanne Jackson

There is the Pomeroy Chamber of Commerce and Veterans of Foreign Wars (VFW). The Community Action Council, formed in the 1980s, focuses on special community projects. There were also a handful of new organizations including the Eagles, formed in the 1970s, which has converted the bowling alley into its lodge hall. The Spinners and the Pomeroy Service Club have replaced the Jaycees and Kiwanis as the key community service organizations. There are also four garden clubs, several of which tend the Pomeroy public gardens.

Community Celebrations

Just about every community has at least one celebration or special event every year that has widespread community participation and often pulls in hundreds or thousands of outsiders. Each festival has its own focus and flavor, but they tend to be built around the community's history or the local way of life — for example, a wheat or other dominant crop, ethnic origins or a rodeo. Some community events are whimsical, such as the Kettle Falls' Annual "Town Grouch" election, when ballots are cast for 25 cents each to select the most popular "Grouch," who reigns for one year. The festivals often originated in the early days of the community and are first and foremost held for the people of the town and those living in the surrounding countryside. Visitors are welcome and real effort is often made to advertise in the nearby towns as well as throughout the region.

At Loon Lake in Stevens County, the early summer event is Loonsday, a volkswalk event where people get out and take a long walk together. It is held the first Saturday in June and as many as 1,400 people have participated. The community also holds an annual Old Schoolhouse Summer Festival with the focus on history and its crafts. Okanogan Sunny Days bring the community together, as do the annual Pioneer Days in Deer Park. In the late 1990s the Omak Stampede (rodeo), with its famous (or infamous) horse race, became the focus of great controversy as animal protectionists across the region and nation challenged the race as cruel to animals. Indeed, many years some horses were injured and occasionally one is killed

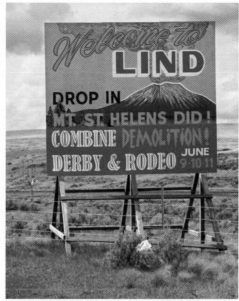

■ (Far left)
Fairfield holds a Flag Day
celebration every June.
*Spokesman-Review
Photo Archives*

■ Lind, Washington, holds a
combine demolition derby each
summer. When Mount St.
Helens erupted on May 18,
1980, Lind achieved
statewide notoriety for one
of the heaviest deposits
of volcanic ash.
Carol Kelly

by the dangerous race course. The festival in 1999 was further complicated with funding and space allocation issues between the Native Americans and the event coordinator, so the stampede was not held. In 2000 the event resumed with the race included.

In Odessa, founded by German-Russian immigrants, the primary community celebration is the September Deutschesfest, during which community organizations prepare and sell authentic German food. A highlight of the festival is a German-style Bier Garten with its lively Oom Pa & Ma Polka Band. There are also handicraft booths and entertainment ranging from humor to folk dancing. The festival is very popular and has drawn up to 20,000 out-of-town visitors.

In the Palouse the festivals begin in April when Colfax holds a history-themed Plow Day with the earth plowed with antique hand-guided and horse-powered equipment. As one farmer dryly observed, after spending some time guiding the plow, "Trying to plow a straight row with that hand-guided plow sure makes me appreciate my power equipment. Those early farmers were really skilled." In May the Uniontown German Sausage Festival is popular with the women because the men cook the food. Being held in May, when there is a pause in the wheat farm work, it brings people to Uniontown from all over the Palouse. May festivals are also observed at Oaksdale

■ "Bailadores el Sol" dance
troup from Yakima Valley has
been performing together
for nearly 25 years.
*Carlos Maldonado/EWU
Chicano Education Program*

and the town of Palouse. Ritzville puts on a Blues Fest in July and a Rodeo Fair on Labor Day weekend. Since 1972 Davenport has observed Pioneer Days the third Saturday in July. The festivals and celebrations across the region are as individual as the towns themselves.

The Churches: Spiritual Guidance and Social Service

Religion and active church membership were highly valued by those who settled in the inland region. Building the church was among the first things the people undertook when they founded their community. More often than not building the church was a great cooperative community effort with both the construction materials and labor being donated by those wanting the church. Often a lay pastor served for years before an ordained minister could be attracted to the community.

■Idaho's oldest building is The Mission of the Sacred Heart in Cataldo, built between 1848 and 1853. *Old Misson State Park*

During the second half of the 20th century, the United States experienced a substantial decline of interest in and support of organized religion. All over the country pastors reported a radical decrease in church membership and ever more gray-haired congregations. Across the inland region the trend followed the national pattern. By the 1980s, formerly well-established community churches, some dating back to the 1880s, were struggling to keep their doors open. The following discussion is based on responses to questions asked of ministers and church members about the community role and activities of their inland community churches in the early decades of the 20th century through the 1950s and the late 20th century.

Traditionally, providing spiritual guidance and a place to renew the spirit was the first objective of the church. The second objective was providing religious education and supportive activities for church members. Outreach to the greater community and support for the indigent was a third priority. By the 1980s there was noticeable change in the churches' objectives and priorities. Spiritual guidance remained in the first place; however, community outreach moved to the

second place with religious education and social activities for church members being a third priority. There are certainly exceptions to these generalizations; however, the small communities in the region reveal a common pattern of change.

As a whole, the older prosperous regions with a stable population, such as the Palouse and Walla Walla, have been less severely impacted by these trends than the districts where there has been aggressive consolidation of farm land into larger and larger farms with a parallel drop in population. Churches in the Palouse report fairly good participation by young people in church services and youth group activities. Towns located close to growing cities, like Moses Lake or Tri-Cities, are increasingly populated with city workers, including former farmers who live in the town but commute to city jobs, and are less invested in their bedroom community than those who earn their living locally.

The diminishment of the church as a community institution was most evident in the traditional old-line churches, such as the Methodist, Lutheran, Episcopalian and Congregational. Church membership dropped

The Mennonites

The Mennonites trace their roots to the Anabaptist (adult baptism) branch of the 16th-century Protestant Reformation. They are pacifists and declare themselves conscientious objectors when asked to fight in wars. They are also of Germanic origin and in the early 20th century maintained the German language. In the 1990s there were 23 Mennonite congregations in Washington, five of which were in the Inland Northwest in Ephrata, Ritzville, Spokane, Newport and Warden.

The Menno Church near Ritzville is the oldest congregation in the region. In 1899 the country church was built among the members' fields, 20 miles from Ritzville, by a group of Volga Germans (Russian Germans) who came from South Dakota by way of Oregon. After more than a century most of the members of the Menno congregation are related, which is the strongest force in holding the church together. It has about 140 members, 60 of which regularly attend Sunday services. Many people maintain their membership, although they live outside of the inland region, e.g. Seattle or Portland. The church always had a very strong commitment to service, especially overseas. The congregation distinguished itself for dynamic leadership in supporting Mennonite congregations across the Northwest, many of which are smaller. The Menno Church maintains Camp Kamrak in Leavenworth for youth and adult conferences, retreats and summer school. An important annual event is the autumn Mennonite Country Auction and Relief Sale, which draws thousands of people from across the Northwest, church members and the public. It is not unusual for up to $100,000 to be raised. The money is used to support overseas church work.

The Newport Spring Valley Mennonite congregation was formed by a group that moved to eastern Washington around 1924 upon invitation by the Great Northern Railroad. In 1999 the congregation of the Mennonite Church of Newport, many of whom are descendents of the original group, was the largest it had ever been, 75 in all. "People from the Back-to-the-Land Movement were making inroads into the Newport Mennonite community," said Agnes Goertzen, whose grandfather was a leader in the original group. "People are attracted [to the church] by the fellowship." Goertzen emphasizes that "It is our hope that what we do in life and in our hearts, and how we live our lives will testify to our beliefs. We really do believe that we need to live our beliefs and Christ's teachings in how we conduct our everyday business." Her group is strict in adhering to traditional beliefs, but externally live as their mainstream neighbors with no special clothing or other lifestyle customs. They have never formed colonies in the Northwest. The church does not maintain its own schools. While out-marriage was a serious break from the Mennonite group in the early days, by the 1980s it was accepted and occurred more frequently than previously. Evelyn Reed expresses the feelings of many Newport residents toward their Mennonite neighbors when she says, "I have gone to school with them, known them and respected them. They are very much a part of our community."

radically and the remaining members are generally older people. This has been less true for the Catholic churches throughout the inland region because most of the churches recognize they are rapidly becoming churches of senior citizens, they are working very hard to understand what young people and young families want and need from the church. They are working with new programs designed to meet those needs. One thing is clear: people have less time available and the full schedule of church activities that characterized these churches earlier in the century has almost disappeared. An example of this is the tradition of

Wednesday night being "church night" with services, Bible Study and social activities. The new fundamentalist churches and Church of Jesus Christ of Latter-day Saints are the most successful in carrying on church activities throughout the week with good turn-outs.

A significant change in the churches has been the gradual replacement of the traditional male pastors by women. Through the 1970s in most small towns the minister was always a man, but that all changed in the 1980s and 90s. As the hometown church pastors retired they were replaced with well-trained and dedicated women ministers who were happy to take a rural pastorate. After some initial resistance from more conservative church members, church members report that the women pastors have come to be not only accepted but highly esteemed and loved for their dedication to the hometown church and conscientious ministering to the needs of the people and their community.

The newer churches tend to be fundamentalist and have a younger membership. For example, Ritzville has had no churches close in recent decades. However, in addition to the seven old-line churches established well before 1950, there are seven fundamentalist churches, all established between 1960 and 2000. Moreover, there are the Mormons, Mennonites and Hutterites, making a total of 17 churches. Newport has had a similar experience with the traditional old-line churches mostly surviving with ever-dwindling membership. In the last two decades the seven new churches that have opened their doors in Newport are basically fundamentalist in belief and are attracting younger people. There is also a new Church of Jesus Christ of Latter-day Saints that is growing fast.

Marty Montovani, president of the Davenport Ministerial Alliance, observed in 1999, "Churches certainly do not have the 'social power' they once wielded. Today the churches are responding to the changing social conditions found in the community and the world." One such change reported by virtually every community is the cooperative spirit among the churches that emerged in the latter decades of the 20th century. Church spokespeople describe this as an ecumenical interfaith cooperation approach to everything from use of church buildings, outreach to the needy, and religious education and social activities. Many openly admit that cooperating and working together has been a practical survival strategy for small churches in small towns that seem to be getting smaller decade by decade. Typically the ministerial alliance group meets monthly, or more often when there is a special problem or project. They discuss common and individual problems and work together, pooling their resources to come up with solutions. In some communities the ministers take turns writing a spiritual values and church activities-oriented column that is a regular feature in the weekly community newspaper.

A quick look at some of the ways that the interfaith alliances are working across the region shows how positive and creative the religious leaders and their congregations are in their determination to keep their churches going. For example, in Pomeroy, the Methodist, Episcopal and Catholic churches jointly sponsor an annual Vacation Bible School which has a large number of children from all three faiths participating. In numerous communities it is commonplace for old-line and fundamentalist churches to participate in occasional worship services together. The newer, larger Nazarene and Christian churches conduct their own bible schools.

Using one another's church buildings is not uncommon. For example, whenever there is a large Episcopalian wedding or funeral in Pomeroy it is held in the Catholic Church since it is much larger than the small 1883 Episcopal church building. Another interesting example of this kind of cooperation is in Davenport, when the Christian Church had to close its doors because of dwindling membership in the 1980s; the remaining members joined the Presbyterian Church, which was still stable. However, funerals for former members of the Christian Church were often held in the old Christian Church building, which was standing unused. On such occasions women from the Presbyterian Church hurriedly cleaned, dusted and polished the pews of the closed church so that is was presentable for the last rites service.

Rural Health Care in Eastern Washington

Having to travel long distances for hospital-based health care has always been a serious problem for small communities throughout the Inland Northwest. After the war Ritzville built and maintained its own hospital, Ritzville Memorial, which served eastern Adams County. In the late 1980s the hospital faced closure. Medicare reform, advances in technology and physician shortages, as well as staff turnover conspired to threaten the health care system in this dry land farming area. Deeply in debt and with little market share the hospital appeared doomed. The closure of the Ritzville Hospital would make the closest hospital 50 miles away or more for many communities.

Once again the cooperation of the people came to the fore. Those living in the rural communities of east Adams County banded together to form the East Adams County Healthcare Foundation, which became instrumental in recruiting physicians, promoting special tax levies and raising much-needed capital for the hospital. With the foundation's leadership, the communities of Ritzville, Lind, Washtucna and Benge were able to save and expand their much-needed health care system. Now the East Adams County Rural Hospital (formerly Ritzville Memorial) and associated clinics located in various towns serve East Adams County residents by providing acute care, long-term care, ambulance, clinic emergency and visiting specialist services. The hospital is financially sound and capable of adding services to meet the needs of area residents.

Part II:
The Hometown School: Consolidation and Community Identity

In the 20th century Inland Northwest hometown schools have, in a sense, come nearly full circle from their beginnings in the 19th century when there were many children, but a lack of nearby schools. At the end of the 20th century some small towns had schools but lacked sufficient students, especially on the secondary level, to keep the schools open. Communities across the region are dealing with the situation in a variety of ways.

Consolidation of the original rural one-room grade schools (grades 1-8) took place in the Inland Northwest in the 1930s and 1940s. The consolidation of the high schools began in the 1950s and continued up to the end of the century. Because each school constituted a school district under the original rules, consolidation of the schools involved drastically reducing the number of school districts. For example, Lincoln County's 150 school districts were reduced to eight. In the 1960s the Edwall schools consolidated with Reardan (population 474, 1960). In 1965 Long Lake and Little Falls schools (14 miles apart), which had consolidated earlier, again consolidated, this time with the Reardan School. Lacking enough students to make up a ball team, Harrington and Sprague High Schools, 22 miles apart, and each with a population of around 450, combined their sports teams in 1990 so they could participate in the high school game circuit.

Often consolidation was not accomplished in one action but dragged on for many years. The consolidation process was often complex with numerous districts consolidating at different times, school locations changing and new schools being built. These changes often required the school — students, teachers and administrators — to move to temporary quarters. Such was the case in the consolidation of schools in the communities in the Grand Coulee Dam construction area. Joyce Justice was a high school student at Mason City High School at the end of the dam project. Since her school was slated to be demolished, the students were transferred to nearby Coulee City High School.

STEVE LESLIE
PRESIDENT — ASB PRESIDENT

MARY ELLEN LESLIE
SECRETARY — ASB SECRETARY
SALUTATORIAN

GAROLD COCKLE
TREASURER — ASB TREASURER
VALEDICTORIAN

RICHARD COCKLE
VICE PRESIDENT

She remembers, "It was upsetting to be moved to a different school and the school was very poor."

Jim Green, retired teacher from Lake Roosevelt High School, lived through the entire process in the Grand Coulee Dam area:

"Consolidation [in Grant County] came... after the war ended. They pulled the high school in Coulee Dam to replace the one in Mason City. At the same time they built a new school two miles away. In 1973 they finally combined the schools and named the new school Lake Roosevelt High School. It made us a much more unified community because the kids were merged together and unified more than when they were separated. Some didn't like it and a half dozen teachers resigned from the Lake Roosevelt High School."

As the baby boomers finished school some of the towns found that in the late 1960s their school buildings were too large. Buildings constructed in the late 1940s and early 1950s were built to accommodate not only the full classrooms of that era but anticipated increases in the student body based on past growth. As Nancy Burke of Ritzville observed in 1999, "The future student size calculations were made before people began making so many modern choices accompanied by the [family planning] advantage of 'the pill.'" As couples elected to have two or three children rather than the four to six typical of their parents' generation, the new schools built after 1970 were smaller.

Ritzville, (population 1,736) like most small communities, dreaded the expense and disruption that building new schools involves. In the 1970s school districts all over Washington were under pressure to bring their schools into line with the new building and education standards. Substantial modification of the administration and teaching staff was also necessary to comply with the ever-broadening state-mandated public school services and programs.

The first new school built was for the elementary and intermediate levels. During the remodeling year the Ritzville School District rented the Ritzville Community Center, conveniently located adjacent to school property. It became the kindergarten classroom. The Community Center's cement floor concerned many parents, who feared it would be too cold for young children. The parents soon learned that there were no funds for improving the situation. Nancy Burke remembers that the parents got together and worked out a solution. "Families donated carpeting that they salvaged from home redecorating projects to cover the concrete floor. Since no two carpets were alike it created a great patchwork floor covering. This turned out to be a useful tool in that specific areas of play and learning were defined by the color of the carpet — building blocks on brown, reading circle on green, desks on blue, etc. In the beginning there was concern about isolation from the rest of the school, but as with most things it turned out fine."

After the new school for the lower-level grades was opened, the high school closed and the faculty and student body moved into the two buildings just vacated by the elementary and intermediate classes. Space was at a premium that year and all classes shared a single library and music room and other resources.

Most Inland Northwest communities were greatly divided on the issue of consolidation before and while the consolidation process was going on. After the transition disruption was over and things settled down, attitudes changed and the consolidation was generally seen as positive. Often how the consolidation was viewed broke down along generational lines with the older members of the community feeling the greatest loss from consolidation. Emmalyn Gerhauser of Fairfield, Spokane County, expresses how they felt.

"For the older folks it was a bigger blow than for the younger ones because young people transfer loyalties quicker. Some towns wanted to hold onto the school because it draws everyone together. You attend events at the school, know more about education — there were fewer students, parents were more cohesive. There are too many schools consolidated now to say anything bad, but if we could have just held onto that school.... Many people age 60 and older wish that consolidation had never happened because schools were what brought people together when the area was settled. The school and church were the first things erected, often in the same building."

The Home Team:
The Heartbeat of the Community

When small-town people are asked what brings their town together more than anything else, the almost uniform answer is, "the high school team." This is immediately followed by an energetic spiel on the best team in recent years, a memorable coach that kept the school at the top or a lament over what is keeping the hometown team from excelling as it should.

Everyone is in the stands when the hometown team is playing, from grandparents right down to newborn babies carried by their parents, who are not going to miss the game. Besides, it is a good chance to show off the baby. Getting together in the stands at the game is about more than just watching the kids play. Many people attend who do not have a relative playing on the team or in the band, but they know who the players are and the game is a grand social occasion to catch up

Children board the school bus for the long commute to St. Mary's Mission School, Omak, 1959. *Northwest Museum of Arts & Culture*

Members of the 1952 Wilbur Yell Club show their school spirit. *Big Bend Historical Society*

Marching bands are often at the heart of high school athletic events. *East Benton County Historical Society*

with neighbors, old friends and acquaintances on the home team's side as well as the opponent's side — after all it's just the next town up the road. Julie Galbreath of Ritzville puts it simply, "The ball teams bring pride to our community and the individual families."

While small-town high schools may have some disadvantages over their big-city counterparts, there are real advantages when it comes to extracurricular activities. Mildred Deife of Odessa (population 957) tells how the "young people in the small towns get a chance to do just about everything — whether they want to or not."

"The kids in school participate in everything. They do all the plays and several school sports. They get to do it because there just aren't enough kids to do it. In the small school you are an outcast if you don't play sports. There is so much pressure to play at least one sport. When the school is small, it doesn't make a difference if you have skill. If you are tall, you play basketball. One basketball game with Reardan, a player fouled out and there weren't any other players to take his place. So, they had to grab a boy from the stands to fill in."

LaDona Madison, who attended Pasco High School, remembers, "Football had enormous support in my town. People would walk across the train bridge to play the games with each other and all the stores downtown would close so that everyone could go to the game. Our biggest game every year was on November 11, Veteran's Day. On this day we played our biggest rival: Kennewick High School!"

John Evans, who played on the State Champion Prosser High School football team in the 1990s, vividly recalls the excitement of the hometown team winning "big time" when the team from a town of 5,000 beat the big Seattle school team.

"Football was the biggest sport for seven or eight years (late 1980s through 90s). In the early 90s we won three or four State Championships in a row. In 92 and 93 I played in the Championship games, which we won. In 92 we beat O'Day, our big rival from Seattle. They are a big, private, all-boys school. Playing them caused a huge uproar because of their size and because they recruited boys from all the Seattle Jr. Highs.

"Everyone was really excited at the football games, but we had a suspicion it was unhealthy. I remember my senior year (1994-95) at the playoff game versus West Valley, our big rival from Yakima. It was 4th and 1, and the coach called punt because we had too far to go. The star player's father got mad and came onto the field yelling at the coach. The parents were pretty intense about football. I guess it is because they had their normal work that they did everyday, and football is their extra curricular activity. They throw themselves into the games. Parents push their kids, even when they are young, so that they will be good football players in high school. Then, once they get into high school, they push them even harder."

A big part of hometown sports is the fun of the traditional rivalries and rituals that have developed over the years. Often no one can remember what started the ritual, but it is faithfully carried on generation after generation. Al Kamp fondly remembers the traditional rivalry between Omak and Okanogan High Schools.

"The rivalry between Omak and Okanogan had been around for a long time, since before the thirties, I would say. You never know who is going to win, and a team's record doesn't mean a thing. One team can be riding high where they are undefeated and the other

REARDAN HIGH SCHOOL

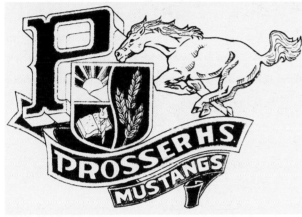

will come in with a low record like 2-5 and they will win. It just gets the kids fired up.

"After the game, there is a tradition where the principal of the losing school takes the principal of the winning school the length of the field in a wheelchair. All the kids from the winning school gather around the wheelchair and cheer the whole way. Then, there is the trophy that they exchange back and forth, depending on who wins that year."

Part III:
Room for Everyone — Alternative Lifestyles Inland

In 20th-century American history the turbulent 1960s and 1970s will be remembered as the time of intense political, social and cultural protest. A number of people felt it was too hard to live within the mainstream and follow their convictions. Thus, like many idealists in American history they decided to withdraw from society and build an alternative life. Prominent among those choosing to withdraw from mainstream

were the followers of the Back-to-the-Land movement (a.k.a. Landers). Many believe that the Back-to-the-Land movement was one of the most forceful and successful of the groups embracing an alternative lifestyle based on philosophical outlook because of its longevity and noticeable influence on mainstream thinking. Landers formed communities across rural America, including in the remote communities of Okanogan, Ferry and Stevens counties in Washington and in northern Idaho counties.

In approximately the same period as the Landers were establishing themselves in the inland region, the Hutterians came to Inland Washington to establish their own type of idealistic community. Unlike the Landers, who represented the rebirth of an old idea — the best life is based on living in close harmony with nature — the Hutterians were followers of religious beliefs reaching back to the 16th century. There are other groups that have moved into the inland region to establish alternative lifestyles away from the mainstream; however, they will not be discussed here. A brief look at these two groups pursuing alternative lifestyles reflects the tolerant attitude of many inland residents toward others whose philosophy and behavior is not anti-social or harmful to the common interest.

Back-to-the-Land Movement

By the 1950s Americans had been steadily moving off farms and into the city for over 30 years. This pattern of steady decline in farm population broke for about 10 years between 1975 and 85. The reason for this was a revival of interest in nature and the agrarian lifestyle. The romantic image of the wholesome natural life of the farmer caught the national imagination. For most people their attraction to farming was more social and lifestyle than economic. For some people this interest was expressed simply as having a few acres, a "hobby farm," where they could pursue a vaguely rural lifestyle in their off hours while they made their living with an urban job. Others interested in making a more substantial commitment aligned themselves with the Back-to-the-Land Movement.

In their quest to forge an alternative lifestyle that was healthy, wholesome and close to nature, the Back-to-the-Landers retreated from mainstream America. To build their own society based on subsistence farming and self-sufficiency, they sought inexpensive land in remote areas that they could afford and where they would be left alone. The top tier of counties in north-eastern Washington, Okanogan, Ferry and Stevens, met their criteria.

Notices of the availability of affordable land in eastern Washington began to appear in the *Whole Earth Catalogue, Mother Earth News* and other counter-culture publications of the time. Idealistic young people from all over America began making their way to the Inland Northwest to establish a better, simpler, healthier way of life.

Jennifer Rosse remembers those early days:

"We were all hippies, back-to-the-land people. I was disillusioned and moved to the country. Everything was really cheap — $300 an acre [for land]. People came for years after we came in 1973.... I wanted to be healthy and I am athletic. So many chemicals are added to our food and people are getting sick. Biggest benefits of taking up the 'hippie' lifestyle — physical health and mental health. No traffic, no stress, you [can save] money because of the lack of expensive entertainment."

The most typical approach to acquiring land was a group of people who bought small 20-acre parcels in the same general area. Mostly they bought their parcels from some fast-moving real estate entrepreneur who had bought a tract from a large ranch and subdivided without telling the locals what he was up to. Not everyone was happy when they realized that the buyers were "a bunch of hippies."

Madilane Perry recalls that the commonplace attitudes of locals in the Republic area back in the 1970s was generally not very favorable toward the Landers. They were perceived as "dirty, drug users and a threat to the established order of things." Of course, Perry notes, "in some cases some or all of these things were true, in others none of them applied." As people got over their anxieties and prejudice toward the Landers and became comfortable with them as a part of the community they replaced "hippie" with "Hill People" because they lived back in the hills.

Joseph Barreca, a Lander who settled in the Republic area, describes how it was in the early days.

"Having deliberately settled on remote land, we didn't establish many community places. There were a good number of 'communes.' This term can cover anything from very structured and organized [group] ventures to lands purchased as undivided interests in some large parcel. The title sheets to these now read like a Peyton Place of divorces, re-marriages, exchanges and defaults."

The Back-to-the-Land lifestyle was based on a communal approach to farming and daily life, nourishing themselves with wholesome, healthy food and raising their children in a healthy environment. Over the past 40 years things changed — some left, others gradually became more mainstream in their way of living. Eventually there were marriages between Landers and locals and more between their children and the locals. By century's end the Landers were somewhat integrated into the larger community and served on school and community committees and occasionally appeared on the ballot in local elections.

An important part of the 1960s counter-culture philosophy was returning to "natural foods" — i.e. unprocessed food that had been raised without pesticides, hormones or other chemicals — and Landers established food co-ops. The Landers who settled in the Colville area started their co-op in the late 1960s with just a group getting together and ordering in bulk quantities — 50-pound bags of whole-wheat organic flour, dry beans, rice and other staples. Since many people were vegetarians there was an emphasis on high-protein beans and peas, brown rice, bulk cheese and lentils.

So many people asked for the organic whole foods that they opened a store, the North County People's Co-op. The group had very little money to invest, but they found an old building behind an optometrist's office next to the Goodwill Store in Colville. Everyone worked together and for years ran the co-op successfully from that location, which had a place outside the building for the children to play. Later the co-op was moved to an old church building.

In 1999 the North County People's Co-op was in a crisis. Laurie Quinn, who has been actively involved with the North County People's Co-op from the beginning, recalls:

"We almost went out of business in the spring of 1999. We called a membership meeting and voted whether or not to close. The overwhelming vote was to

stay open and our members donated $9,000 to pay the bills to keep us open. People came out of the woodwork to save the Co-op. Now we have a manager who is helping us with marketing, increasing sales. There is a lot more competition now. There are lots more health food stores now. The Co-op is so much a part of the community closing it would be a horrible loss. We have good lunches; we have a real regular group of people who meet here."

The Natural Food Co-op evolved from "the hippie store" into a well-established and respected place on Main Street. Jennifer Rosse, who has been active with the Co-op from the beginning and was one of the managers in 1999, comments with a laugh, "It used to be, 'Oh those dirty hippies!' But when people were introduced to natural foods through mainstreaming — loggers, ranchers, senior citizens — a little bit of

everything started coming in." Rosse says that it has been easier and easier to find volunteers. There is a "hard core" of about 400 members. At lunchtime people crowd into the Co-op to enjoy the day's healthy and tasty luncheon special. Rosse observes "a lot of people come and eat here who I wouldn't expect to see in a Co-op. I guess we are seen as a 'good place,' which we are!"

By the late 1990s the Co-op building badly needed sprucing up and there wasn't enough money to do the job. Co-op members and non-member customers worked together putting on a community dinner and auction and raised $3,000 in one evening. Materials were bought with the money and volunteers built shelves, painted and tiled the floor. Rosse is proud when she says, "People feel like it's their store."

The food co-ops serve as community centers with public bulletin boards and regularly published newsletters. Joseph Barreca of Kettle Falls observed in 1999, "the one kind of community place that still exists for us [original Landers] in Okanogan, Ferry and Stevens counties is the local food co-op. These are the places where we have worked together to promote organic foods and lifestyle, practiced politics, learned alternative medicine and herbs [at the Co-op] and our kids grew up knowing other kids they could relate to."

After about 40 years living in the upper tier of counties the Landers have generally assimilated. The locals like to say, "The weak ones froze out." The communal life is a thing of the past and most Landers live in conventional nuclear families. There are still some distinctions in dress and lifestyle. Many have "dropped back in," gone off to college and returned to the community with credentials that enabled them to get qualified jobs in their adopted hometown. Long-term Colville resident Tom Dodson observed that, "Many of the [hippies] have stayed on and have become part of the mainstream of the communities in the county." After living alongside the Back-to-the-Landers for decades many local people agreed with Madilane Perry's opinion that the Landers have "given Ferry County an influx of creativity and broadened world view that it badly needed... In addition, there seems to be a flow of 'hippie' ideas into the community. This is particularly [noticeable] in the areas of nutrition, medical and health practices, and desire for self-sufficiency."

The Hutterian Colonies

Beginning in the 1950s the Hutterian Brethren have made their homes in the Washington Inland Northwest, where they live as a religious minority apart from the surrounding community, yet participating in various ways. They have settled in Spokane, Pend Orielle, Lincoln, Grant and Adams counties. They are of Germanic origin and some groups maintain German as a second language.

In order to appreciate the colonizing activities of the Hutterian Brethren it is useful to understand the history and beliefs of this old religion. The Hutterite religion emerged in Austria and Czechoslovakia in 1528 during the 16th-century Protestant Reformation. Like the related Old Order Amish and Mennonites, in the 470 years since their founding, Hutterians have been frequently persecuted for their beliefs, which include refusing to belong to a state church, rejection of infant baptism and pacifism. The men declare themselves conscientious objectors when called up to fight in wars. Communal ownership of property, pursuit of a colony lifestyle and isolation from the mainstream has set them apart from their neighbors.

The agrarian colony, or Bruderhof, is the key to Hutterite life and culture. Once a colony's population reaches 110 it must divide into two. The Bruderhof has a two-fold role, first providing a safe refuge from the outside world, which tradition defines as filled with temptation and sin, and functioning as an economic unit that supports the colony. A Hutterian woman or man must live within the colony to maintain God's order and receive eternal life. It is not possible to be a Hutterian in good standing and live outside of a Bruderhof. With a birthrate up to four times the national average, Hutterian colonies quickly reach the prescribed maximum 110 souls and the process of establishing a new daughter colony begins again.

Between 1955 and 1999 a number of Hutterian colonies were established. In 1999 the following colonies were thriving in the Inland Northwest: Grant County at Marlin, north of Ruff; Warden, near the old town of Warden; Stahl and Schoonover; Adams County near Lind; Odessa; Ritzville; and Lincoln County near Lamona and Reardan.

When a handful of Hutterians bought land near the town of Lind in the early 1960s the local residents took a wait-and-see attitude toward their new neighbors. Irma Gfeller of Lind recalls that the local people were interested in their communal way of life. In the following years the Hutterians acquired thousands of acres of dry land and irrigated farmland. Gfeller comments:

"They are excellent farmers. They now farm a vast number of acres in the county and have the ready cash to purchase land whenever it comes up for sale. There is some animosity from locals who see them as 'land grabbers'... One of the perceptions of them is that they own too much land and squeeze out the smaller farmers. [Because of their communal approach] they are very powerful. [Working together] they can get the best price on equipment, fertilizers and pesticide sprays. These options are not available to the farmer working alone."

Throughout the 40 years since the founding of the first Bruderhofs near Lind, the Hutterians have maintained a separation from the local community, although they are cordial to all and make personal friends with non-Hutterian neighbors. The children attended the Lind public school until they established their own elementary and secondary schools. They have their own church and cemetery, but use the community doctors, dentists and hospital. Irma Gfeller notes that, "They tend to keep to themselves and only seem to venture out for parades and special community events. They seldom shop at the small local stores, preferring to buy in bulk at large discount and department stores."

In the Odessa area there are four Bruderhofs. Two of the colonies send their children to the public schools and two maintain their own schools. The Hutterians often speak German among themselves but are bilingual and use English in the greater society. The Bruderhofs near Odessa have thrived and share German ancestry in common with their neighbors, many of whom are descendents of Russian Germans.

The Hutterians, men and women, use modern technology in their work; they have computers and cell phones. There is a Hutterite Web site that helps the Inland Northwest Hutterite colonies share information and stay in close touch. All members of the colony dress alike for church and social occasions. Sometimes the men wear cowboy boots and hats to church. They wear these clothes for everyday. The women live very frugally. The women wear dark dresses and scarves cover their hair. Young girls wear caps to cover their hair.

Like many others in her community of Lind, Carol Kelly has good friends who are Hutterians. She finds them to be very warm, friendly people. She and her husband have been invited to many social events including weddings and funerals. She says, "they are great gardeners and we love it in the summer when they share all of their fresh vegetables with us. They are good neighbors and we are glad to have them close by."

No one would have predicted in 1900 that the arid Washington Inland Northwest, with the Great Columbia Desert at its center, would become a water-lover's Mecca by the end of the century with hundreds of lakes to choose from. Indeed, by the 1980s most people living in the region were one hour or less away from a lake. Many of these lakes, of course, are human made, the reservoirs of the numerous dams constructed after 1934.

Use of the dam reservoirs as recreational lakes was not a part of the original Army Corps of Engineers master plan developed in the 1930s. In the beginning the federal dams were geared toward producing hydroelectric power, irrigation and water transportation. Recreational, social, cultural and environmental issues were not considered. However, after the war many things changed including the leisure and recreational activities of Americans. Reflecting an understanding of the recreational potential of the

Chapter Four

Recreation and Leisure in the Inland Northwest

reservoirs, in 1946 Lake Roosevelt, extending 150 miles from the dam itself to beyond Kettle Falls, was designated the Coulee Dam National Recreation Area. In 1966 it was renamed the Lake Roosevelt National Recreation Area.

Jim Pope, who managed the recreation program for the Chelan County Public Utility District in Wenatchee for many years, has vivid memories of how folks spent their leisure time earlier in the century. Pope said in 1999:

"Family outings where I grew up in Latah County, Idaho, in the 1950s were limited to local places because of transportation limitations and lack of extra money. We didn't have the good cars and roads we have now. Our recreation in those days was simple, close by and inexpensive — swimming in the river or creek, bird watching, playing baseball in a field or going to a neighbor's house for a potluck supper. A lot less money was spent on recreation. The prolonged peace since World War II has provided the prosperity to develop the recreational expectations we have today."

Extra time and extra money were two key factors that radically changed American's ideas about leisure

and recreation. In the boom years after the war, pay rates were high. The five-day, 40-hour work week became the national standard and a significantly larger proportion of employers gave their workers a paid vacation. With a two-day weekend and a paid vacation, many people had leisure time. Moreover, postwar prosperity made people feel that they could spend money on recreation with a clear conscience for the first time in their lives.

Improvements in the roads and automobiles were also significant factors in changes in leisure and recreation-time activities. In the Inland Northwest, as across the nation, the decades following the war were a time of major road construction. Part of the federal interstate highway system, I-90 was completed across inland Washington and Idaho in the mid-1960s. New state and county roads were built or improved for all-season travel from the 1960s into the 1990s. Finally, automobiles were better built and more reliable. There was a definite evolution of the automobile as a recreational vehicle between 1950 to 2000. At mid-century most people traveled in the family sedan. In the 1970s the recreational vehicle (RV) made its debut and rapidly became common-place. The typical RV was a pickup truck or van that was used principally for recreation rather than work. By the 1990s one out of three vehicles purchased was in the sport utility vehicle (SUV) category, thus testifying to the importance of the automobile in people's recreational activities.

Official recognition of the growing recreational interests and needs of Americans was verified in the early 1960s Outdoor Recreation Report, commissioned by Congress under Washington Sen. Henry "Scoop" Jackson's sponsorship. The study found that Americans' social and recreational patterns were changing and boating was fast becoming a popular activity as more people could afford boats and had the leisure time to use them. In the mid-1960s the Bureau of Outdoor Recreation was created to administer federal funds supporting development of recreational facilities across

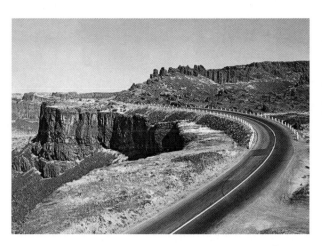

■US Highway 10 climbed through Grant County from the Columbia River to Quincy Flats before the road became Interstate 90. *Northwest Museum of Arts & Culture*

America. By the late 1960s dam construction master plans included recreational facilities such as boat launches, docks and shoreside parks. Sen. Jackson's lead in this matter was not accidental. He had been a strong advocate for the big Inland Northwest water resources projects from his first years in Congress including the Columbia Basin Project and the massive working rivers dam construction plan.

■Lewis and Clark Trail along Highway 12

Sparkling Water

The natural lake district of the western side of the region is in the lower Grand Coulee area. Most of the lakes are the result of geologic features created by water in earlier epochs. A unique example of this is a chain of small and large lakes that are, in fact, plunge pool basins formed by a tremendous waterfall on the Columbia River slowly receding upstream. The chain of lakes drain south into one another and finally into Soap Lake, which, lacking an outlet, is high in both minerals and salts, which makes the water feel soapy and form masses of foam-like soap suds on windy days. Because most of the lakes accumulate rain water and lack outlets, the water is not refreshing and pleasant but bitter and soapy. There are about 35 natural lakes in the Columbia Basin district. In the Channeled Scablands numerous hollows and basins were scoured into the volcanic basalt by the fierce Ice Age Floods that appear today as ponds and small lakes in low places. Again, lacking

outlets, these lakes tend to be brackish. However, the Scablands are scenic and a favorite haunt of hikers and wildlife watchers.

The dams were built sufficiently close to one another in many sections on the Columbia, as well as the Snake and their tributaries, that the rivers are reduced to essentially a series of great lake-reservoirs with short sections of relatively slow-flowing water linking them. Some of the reservoirs affected the natural lakes by raising the underground water table. For example, Potholes Reservoir, created by the O'Sullivan Dam south of Moses Lake, has raised the level of Moses Lake, a natural body of water, and flooded a tract of sand dunes.

The Columbia Basin Project transformed the former Great Columbia Desert into a vast water recreation area beginning at the Canadian border on the north, sweeping south to the Columbia River, a total of 400,000 acres of water surface available for recreation use. The sunny, dry summer days with temperatures ranging from mid-70s to 100 degrees Fahrenheit and evenings of 50 to 60 degrees are a magnet for people

from the cool, wet side of the Cascades. Every weekend RVs towing boats and campers pour over Snoqualmie, Blewett and Stevens passes and down into the basin heading for Grand Coulee Country. In the late 1990s over 3 million people visited the Columbia Basin every year for recreational purposes.

The centerpiece of water recreation within the Columbia Basin Project is the Roosevelt National Recreation Area, which is immensely popular with boaters, water skiers and fishermen. The visitors pull into one of the numerous modern campgrounds, many with hook-ups for campers and motor homes. On a typical summer day thousands of people are enjoying a wide variety of leisure activities including boating, fishing, sunbathing, hiking, picnicking and photographing the scenery. However, with 700 miles of shoreline the lake rarely appears crowded. There are a half dozen lifeguard-protected bathing beaches where swimmers enjoy 70-degree water by August.

Scattered along the shores of the great reservoir are more than 15 boat launches. Rowena McIntosh, who lives in Kettle Fall's second townsite (the original site is under water), knows Lake Roosevelt well. She says, "There are hundreds and hundreds of people who use the lakeshore during the summer. For some people it is has become a tradition to rent a houseboat from the Indians for a weekend every year. Twenty or so people will get together and go out on the lake. Just about everyone up here [Kettle Falls] has a boat that they use on the lake. Two hundred boats can leave the shore at the same time and in fifteen minutes you will see no one, it's such a big lake."

McIntosh, like many locals, has a sense of the lake being "her lake." Reflecting on how her life and that of her family have been entwined with the lake, she comments:

"Our kids have grown up there and now our grandkids. I take my grandkids down there quite often and just they and I go camping. It's a fun thing. A lot of hiking, looking at rocks, tracks.... I teach the kids respect for nature and give them a love for land and for nature. This is one way that I bond with my family. Everyone who uses this lake appreciates it. Litter is a very rare thing."

In the winter people continue to point their vehicles toward Lake Roosevelt, only the activities change. Ice fishing, cross-country skiing and snowmobiling draw the outdoor sports enthusiast. Banks Lake, where irrigation water is held, fills the ancient Grand Coulee and is breathtakingly majestic with the cliffs of the coulee rising high above the lake's surface. All of the major reservoirs, including those on tributary rivers, have some recreation facilities, such as boat launches, picnicking and restrooms, at the very least. Many of the reservoir facilities are similar to those on Lake Roosevelt including bathing beaches, fish cleaning sinks, camping, RV hook-ups, children's play equipment and sun-sheltered picnic tables.

In some cases the reservoir's role as a recreation resource has diversified. Lake Wallula, the reservoir of McNary Dam, is an example of this. Bird and wildlife observation is offered at nearby McNary Wildlife Refuge. A short drive northeast takes hikers to the Juniper Dunes Wilderness where they can enjoy desert hiking. The 61-mile-long reservoir has 12 parks, the largest of which is 609-acre Columbia Park, which has, in addition to the usual water facilities, an18-hole golf course, tennis courts, over six miles of hiking and biking trails, interpreted nature trails, and picnic and camping facilities. Like most of the reservoir lakes it is open seven days a week, year around. Other non-water recreation resources developed close by river reservoirs include the Quincy Wildlife Recreation Area, Saddle Mountain Wildlife Refuge and the Desert Wildlife Recreation Area.

Hunting with Camera or Gun

The Columbia Basin is on the Pacific Flyway, a major waterfowl migration route, and hundreds of acres of wetlands within the basin project are traditional resting areas on the migration journey for numerous bird species. A portion of the Potholes Reservoir area, which includes 2,500-acre Potholes State Park, has been included in the Columbia National Wildlife Refuge. Year-round the refuge attracts birders, but the spring Sandhill Crane migration is of special interest.

Look, Mom! We've caught supper!! *Northwest Museum of Arts & Culture*

Beginning in 1998, every March, Othello, located 14 miles from the Columbia Wildlife Refuge, observes the Sandhill Crane Festival. The festival focuses attention on the approximately 25,000 Sandhill Cranes that stop for about six weeks at the wildlife refuge, resting and fattening up for the long flight to Alaska where they mate and raise their young. Originally the people who boarded the yellow Othello School buses for the two-hour tour into the refuge to see the cranes were mostly from Seattle, but each year more birders come from across the nation and abroad. Bob Flores, refuge manager said, "[The festival] has definitely put Othello on the map. I'll be on a plane sometimes and someone will say, 'Oh, Othello, isn't that the cranes?'"

From the beginning the Sandhill Crane Festival was a major community project with local farmers and townspeople alike serving as bus-driver tour guides. On the trip out to the refuge the driver fills the visitors in on local history, crops and farming practices. He or she stresses how irrigation-flooded potholes and crop residues have increased biological diversity in the Columbia Basin. During the Sandhill Crane Festival Othello is a busy town with every motel and restaurant doing a brisk business.

The brushy undeveloped areas and wetlands in the north central part of the Columbia Basin project have traditionally offered excellent hunting, and pheasant, a favorite upland game bird, is regularly stocked throughout the region. Hunters are permitted wide access to private land in Grant County and every fall they arrive in droves. It is commonplace to see

signs posted at Moses Lake motels during the hunting season: "Dressing out of game is not allowed in the motel rooms." Because of overhunting the game bird population had dropped noticeably by the 1980s. Grant County, working with the State Department of Wildlife and Fisheries, launched a vigorous program to bring back the birds.

The northeast corner of Washington and northern Idaho offer a very different type of lake experience than the arid central region. There are scenic rushing rivers like the Pend Oreille where one can fly down the canyons on a jet boat. The summer weather is similar to the central inland region — sunny, dry and warm to hot. However, with higher rainfall the district is wooded and peppered with hundreds of small lakes. Many of the lakes are circled by summer cabins, modest year-around homes, or low-budget resorts and RV parks. In addition to outdoor and aquatic fun, the lakes represent a place of peaceful retreat for harried urban-ites, especially from Spokane. One Spokanite expressed the tradition of the lake for restoring one's soul. "The wonderful forest lakes of the Pend Oreille area are where we all go 'to get away from it all.' Staying at the lake cabin is a tradition. It is very tranquil and natural there."

The beauty of the natural lake district continues into northern Idaho. The Panhandle offers the boater and water skier a unique opportunity for a waterway adventure exploring four lakes and three rivers, all

connected. From Lake Coeur d'Alene to the end of navigation on the St. Joe River, the highest navigable river in the world, there are nearly 80 miles of smooth inland waters ringed by beautiful mountains. Small, family-run resorts scattered around the lakes provide pleasant places to stay. There is excellent fishing for trout, bass, northern pike and panfish.

Part II:
Retirees' Shangri-La

As the Inland Northwest became more widely known as a recreational haven, retired people from the wet side of the Cascades began moving east of the mountains. High on the list of the region's many attractions mentioned by those who have chosen to live there in retirement is the wonderful, clear, sunny, dry climate and short, mild winters. Nancy Ellis told of how she and her husband made the move to the Eastside.

"I ended up on Hawk Creek because my husband loves trees — eastern Washington trees. He graduated from Ephrata High School and never lost his enthusiasm for sunshine and duck hunting. Although we lived near Poulsbo on the Olympic Peninsula for some 30 years we spent all of our recreation time east of the mountains. The day came we had some extra dollars [and] we came to Lincoln County and found his trees. The land had been settled by Back-to-the Earth folks and it had a little cabin so we had our own place to stay. We had such a good time here and everyone was so friendly and welcoming that we decided to make the big move. We sold our house on the coast, added on to the 'hippie' cabin that came with the trees and have never looked back."

Dayton resident Margaret Jayne observes, "since the 1980s and 1990s retirees from the Coast and the Spokane area have arrived in good numbers... [they live] along Lake Roosevelt at Lincoln, Seven-Bays and Deer Meadows. Many of them go south for the winter."

Nudists Find Refuge in Stevens County

In 1939 The Kaniksu Ranch Family Nudist Park was established on 240 acres of forest in the vicinity of Deer Lake north of Spokane. The member-owned landed club is affiliated with the American Association of Nude Recreation, the Naturist Society and the Northwest Nudist Association. The Kaniksu Ranch has extensive recreational facilities ranging from ping-pong and volleyball to swimming and horseshoe. The property has mountain terrain hiking and biking trails. Nude recreation enthusiasts from the Northwest and beyond regularly come to Kaniksu to get away from their hectic lives in the city.

The annual big event is Kaniksu's 5K Original Bare Buns Fun Run — clothing optional — held since 1984. Approximately 500 runners participate including runners from all over the United States as well as around the world. There are men and women division winners in nude, clothed and wheelchair events. There are also age group awards. Winners receive the coveted "NUDE FINISHER" or just "FINISHER" for those opting for running clothed.

Florence Stout said in 1999, "Odessa [population 957] is advertised around the country as a 'retirement community'. In recent years this has brought in people from California, Arizona and West Coast cities, who wanted to live in quieter surroundings and pursue a relaxed life style not possible in their home cities."

Lifetime resident of the town of Grand Coulee, population 897, Bill Gould has watched his town evolve from a dam construction boomtown into a retirement leisure community.

"I moved from Tonasket in 1946 to Grand Coulee when I was 23 years old. I went to work for the furniture store that I eventually owned. I enjoyed hunting and fishing. The community of Grand Coulee has been up and down with the construction of the third powerhouse. Now the [young] population is decreasing. A lot of the newcomers are people retired from Boeing — makes for a slower going community ... makes it easy to make friends. Just a nice community."

■ Water-skiing is a popular sport on Loon Lake, one of a myriad of natural lakes in northeastern Washington and northern Idaho. *Spokesman-Review Photo Archives*

■ Inland Northwest ski school *Jack Fix*

■ Camping is a favorite pastime at Priest Lake, Idaho. *Northwest Museum of Arts & Culture*

The Art of Retirement in Sunny Inland Hometowns

In the final decades of the 20th century, communities designed as leisure and retirement communities began cropping up along the Columbia River. Affordable waterfront and water-view properties, strung along the river from a few miles below Rock Island Dam south to Priest Rapids Lake, average one-half to three-quarters of an acre. All amenities are provided by the developer, which at Desert Aire includes a 3,600-foot-long airfield for residents' use. Recreational facilities are a key feature and usually include swimming pools, golf courses, tennis courts, water skiing and boat marinas on the nearby river or reservoir. More leisure communities are expected to be developed in the coming decades as the Baby Boomers retire.

In 2000 there were 1,200 residents, up from 400 in 1998. Most were retirees from western Washington. "The trend toward leisure communities is a natural," says Tom Truax of Desert Aire. "The great inland climate, the water recreation provided by the reservoir-lakes and the affordable, high-quality standard of living will just bring more and more people into the inland area for retirement, especially from the high-priced, gray-weather west side of the state. More people are buying a place to use on the weekends while they are still working and retiring to later."

Looking for ways to strengthen the local economy and counteract the continuing loss of population, in the mid-1980s some small Inland Northwest communities turned to the idea of encouraging retired people to move to their towns. They received help in this venture from the Washington Department of Community Trade and Economic Development (CTED), which fostered a self-help model. The town of Goldendale (pop. 3,760) on the Columbia was selected as a test community. Advertisements describing the quality of life in Goldendale as well as the attractions of the region were placed in California newspapers. The resulting 400-plus inquiries eventually resulted in more than 40 retiree households relocating to the community.

Encouraged by the success at Goldendale, a state program was launched in 1988 whereby direct assistance was given to small towns to attract retirees to relocate in their community. Under the Team Washington Project, a state program in the 1980s, the Art of Retirement Task Force was formed, composed of representatives from both the private and public sectors, including the state's economic and community development agencies. The principal objective was to assist rural Washington communities that were interested in attracting urban retirees.

When asked to draw up a list of their community's attractions, the top of the list was inevitably "wonderful sunny climate with warm summers and mild winters." Reasonably priced housing, friendly community, peace and quiet, and an abundance of leisure recreation resources nearby, especially water-recreation offered by the region's many lakes, were also high on the list. Living in the local hometown, retirees could be assured of finding peace and quiet in an affordable community, no small attraction for people living in hectic big cities. To help the communities with their local retiree-attraction program, the Task Force produced a practical self-help guidebook in 1987, *The Art of Retirement: An Economic Development Program for Rural and Distressed Areas.* In 1990 the Washington State Rural Economic

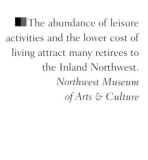
■The abundance of leisure activities and the lower cost of living attract many retirees to the Inland Northwest.
Northwest Museum of Arts & Culture

Assistance Project put out the more comprehensive *Economic Expansion Using Retiree Income: A Workbook for Rural Washington Communities.*

In 1990-91 Chewelah (pop. 2,186), located 40 miles north of Spokane in Stevens County, launched its local retiree-attraction program. A plan was developed with help from the Team Washington Art of Retirement Program and consultant Lee Fisher, who had been hired with federal funds to assist a number of communities around the country in developing programs to attract retirees. Chewelah hired an administrator to run the program, with the headquarters in the Chamber of Commerce office.

The Chamber of Commerce took the initiative in generating funding through partnerships with local companies. Before long almost everyone in town was involved. The Chamber of Commerce spent $6,500 on a promotion brochure. Chewelah High School students used the school's new video equipment to make a promotional video for a total cost of $167.50, which was professionally edited in Spokane. No one in town could have predicted what was about to happen next. Fisher had contacts with CBS Television and arranged to have Chewelah featured on Dan Rather's "Eye on America" report. Chewelah got 3.3 minutes in June. Gloria Davis, who orchestrated the project, reports, "five minutes after the segment aired the telephone in the Chewelah Chamber of Commerce office started ringing." People said, "We just heard about you on CBS, can you tell us more about what's the deal in Chewelah?" The town was ready and in the following year between 50 to 60 relocation packets and as many videos were sent out each month.

That summer the town was busy with people showing up to "look the town over" as a place to retire. Mark Bingham recalls that one day in July he looked down Main Street and saw license plates from all over the United States. A couple from Minnesota walked up to him and started talking about the idea of moving to Chewelah. They said, "We heard about Chewelah on the evening news and decided we would drive over and check it out." People didn't just window shop, they bought lots in town or acreage close by and moved in. In the first year there were 27 new homes built in Chewelah and the population expanded by 150, mostly retirees.

Promotion of the town continued in 1992-93. A multi-county board paid for $3,000 worth of advertising in regional and national publications, including the *National Farm Journal, Modern Maturity, Stars and Stripes* and *Sunset.* Ads were also run in Colorado and California newspapers under the title "Ready to Retire?" A *Seattle Times* reporter, a hometown girl, wrote a story about her hometown's project for the Seattle paper that was picked up by the *New York Times. Kiplinger's Personal Finance* magazine featured Chewelah in the spring of 1992. With all of this high-level free publicity the project really took off. The phone continued to ring all day, and letters of inquiry jammed the Chamber's Post Office box. The tally showed that in the first three years approximately 2,500 to 3,000 packets and 600 videos (based on the high school project) were sent out.

Chewelah promoted itself as a leisure community located close to an array of outdoor recreation resources. In the early 1990s the community enhanced its in-town recreation by building a 27-hole golf course, swimming pool and tennis courts. The Spokane Tribe opened a casino and the 49° North Ski Resort is a short drive away. Spokane, with its international airport, is 45 minutes away. By 2000 Chewelah's population had increased by 30 percent, 750 people, counting those who had bought property inside the city limits and those living in the new suburbs just outside of town. As the community prospered and the services available expanded, young families have been moving to Chewelah. Some of the young people are the children and grandchildren of the retirees.

Noticing the economic and population boost enjoyed by communities attracting retirees, at the beginning of the 21st century more inland communities were considering promoting themselves as "just a good place to retire to." In addition, planned retirement communities were proliferating, especially in the environs of Spokane-Coeur d 'Alene, the Tri-Cities and along the Columbia River.

City of Spokane

Throughout the 20th century Spokane continued its official role of capital of the Inland Northwest (a.k.a. Inland Empire). Considering the size of the city, the extent of its resources often surprises newcomers. The fact is that Spokane serves a much larger population than the 195,629 who live in the city. It has been estimated that 1.7 million people live within a 200-to-300-mile radius from Spokane. For people living 100-to-300 miles away, Spokane is "the city." Spokane ranks 94th in the nation. Spokane has a small-city feel with a big-city level of activity.

Spokane is a city that knows and treasures its history. In the 1970s through the 1990s many vintage buildings were restored. At the end of the 20th century, the downtown business district carried a sense of continuity with the past with an interesting mix of historic and contemporary buildings. John Abell, professor of Architecture and Urban Design at Washington State University, Spokane Campus, said, "One of the real strengths of downtown Spokane is its wonderful collection of well-preserved historic buildings." The National Trust for Historic Preservation has observed that Spokane is "one of the greatest architectural and preservation surprises in the West."

Spokane is a place of distinctive neighborhoods. Notable among these is Carnegie Square, named for the old Carnegie Library, the district's centerpiece. In the beginning of the 1990s, this neighborhood was a prime example of urban decay. After several years

Chapter Five

A Profile of Select Cities

■Spokane has been the trade center of the Inland Northwest since the early days of mining and railroads. *Northwest Museum of Arts & Culture*

of vigorous renovation and restoration of the collection of vintage buildings, the neighborhood came to life with attractive antique galleries, restaurants, cafes, professional office space and several apartments.

The old blue-collar Hillyard district, which originally grew up around James J. Hill's locomotive production plant, an operation that employed 6,000 people, had become a run-down, seedy part of town. But at the end of the 1990s the district was taking on a new life. The streets in the colorful old neighborhood are now attractive and the old storefronts were restored. New businesses moved in, including antiques and collectibles, hobby shops and cafes. In the 1990s a group of business owners launched a railroad-themed mural project as a way to connect the old railroad community to the contemporary life of the district.

As Spokane evolved into a sophisticated urban center with its old inner-city areas gentrified into upscale neighborhoods, it has become increasingly difficult for people with low incomes to survive in the city. Economic statistics reveal that in 1997, 32 out of every 100 Spokanites lived in households with under $20,000 net income. By contrast, 25 out of 100 city residents enjoyed household incomes of $50,000 or more. Compared to other cities of its size, Spokane has remained relatively homogeneous. For every 100 residents, three are Hispanic, two are African American,

■ Riverside Avenue in Spokane. Visitors are attracted to Spokane's historic downtown buildings and streets, which are now undergoing a revitalization after a decade of exodus to suburban malls. *Northwest Museum of Arts & Culture*

two to three are Asian and one is Native American. In the average American city of Spokane's size, 30 people out of every 100 are non-white or Hispanic.

A major change for Spokane since 1950 has been the replacement of farms in outlying areas with extensive suburbs. By the 1990s much of the Spokane Valley was urban in density and character. Some subdivisions consist of small acreage where homeowners keep horses. Some areas in the far southern section of the valley, such as Otis Orchards and Greenacres, remained rural in nature, with the land zoned for farming activities.

If one were to select three special qualities of Spokane, the first would have to be the abundance of parks and gardens. The Spokane Parks Department says that there is a park within a 10-to-15 minute walk of virtually every home in the city. There are numerous neighborhood parks with recreational equipment. Other parks feature lovely gardens, ponds and scenic views and are designed for walking. Spokane's city park system plan was drawn up by the Olmsted Brothers, the nation's leading landscape architects in the early 20th century. With over 3,500 acres of developed recreation facilities and protected green space, Spokane has one of the most expansive municipal parks systems in the entire country.

In addition to the city parks, Spokane is greatly enhanced by an abundance of beautiful home gardens. Marilyn Smith, president of the Floral Association in the mid-1990s, said, "There are beautifully tended gardens in every neighborhood, not just the fancier parts of town. People here take real pride in their homes, their neighborhoods and their community."

Spokane has traditionally been considered a conservative place. However, there is abundant evidence in the late years of the 20th century that this description is no longer appropriate. For example, Spokane, where more than 90 percent of the population

Spokane experienced a boom in population and housing after World War II, with new suburbs growing both north and east. *Northwest Museum of Arts & Culture*

is white, was one of the first Western cities to elect a black mayor, James Chase. Following Chase two different women served as mayor, Vicki McNeill and Sheri Barnard.

When Spokane was selected as the site of Expo '74, it was the smallest city ever to take on such a major event. In retrospect, Expo '74, which brought 5.6 million people to Spokane, marked a turning point for the city. Spokane saw itself in a different light after Expo. Many people learned from the responses of the visitors that they had a great city. The extensive city restoration and beautification projects executed for Expo, as well as the new public construction, left the city a legacy that makes it one of the most beautiful and well appointed in the Far West.

An ongoing major city concern is restoring the Spokane River to a clean and healthy condition. In 1940 the state health department deemed the river "a serious health hazard and grossly polluted." By 1970 the sewage processing issue was resolved with adequate capacity facilities. However, there are high lead levels in the river water as a result of Silver Valley mining in nearby Idaho.

Spokane continues to be a regional transportation and commercial center as it has been throughout its history. Spokane has what business and industry want: abundant and inexpensive electrical power, reasonably

■Spokane is home to many beautiful parks. Riverfront Park in downtown Spokane was created for Expo '74 from former railroad yards along the Spokane River. *Northwest Museum of Arts & Culture*

priced industrial land, good infrastructure, and a motivated and well-educated work force.

Health care is a significant industry in Spokane, which has six major hospitals, including the second- and third-largest in the state. The Heart Institute of Spokane is a diagnosis, rehabilitation and research center for heart patients. In 1999 Sacred Heart Medical Center was ranked No. 3 nationally by the Health Care Finance Administration. Medical services available include heart, lung, renal, neonatal, and women's health. As an industry, it is the largest sector in employment. Approximately one out of every 10 working people earn their living in health care. Spokane is the largest medical center between Minneapolis and Seattle. The size of the health care market served by Spokane's resources is about the same as Seattle's, as people come to Spokane for medical treatment from across the Intermountain West.

In the latter decades of the 20th century Spokane had an increasingly diversified industrial base. In 1979 Hewlett-Packard built a major research and manufacturing facility in the Spokane Valley which, in turn, attracted other high-tech companies. Hewlett-Packard eventually left but others stayed. In 1999 these included Altech, Telect, Olivetti, Northern Technologies, Itron, Screentech and Egghead Software. Kaiser Aluminum and Boeing also have major operations in the Spokane area. A rapidly growing corporation that reflects the widespread regional orientation toward outdoor recreation is Mountain Gear Inc.

Since its establishment early in World War II, Fairchild Air Force Base has been a significant presence in the city, and in the 1990s it was the city's single largest employer with nearly 5,000 people working at the base. The base's economic impact on the community in the 1990s was estimated to be $260 million. Fairchild is home to the 92nd Air Refueling Wing, with five squadrons of KC-135 Stratotankers, the most of any military base in the world. It also maintains the nation's largest and oldest U.S. Air Force Survival School.

Six institutions of higher education make it possible to achieve a basic education as well as pursue advanced degrees or career-change oriented studies in evening

and weekend classes. Gonzaga University, founded in 1887 by the Jesuits, is the oldest. Whitworth College was established in 1890 by the Presbyterian Church. In the 1990s Washington State University opened a Spokane branch campus and Eastern Washington University, located in Cheney, shifted entire programs to a new city campus. All six colleges have joined together and collaborated with government, local business and industry in launching the Spokane Intercollegiate Research and Technology Institute as the anchor point for the Riverpoint Higher Education Park, which was developed in the 1990s on the eastern edge of the city center.

Spokane's appeals have not gone unnoticed by the nation as a whole. In the mid-1990s Spokane was the focus of national attention. *Newsweek* pronounced Spokane a "Pacific Northwest paradise." *Outside* magazine featured Spokane in a cover story on "Dream Towns — Where to Find It All — a Real Job, a Real Life and the Big Outdoors." The articles in the national magazines pointed out that Spokane is rich in the qualities and resources that people seek in a good place to call "my hometown."

■ Nike Ajax surface-to-air missiles guarded Fairchild Air Force Base during the Cold War.
U.S. Army

Latinos in Spokane, Washington

Carlos S. Maldonado, Ph.D.

In 2000 approximately 4,000 Latinos resided in Spokane and about 10,000 in Spokane County. Spokane's Latino community differs from other such communities in the inland Northwest in three ways. First, there is the cultural isolation arising from the fact that there are no nearby cities with a substantial Latino population. Second, Spokane is not the type of agricultural area, like the Yakima Valley, which have historically attracted Latinos. The Latinos' sense of community is diminished because of their spatial dispersion in the city.

A portion of Spokane's Latinos originally came to participate in a World War II pilot instructor's training program at Calkin Air Terminal. Some of these men married locally and stayed. During the 1940s and 50s skilled and semi-skilled Latino workers from the Yakima Valley moved to Spokane to work in construction and industrial plants like Kaiser Aluminum.

During the 1960s more Latino businesses were established in the Spokane area, such as "El Comal" and "La Copa de Oro" restaurants, which catered to both the Latino military personnel and the growing local community. In 1969 the Mexican-American Organization of Spokane was established. Other community organizations followed. Local Latinos were represented in Expo '74. The national Chicano Movement of the late 1960s contributed to the establishment of the Chicano Education Program at Eastern Washington University in 1977.

In the 1980s and 90s the Latino community in Spokane continued to grow in size and visibility. An organization calling itself "La Comunidad Catolica de Spokane" began staging religious and cultural activities including "Las Posadas" and "La Procesion de La Virgin de Guadalupe" and a regular Spanish language mass at St. Joseph Catholic Church. In 1991 "Que Pasa" began airing on public-access television on weekends. A short-lived radio program followed. "La Tiendita," Spokane's first Mexican food specialty store, opened its doors in 1995. In 1996 the Cheney Cowles Museum staged a photographic exhibit, "Mexicanos In Spokane County," which highlighted the history and presence of the local Latino community.

Flight instructors from Mexico and Latin America trained at Spokane's Calkins Air Terminal during World War II.
Carlos Maldonado/EWU Chicano Education Program

Authentic corn tortillas are handmade at Tortillaria Lourdes.
Spokesman-Review Photo Archives

At the beginning of the 21st century, a number of annual celebrations highlight Latino culture, including "Cinco de Mayo," sponsored by Eastern Washington University's Chicano Education Program; "La Virgin de Guadalupe," sponsored by "La Comunidad Guadalupana de Spokane"; and the Hispanic Graduation Recognition Banquet, sponsored by Spokane's Hispanic Professional and Business Association. Latinos in Spokane are employed in diverse fields including teaching (K-12 and higher education), business, health, government agencies, food and service industries, and others. Latino-owned businesses are increasing. A new edition to local Spanish-language media is "La Prensa Bilingue."

The greater community as well as the Latino community has been enriched by the diverse Latino community culture, which is expected to continue to expand.

The Tri-Cities, Hub of the South Central Inland Northwest: Kennewick, Pasco and Richland

Since 1950 the communities of Kennewick, Pasco and Richland have become collectively known as the Tri-Cities. Although the three incorporated cities routinely collaborate on many activities, and the possibility of merging has been discussed, it appears unlikely in the foreseeable future. The attitude of the three communities that make up the Tri-Cities has been humorously described as "coopetition" — a mixture of cooperation and competition. The cities are 10 miles apart, a distance that seems to diminish year by year as each city expands its suburbs and outlying industrial areas. Each city struggles with the reality that while they are in fact three separate urban entities; they are tightly bound by a common destiny.

While each city has a unique history, the focus here is on how the three cities share their resources and work together to achieve their mutual goals. By the end of the 20th century they had an extensive history of working together for economic development as well as expanding cultural and social amenities. The close proximity of the burgeoning urban centers has proved a real advantage in transportation. Pasco's strong agricultural and industrial background helped it grow into the region's agribusiness and food-processing center.

While there are three ports in the area, the Port of Pasco, a municipal corporation organized in 1940 to utilize barge transportation on the Columbia River, is the principal commercial port. Since the 1970s the port has been one of the largest container barge terminals on the Columbia. In 1999 a record-breaking 4,200 containers were barged from Pasco to Portland. The Tri-Cities Airport, the former U.S. Naval Air Station, is located in Pasco. Through the Tri-Ports Association, the three ports collaborate on issues including marketing, participating in business and industry organizations, and lobbying.

The Tri-Cities' function as a shipping and a distribution retail center for the south-central inland region substantially benefited from major road improvements

■The stunning and graceful cable bridge spans the Columbia River at Pasco, the confluence of the Columbia, Snake and Yakima rivers. *Lon Martin/Franklin County Historical Society*

■The Port of Pasco includes river, air and rail transportation routes. *Northwest Museum of Arts & Culture*

1956 Columbia Basin
Water Festival parade
*Ralph Smith/Franklin County
Historical Society*

in the 1980s and 90s. In the early 1980s I-82 was built, linking the Tri-Cities with Prosser, Sunnyside and Yakima, and Umatilla, Oregon, and I-84 to the south. In 1986 I-182 was completed, greatly improving travel between the three cities and directly connecting

the Tri-Cities to I-82. U.S. 395 from Pasco to Ritzville was a much-traveled two-lane road with serious safety hazards and many accidents. In the 1990s it was improved to four-lanes, thanks to support from former Speaker of the House Tom Foley from Spokane.

When the Columbia Center was constructed in Kennewick in 1969 with 100 retail spaces, it was the largest covered retail shopping mall in the Inland Northwest. But Pasco and Richland soon caught up with Kennewick. In the 1990s all of the cities offered a wide array of retail shops.

Radio announcer Herminia Mendez aired Washington state's first Spanish radio program from Sunnyside in the 1950s.
Carlos Maldonado/EWU Chicano Education Program

In their push to become a significant business and population center, the Tri-Cities have not overlooked the cultural, social and recreational needs of a balanced community. In 1989 the 6,000-seat Tri-Cities Coliseum was built as a public/private enterprise. It is home for the Tri-Cities Americans, a Western Hockey League team. Many out-of-town celebrity acts are booked at the Coliseum. In the 1990s a major sports complex capable of hosting national soccer, softball, baseball and arena events was built in Pasco. Tri-Cities residents have many opportunities each year to enjoy a variety of concerts — from classical to rock — as well as theatrical and variety programs.

Recreational facilities in the Tri-Cities have been a priority for several decades. A regional resource is the 570-acre Columbia Park, stretching along the west bank of the Columbia River in Kennewick for about five miles. Across the river on the Pasco side is Chiawana City Park. At the end of the 1990s, Kennewick was working closely with Richland in developing a plan for improving Howard Amon Park, Richland's riverfront park. All of the riverfront parks have a wide array of summer water sports facilities, as well as picnicking, jogging paths, tennis courts and golf courses. Each city has its own festivals such as the Columbia Cup Unlimited Hydroplane Races in Kennewick and the Fiery Foods Festival in Pasco. The two main cooperative events for the Tri-Cities are the Benton-Franklin County Fair and the Tri-Cities Water Festival.

Other important shared resources are media and education. The daily *Tri-City Herald,* which evolved from the weekly *Pasco Herald* in 1947, serves as the regional newspaper. Opportunities to pursue higher education were available in the 1950s through the General Electric School of Nuclear Engineering with several regional universities cooperating. This program evolved into the Joint Center for Graduate Study. In 1989 the Washington State Legislature created a branch campus, Washington State University-Tri-Cities, which offers 24 degree programs and has more than 1,200 students. The university branch is located in the Columbia Basin Community College, located in Pasco, which offers a two-year associate degree, college transfer credits and vocational training. Tri-Cities Science and Technology Park is a 2,600-acre campus in north Richland that houses more than 50 businesses and technical organizations.

During World War II the Tri-Cities-area population skyrocketed. Richland metamorphosed in less than a month from a rural village of 200 souls to 17,000 and it kept growing. At the peak of activity there were as many as 45,000 people working at the Hanford site. During this period Kennewick grew from 1,918 to 10,106 while Pasco increased from 3,913 to 10,228. Between 1950 and 1960 both Kennewick and Pasco increased by 50 percent. Richland hovered around 20,000 to 24,000. The following decade was a stagnant period with Pasco actually losing population, although Richland and Kennewick remained stable. In the 1970s Kennewick's population more than doubled, and it became the largest city of the three. Richland grew by 24 percent but then lost population as a Hanford site project failed. Kennewick and Pasco continued to grow throughout the 1980s and 1990s. Since the 1970s the Tri-Cities area has been the fastest-growing urban area in the entire state, second only to Seattle.

Economic Diversification Brings Stability

In the decades following World War II, the economy of the Tri-Cities was closely tied to what was going on at Hanford, which made for a boom-or-bust pattern. Things began to change in the 1980s as business and municipal leaders came together, determined to develop a plan for broadening the Tri-Cities' economic base. Perhaps the most dramatic expression of the shift in thinking was the transformation of the Tri-City Nuclear Industrial Council (TCNIC), which had been created in the early 1960s for the purpose of protecting the Hanford Site from congressional budget cuts. In 1985 the council got a new name, the Tri-City Economic Development Council (TRIDEC), and a new mission — guiding economic development for the Tri-Cities with the focus on attracting diverse industries as metals, manufacturing, food processing and high-tech companies.

■ A Hanford worker in a protective suit stands near the radioactivity warning sign. *Noel Buchner/The Documentary Guild*

When two major Hanford programs were cut in 1988, causing major layoffs, something happened that was different from the results of previous cutbacks. Local governments and business leaders, under the guidance of TRIDEC, came together to save the local economy. A master plan for revamping the Tri-Cities' economy was developed based on technology, agriculture, and health and leisure. Financial assistance flowed in from the state and federal government. In one year TRIDEC had an office with a staff of 10, plus eight loaned executives provided under a federal program. It had an annual operating budget of $1.5 million and quickly became the largest Team Washington program in the state.

Although Hanford was not functioning as a nuclear site in the 1980s and 1990s, many who had made their careers at Hanford remained in the Tri-Cities and constituted a large reservoir of high-tech workers. TRIDEC estimated in 2000 that the Tri-Cities had enough available workers to employ twice as many people in engineering and the high-tech research and development industry. In addition there were sufficient qualified people available to triple the manufacturing work force. The goal is to bring in companies that will keep people working at their training level and experience, and not below them, which was most often the case. At the end of the 1990s TRIDEC was instrumental in bringing in a number of companies including the International Hearth Melting titanium plant to Richland, and Twin City Frozen Foods and Reser's Fine Foods fresh potato processing plants to Pasco.

The Hanford site continues to play a major role in the Tri-Cities' economy and the world scientific community. Facilities once dedicated to nuclear energy have shifted to research on how to contain nuclear waste. In the 1990s the Hanford Nuclear Reservation was in the midst of a multibillion-dollar environmental and hazardous waste cleanup. A number of scientific organizations maintain research facilities at Hanford including Battelle Pacific Northwest National Laboratories, the Laser Interferometer Wave Observatory and Environmental Molecular Science Laboratory.

As a part of the local diversification plan, the Tri-Cities Visitor and Convention Bureau was established with the mission of expanding tourism and visitor services. In 1999 the bureau helped bring 92,000 people to the Tri-Cities for conventions, more than twice as many as five years earlier. One of the 1990s issues that brought out the competitiveness between the three cities was vying for the Convention Center.

In 2000 the rivalry between the Tri-Cities was probably most evident in high school sports. Steve Potter, director of athletic programs at Richland High School, commented in 1999, "We have tons of rivalries. Friday night, going to football games is still the thing to do, and watch one Tri-Cities school beat another. Small town support has grown even as the cities have grown."

Moses Lake: The Legacy of the Columbia Basin Project

The dramatic changes in the community of Moses Lake since the 1950s are an enormous testimonial to the regional transformations wrought by World War II and, most importantly, the Columbia Basin Project. In 1942 the town of 326 was selected as the location for a major U.S. Air Force training base and the population ballooned. In the late 1940s the Columbia Basin project came on line and by 1950 the community had grown to 2,679.

It was the beginning of a new era. In 50 years Moses Lake, located in the center of the Columbia Basin Project-irrigated area, evolved from a sleepy country town to a dynamic economic and industrial center of the Columbia Basin Project that ranks in the top nine urban areas over 15,000 in inland Washington. In 2000 the population of Moses Lake was 14,953 within the city's borders and at least as many living close by. From 1992 to 1994, Moses Lake made the "America's Best Small Cities" list. The city enjoyed an increasingly diversified economy with agriculture in the lead. However, the transition from 1950 to 2000 was not easy. Good leadership and determination as well as perseverance and good luck had a lot to do with Moses Lake's success.

The good luck started in Moses Lake during World War II when the U.S. Air Force built a 13,500-foot airstrip that 50 years later is still the second-longest airstrip west of the Mississippi. After the war Larson Field was kept active as a Strategic Air Command base into the mid-1960s as part of a Cold War-era defense strategy to protect Grand Coulee Dam and the Hanford Nuclear Energy site. It was a blow to the local Moses Lake economy when the military left, turning the airfield over to Grant County. With the departure of the U.S. Air Force a group of community leaders saw the opportunity to turn disappointment into success by creating, through ballot initiative, the Port of Moses Lake to manage the Grant County Airport. By the late 1960s the Port attracted paying customers. A flight-training center was established at Larson Field by Japan Airlines (JAL) and the Boeing Company. Since 1970 more than 300 domestic and foreign airlines and airplane manufactures have trained at the airport — one of the biggest civilian air facilities in America.

Moses Lake received a major economic blow in 1978 when U & I Sugar Refinery closed its doors and 1,000 jobs disappeared overnight, no small thing for a city of 10,000. The entire region was economically depressed, since sugar beets were the cash crop for the farmers. In 1980 Mount St. Helens blew and dumped a thick layer of volcanic ash over everything. This was the point at which people in greater Moses Lake started calling themselves "a community of survivors." Mayor Wayne Rimple, owner of a steel supply business said, "the 1980s were a real turning point for Moses Lake. Rather than just waiting for things to happen, the community decided that if it was going to survive it would have to promote itself and look further down the road for what it wanted to become."

The Grant County Economic Development Council (EDC) was formed with the mission to represent private business throughout the county and to promote the region's agricultural economy, port districts and emerging industrial base. High among EDC's goals was diversifying Grant County's economy from total dependence upon agriculture. Business leaders knew they had a lot to offer companies including very inexpensive land — in the mid-1990s land averaged one-tenth the cost of land west of the Cascades — low taxes and cheap electrical power, which will be even cheaper after 2005 when existing long-term sales contracts with coastal cities come to an end. The Port of Grant County offers convenient and economical barge shipping to Portland. Truck shipping is also convenient because of Moses Lake's location near the intersection of I-90 and SR 17.

Since the early 1990s the port of Moses Lake benefited from a full-time port industrial development manager. Recognizing the inadequacy of the existing infrastructure in meeting the needs of industry, the city built a new waste-water treatment plant and expanded water, sewer and natural gas capacity. The city government and Grant County government share a pro-business philosophy. There are many instances when the city and county have built utility infrastructure beyond existing lines to accommodate new industries. Major accomplishments by 2000 included an industrial park and free-trade zone at the Grant County Airport. In the 1990s the EDC was especially interested in attracting businesses that would provide winter employment for agricultural workers. By the late 90s the Port of Moses Lake had a variety of non-agricultural companies including Takata Corporation, Advanced Silicon Materials, Eka Nobel, D & L Foundry and Sunstrand Data Control.

In the early 1940s Moses Lake's retail offerings consisted of one or two general merchandise stores. In the 1990s Kmart and Wal-Mart both identified Moses Lake as a growing retail center for the surrounding region and built major stores. Douglas Sly of Big Bend Community College, who monitors the community's growth, said in 1993, "The new retail development is a direct result of the industrial development of the past 10 years."

■ Open-air concerts are held at the Gorge Amphitheater, a dramatic setting on the Columbia River in George, Washington. *House of Blues/Standard Photo*

Moses Lake community leaders understand that the city must have good schools, health care and recreation to attract people who want to work and live there. Health care is available at eight hospitals. Keith Baldwin, Samaritan Hospital administrator said in the mid-1990s, "We have enough specialists to provide 80 percent of the medical needs." He noted that the slower pace of life and possibility of being able to go fishing or duck hunting at 5 a.m. and be in the office by 8 a.m. made it easy to recruit physicians.

A wide array of recreational activities for the outdoor enthusiast is close at hand. Potholes Reservoir south of Moses Lake is a water sports paradise. In or near the city there are eight golf courses to choose from, swimming pools and other resources at the city and county parks. In the summer those who enjoy big-name contemporary musical entertainers need only drive a few miles to George, Washington, to the Champs de Brionne Winery 10,000-seat amphitheater overlooking the Columbia, better known as the "Gorge at George."

There is evidence that not everyone is happy with the pro-growth philosophy of the community leadership. A part of the community fears the impact of economic development and is committed to preserving the more leisurely, uncrowded lifestyle that has characterized Moses Lake. The rapid population increase in the 1990s brought on a housing crisis, especially at lower-end prices. Entry-level housing under $60,000 was scarce. The average three-bedroom, 1.5-bath house cost $80,000. Rental property was at a premium. Recently there have been serious efforts to curb big housing-development plans. One such case is the Moses Pointe project. The plan for this ambitious resort-style development on Moses Lake was to include 800 residential units, a resort-lodge, a golf course and a marina. However, it was stalled by lawsuits brought by local residents who wanted to maintain the status quo. In spite of the lawsuit, another residential-resort development, Moses Lake Estates, was already on the drawing boards in 1999.

At the beginning of the 21st century, Moses Lake is still in the throes of transition. The city continues

The Latino Community in Moses Lake

Carlos S. Maldonado, Ph.D.

In the 1940s and 50s Latinos were recruited from the Rocky Mountain states and the Southwest to work in agriculture in Moses Lake. From this beginning their population grew until in 2000 they comprised 20 percent of the population. The story of the Latinos in Moses Lake is in the lives of the people.

Rodolfo (Rudy) Ramirez came to Yakima Valley with his family when he was 15. The Ramirez family had previously worked in Montana, Idaho and Texas. The Yakima Valley was experiencing a labor surplus and Rudy and his wife decided to move to Moses Lake to work in 1953. The Columbia Basin Project was creating an expanding economy with opportunities for good workers. After several years of working in agriculture, Rudy secured employment in non-agricultural work. Soon, Rudy and his wife bought a small lot with a trailer house.

Geraldo Garcia came to Moses Lake from Southern Texas in 1954 with his family. The Garcia family made their home in Wheeler, located on the outskirts of Moses Lake, which became known as "Little Mexico." Geraldo and his family worked for several different Japanese farmers picking potatoes and onions, and weeding sugar beets.

Ramirez and Garcia recall that there were very few Mexicano families in Moses Lake when they first arrived. Our Lady of Fatima Catholic Church was the religious and social center for the families. As more Mexicano families joined the community an annual Mexican fiesta was held beginning in the late 1950s. The fiesta served to raise funds for the church and the needy. Preparing for the annual fiesta brought the Mexicanos together as they made traditional foods, prepared dance performances and handicrafts. The fiesta was well attended by Mexicanos and the greater community. Moses Lake's Mexicano community continued growing. In 1962 Emilio Vela established a Spanish-language program on KDRM radio. The popular program provided entertainment and community news.

By the 1990s the Moses Lake Latino population was about 2,500. Mexicanos are a part of the larger community and found in every kind of work including teaching at the public schools, serving on the police force and working as health care professionals at the local hospitals. The Latino population has been very stable and many of the young Latino professionals are the grandchildren of the first-comers. There are many Latino-owned businesses, some of which cater to the Mexican community. These include a *"tortilleria"*, two Mexicano bakeries and several Mexican restaurants. There is a Mexicano senior center, *"Asociacion Pro de Personas Mayores"* where the elders eat and socialize.

Emilio Vela operated the first panaderia, or Mexican bakery, in Moses Lake. Vela also ran a Spanish radio program on the weekends. *Carlos Maldonado/EWU Chicano Education Program*

to pursue its goal of being a full-fledged business and tourism hub, as well as just a good place to call "my hometown."

Coeur d'Alene

Coeur d'Alene, located on I-90 33 miles east of Spokane, Washington, is North Idaho's largest city. With a population of 27,000 it is the seventh-largest city in Idaho. In 2000 Coeur d'Alene and Spokane already constituted a Metropolitan area that is destined to continue growing. In spite of its location over 300 miles in from the Pacific Ocean, Coeur d'Alene enjoys a relatively mild low-elevation Pacific Northwest climate with maritime influences. The 150-day growing season and a reliable average precipitation of 24 to 25 inches a year plus the rich soil support small farms in the nearby countryside. The city of Coeur d'Alene is the hub of the Idaho Panhandle region, which includes Kootenai, Shoshone, Benewah, Boundary, Latah, Clearwater, Lewis, Nez Perce and Bonner counties. French-Canadian fur traders, who found the native people shrewd bargainers, gave the name Coeur d'Alene, "heart as sharp as an awl."

In its early years Coeur d'Alene was a timber, farming and mining center for the Idaho Panhandle. In the latter half of the 20th century the city developed a diverse economy as an amenity-based residential community and a recreation/tourism center. Much effort has been put into making Coeur d'Alene a beautiful and comfortable place in which to live. The city is noted for its series of waterfront parks, with the largest being Tubbs Hill, a 150-mile natural park with a nature trail. City Park features a wide pathway known as the Promenade. This tree-shaded grassy park is a favorite for picnics and swimming. North Idaho College, the only community college in Coeur d'Alene, is located on the historic Fort Sherman site.

Between these two parks is the new Coeur d'Alene Resort complex — the largest resort in Idaho north of Sun Valley. The resort is the project of Duane Hagadone, who is to modern-day Coeur d'Alene what Fredrick Weyerhaeuser was 60 years ago. The resort symbolizes the transformation of the economy from the old industries to tourism. The resort's golf course was described in *Golf Digest* as "America's most beautiful" in 1992. A unique feature of the golf course is the "floating green" located on the lake. The resort also has a spectacular floating boardwalk, which provides the visitor with splendid views of the lake. Some have seen the resort as a forerunner of the future when Coeur d'Alene will be the "Tahoe of the North."

Coeur d'Alene is the seat of Kootenai County, which was experiencing a population boom in the 1990s with escalating real estate prices. Between 1970 and 1990 the median house price rose from $13,800 to

■ Lake Coeur d'Alene is a haven for fishermen, boaters and vacationers, who enjoy the fresh air and cool waters of the lake. *Northwest Museum of Arts & Culture*

■ Playland Pier once occupied the beach on Lake Coeur d'Alene near downtown. *Museum of North Idaho/Ross Hall*

$64,800. The sharp rise in real estate is caused in part by the growing number of people from Spokane who prefer to live in Coeur d'Alene and commute to work in Spokane, only 33 miles away. Post Falls on the Spokane River just west of Coeur d'Alene is symbolic of the rapid development of the region at the end of the 20th century. In 1970 Post Falls' population was 2,371. In 1990 it was 7,349 and in 1993 9,500 with an additional 15,000 living within five miles. This growth offers new opportunities and an economic alternative to declining material resource-based industries like logging and mining that earlier dominated the region.

The Coeur d'Alene and Spokane regions are economically and socially bound together. It has been predicted that Spokane and Kootenai counties will be declared a metropolitan statistical area (MSA) by 2005. With good roads, the 33-mile drive between the two cities is no deterrent for the growing number of people choosing to live in Coeur d'Alene and commute to jobs in Spokane.

Wenatchee: Apple Capital

Wenatchee is one of the first cities in north central Washington that the traveler encounters when crossing the Cascade Range via U.S. 2, the scenic Stevens Pass Greenway. In the second half of the 20th century, fruit tree culture replaced the region's original natural resource-based logging and mining industries. Apples dominate, but there are also large acreages of pears and cherries and less of peaches, apricots and nectarines. Enormous packing sheds and cold storage buildings are commonplace as are roadside stands where tourists load up on exquisitely delicious local fruit. The Washington State Apple Commission, located in Wenatchee, pursues its mission to assure high production standards and find markets for the more than 2 billion pounds of apples produced annually.

The second half of the 20th century witnessed a radical transformation of the apple industry. Area horticulture experienced a technical revolution when laborious hand methods were replaced with mechanized techniques that greatly improved the efficiency of all of the steps of fruit production from blossom thinning

Skiers enjoy good snow and great vistas at Schweitzer ski area in Sandpoint, Idaho. *Ross Hall/Dann Hall*

Main Streets remain the social and retail hubs of community life, despite the threat from malls and highway bypasses. Wenatchee Main Street, 1950s *Deanne Jackson*

and insect and disease control through picking, packing and shipping to market. A key breakthrough came in the 1950s with the introduction of an atmospherically controlled storage system. The newly picked fruit was put into specially designed storage rooms with carefully controlled carbon dioxide and oxygen levels. Held under these conditions the fruit does not deteriorate but retains the quality of fresh-picked fruit.

After World War II to the 1980s Wenatchee's economy perked along with the fruit industry as the mainstay. Locally owned and managed hydroelectric power, aluminum production — a legacy of the war effort — lumber milling and tourism also contributed. The recession of the 1980s brought economic hardship. Environmental issues were raised about orchardists' use of pesticides and other sprays. The sharp decline in building hurt the lumber industry, and many local lumber mills closed, eliminating jobs. In the 1980s the fruit and wheat industries continued to be plagued by commodity prices that at times fell below production

■ Apples were once individually wrapped in paper before packing into wooden crates.
Northwest Museum of Arts & Culture

■ Carol Lee Jessup represented Wenatchee as the 1954 Apple Blossom Festival Queen.
Parsons Photography/Wenatchee Valley Museum & Cultural Center

diversified one. Apples and tree fruits continued to lead, but manufacturing, health care and tourism are expanding. The city of Wenatchee emerged from the depressed years an even stronger regional hub, especially in medical services and retail trade.

Telecommunication advances came in the 1990s, and a dozen computer programmers operating technology-based businesses launched a small but growing software industry. GTE installed fiber optic cable throughout the area, which quickly had a variety of applications including beaming in classes from Washington State University, Pullman, and Central Washington University, Ellensburg, for students attending Wenatchee Valley College. The availability of fiber optic technology enhances Wenatchee's appeal to high-tech companies. In the 1990s companies began moving into the region, including Pacific Aerospace & Electronics Inc., which quickly became a major Wenatchee-area employer.

In the 1990s downtown Wenatchee was revitalized with an estimated $29 million going into improvements including historic preservation. Significant features of the new downtown include the $3.6 million expansion of the Convention Center and the new $9 million Columbia Station Transportation Center. The arts have not been left out and focal points in the city center are the new Stanley Civic Center with its Bank of America Performing Arts Theater, Riverside Playhouse Theater and the 35-piece "Art on the Avenues" outdoor sculpture exhibit. The North Central Washington Museum, located in downtown Wenatchee since 1939, was renamed the Wenatchee Valley Museum and Cultural Center and rejeuventated with a new mission and expanded programs as well as a $3 million capital improvement plan.

Wenatchee's growth has been attributed to the good quality of life and its proximity to Seattle, about two hours away. However, there have been people working hard behind the scenes to usher in the growth including the now defunct Quest for Development, Inc. which coordinated efforts made by a number of organizations. Development efforts are continued by the Wenatchee Chamber of Commerce, the Chelan

costs. The Alar (a chemical widely used in apple culture) scare of the late 70s decimated the fruit market. In 1993-94 Alcoa Aluminum cut back production at the Wenatchee plant, laying off hundreds of workers.

In the 1990s north-central Washington was in transition from an agriculture-based economy to a and Douglas county port districts and the Wenatchee Downtown Association, all of which are working hard educating residents about the need for economic diversification and healthy growth.

From 1950 to the end of the century, Wenatchee's population grew erratically; however, overall it nearly doubled. A noteworthy portion of the growth is from people moving in from the Puget Sound region, Oregon, California and other states. Attractions they list when asked include the region's natural beauty, outdoor recreational resources, safe streets, good schools and a pleasant small-town feel.

At the start of the new century, economic downturns were becoming evident throughout north central Washington. In the Wenatchee area the apple industry was struggling with high production costs and low market prices. In addition, a series of drought years was having a negative impact on the region's agriculture and hydroelectric power production. In spite of these problems the area residents, independent and committed to their way of life, took these obstacles in stride, as they had in the past, and moved forward with a positive eye to the future.

City of Walla Walla

The 20th century for Walla Walla and the surrounding county could be summarized as a time of transformation from agriculture to diversity. Walla Walla is an old city steeped in early Washington history. Indeed many consider it the birthplace of Northwest heritage. For the first half of the century the city of Walla Walla and Walla Walla County were noted as prosperous farming areas with several small good colleges and the state prison as a major employer. With an exceptionally long growing season — 200 days — and adequate precipitation, Walla Walla was the inland agricultural leader up to the 1970s when the Columbia Basin and Yakima irrigation projects moved into first place.

With an already declining economy Walla Walla was hard hit by the recession of the 1980s. The city and immediate area were facing a devastating disintegration of their traditional industries and hundreds of jobs disappeared. Family income

The 280-square mile Walla Walla Wine Apellation is setting the standard for Northwest winemaking with its Merlots and Cabernet Sauvignons. Experts attribute the excellent soil to the work of the Ice Age Floods, which left behind rich, well-drained soil.
L'Ecole No. 41

Downtown Walla Walla at mid century. It is home to Whitman College and the recently renovated Marcus Whitman Hotel.
Northwest Museum of Arts & Culture

steadily declined and young people were leaving since there were few opportunities. However, the community had a long history of working together and not being overcome by hard times.

In the 1980s the Port of Walla Walla, with the assistance of local governments and business leaders, assumed the role of lead agency in executing an economic development plan designed to diversify the economy of the Walla Walla Valley. The primary focus was to retain and create living-wage jobs.

Successes in the 1980s included retaining the Northwest Book Bindery (55 jobs saved) and Regents Northwest medical claims processing center (25 jobs saved). A comprehensive economic development strategy was adopted to attract industry and encourage the development of small businesses by offering advice and support through a community small-business assistance center. A key component of the new business recruitment element was the development of ready-to-go industrial sites, with infrastructure and improvements in place such as Avery Industrial Park. Significant companies relocating to Walla Walla included Key

Technology Inc., manufacturing food processing equipment, with 420 jobs and over $45.5 million in sales by 1998; Sykes Enterprises Telemarketing, with 500 jobs; Nelson Irrigation; Martin Archery; Continental Can; Boise Cascade; and Ponderosa Fibers of America, the largest recycled-pulp producer in North America. In addition, numerous new business have started in the city and throughout the valley including boutique wineries, like Russell Creek Winery, and light manufacturing such as Clay in Motion, which produces handcrafted pottery with original designs.

Revitalizing Main Street

At the end of the 1990s Walla Walla's historic Main Street, a mix of handsome vintage brick and modern buildings, was healthy and vibrant. Antique streetlights and benches invite leisurely shopping and visiting. The Chamber of Commerce reports that people starting new businesses look for space downtown before they go to the mall and often cannot find anything since there is only a 3-percent vacancy rate on Main Street. The renewed glory of Main Street is the result of community effort. Bruce Buchanan, director of the Downtown Walla Walla Foundation, remembers the numerous vacancies on Main Street in the 1980s. He says, "Back in the fall of 1989 I remember wanting employees and store owners to park on the street so it would look like someone was downtown." Even before the Blue Mountain Mall opened in 89 the locals recognized that Main Street was on the skids with unkempt storefronts and many vacant shops. The Downtown Walla Walla Foundation was formed to guide the revitalization effort. Public and private funds were found and the restoration of Main Street project was launched. In 2000 the centerpiece of the historic preservation effort was the $25 million restoration of the magnificent Marcus Whitman Hotel by a local investor.

People in Walla Walla have a keen sense of their history and no one takes the community's pioneer spirit for granted. As one member of the local historical society observed after the Main Street renovation work was underway: "We feel an obligation to our fathers and grandfathers. They gave their blood, sweat and years to settling this valley. We can't let them down. This town never has been real big on change, but we aren't going to sit back and watch it all die."

Walla Walla Wine Country

Lying within the larger Columbia Valley Appellation, the 280-square mile Walla Walla Wine Appellation is setting the standard for Northwest winemaking when it comes to Merlots and Cabernet Sauvignons. In 1999 vineyard acreage totaled 800 acres and was expected to double by 2001. While the Walla Walla Appellation extends into Oregon, all wineries in 2000 were located in Washington. The most remote of the Inland Northwest official wine districts, it is noted for the esprit de corps of the more than a dozen wineries and their vintners. Martin Clubb, owner of L'Ecole No. 41, located in the schoolhouse in Old French Town, says, "instead of being competitors, the winemakers here are comrades. We are trying to help each other out ... to build and solidify our reputation. The wineries include Woodward Canyon, Canoe Ridge, Seven Hills, Glen Fiona, Three Rivers Winery and Pepper Bridge Winery. Viticulture soil experts attribute the excellence of the Walla Walla Appellation to the work of the Ice Age floods. When the floodwaters retreated they left behind ponds that abounded, as in the Walla Walla region, and fine-grained slackwater sediment deposits. This rich, well-drained soil, combined with the arid, sunny climate and extremely long growing season, over 200 days, create ideal conditions for grapes, producing complex red wines of unusual flavor. A delightful way to enjoy the region is taking a wine tour visiting the many wineries that welcome visitors and offer wine tasting.

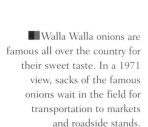

To many people Walla Walla is synonymous with onions, the famous Walla Walla Sweet, which is only available for three or four weeks in the spring. In 1998 local onion farmer Steve Plucker opened Onion World, a store dedicated to selling Sweets and onion products. He said, "Sweet onion relish is the biggest seller. The Walla Walla Sweet is an onion that you can eat like an apple. They aren't too spicy. We sell them as gifts." The Walla Walla Sweet name is said to have originated in the 1950s when a local shipper included a recipe for a "Walla Walla Sweet Sandwich" in the bottom of his customers' sacks of onions. The onion harvest is highlighted by the Walla Walla Sweet Onion Festival put on by the Chamber of Commerce. Stacy Burch

Buchanan of the chamber said, "many families will have their acre or two and grow the Sweets and sell them alongside the road. The roadside onion stands are a part of the local culture. During onion season, people talk onions all the time. Lots of people go out of their way to come here to buy onions. They send them all over the world."

A reflection of the early and continuing prosperity of the farmers in the Walla Walla district, the city has had two private four-year colleges, Walla Walla and Whitman, and the public two-year Walla Walla Community College. In the later decades of the 20th century the community college began offering a wide array of classes serving the regional business community. Thousands of people have been sent to the community college for training and staff development at their employers' expense.

"Walla Walla is being discovered," says Jim Kuntz, executive director of the Port of Walla Walla. "The lure is a well-educated and motivated work force and the promise of peaceful small-town life. We're convincing companies that this is a good place to do business." In the city of Walla Walla, as well as the county, a pro-business attitude prevails. The county commissioners and city council have pledged to support economic development and promised to speed up the permit process for the development of industrial land. Walla Walla has much to offer businesses including low hydroelectric rates and inexpensive land cost.

In the early days of the 20th century, Walla Walla was considered a remote inland place. By the late 20th century that was no longer the case. In 2000 the new Walla Walla Regional Airport was completed. The new airport is a $10.5 million state-of-the-art structure. Considerable thought and effort went into the new terminal to create a gateway facility that reflects the economic diversity image of the region. Valley Transit provides public transportation for an area that reaches from the airport to College Place and Milton-Freewater. Strategically located at the confluence of the Columbia and Snake rivers, barge shipping to Pacific ports is available. Every effort is made to retain light-density rail transportation.

In spite of the significant stresses Walla Walla experienced during a prolonged period of transition, by the end of the 20th century the goal of economic diversity had become a reality thanks to the efforts of community leaders and the port. Agriculture remains an important component, but it only represents 11.5 percent of the labor force. City leaders have a long-term vision of the city becoming the medical, professional and business services hub for southeastern Washington and northeastern Oregon. The population of the city of Walla Walla in 2000 was 29,000, approximately 5,000 more than in 1950. Walla Walla County grew from 40,135 in 1950 to 55,180 in 2000.

Sandpoint

On the west shore of Lake Pend Oreille, 45 miles north of Coeur d' Alene on U.S. Highway 95, is Sandpoint. Begun in 1882, it grew in 25 years into a town of 5,000 with an economy dominated by timber. Three railroads, the Northern Pacific, Great Northern and Spokane International, shipped Sandpoint lumber, poles and shakes all over the United States.

The timber industry provided Sandpoint with a clear sense of identity through its first half-century, but in the mid-1950s the last brail of logs was threaded through the highway "Long Bridge" connecting Sandpoint with the south shore of the Pend Oreille River. By the early 60s a shrinking supply of trees and changing attitudes about the environment began to modify how Sandpoint defined itself.

Sandpoint is an attractive place. The lake, 46 miles long, 1,200 feet deep and surrounded by mountains and deep forest, has drawn visitors for centuries. The Kalispel tribe made its adjacent meadows a summering ground, gathering fish and picking huckleberries in the Cabinet and Selkirk mountains. Since the rail was laid, tourists have come every summer, and to expand upon this, Sandpoint businessmen opened Schweitzer Basin ski area in 1963.

Shortly after, a mixture of "back-to-earthers," hippies and urban refugees discovered Sandpoint. A real estate boom in the early 70s resulted, and the influx of newcomers has continued since, swelling the population of Sandpoint to 6,800 and Bonner County from around 17,000 in the 60s to 37,000 in the latest census.

Sandpoint has emerged as a community focused on arts and recreation. The Pend Oreille Arts Council was begun in the 70s to encourage arts of all kinds. Schweitzer doubled its size and lift capacity. An extraordinarily challenging 18-hole golf course, Hidden Lakes, opened in 1985. In the mid-80s the Festival at Sandpoint began as an outdoor forum for musicians as diverse as America, Dwight Yoakum, Natalie Cole, The Doobie Brothers, children's concerts and classical programs. The vintage Panida Theater became a community-owned venue for local talent and international stars.

Entering the new century, Sandpoint has become a fixture on the list of 100 Best Small Arts Towns in America. Schweitzer has evolved into a multi-season operation. Hidden Lakes has matured into one of the finest golf courses in the Northwest, with a 17,000-square-foot clubhouse on Pack River. Companies as diverse and successful as Litehouse Dressing and Coldwater Creek make their headquarters in Sandpoint.

Timber's legacy to Sandpoint stands in 1900-vintage brick buildings facing First Avenue and logging trucks still rolling through town. Local mills still ship timber products nationwide, but the Spokane International tracks that once ran through the center of town have been moved and replaced by a green strip and bike path. Caulk boots are replaced by the sandals of summer tourists and the shoes of recreationalists who come to enjoy all seasons in the forests and mountains of Idaho.

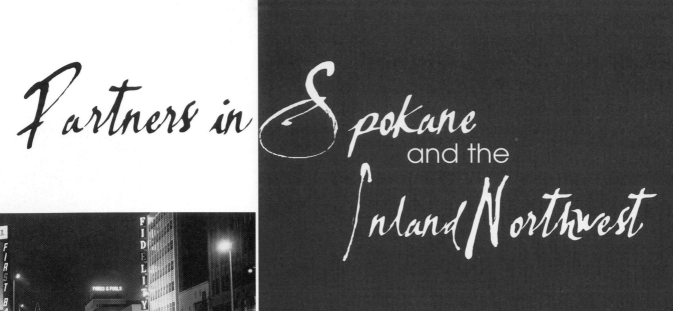

Professional Services

Quality of Life

Patron: Cowles Publishing Company

Edgewood Log Structures, Ltd.

An ancient structure of Europe and Scandinavia made its way to the New World with an iron ax wielded by explorers and colonists who introduced log construction to the Americas. Log cabins were first shelter for pioneers from Massachusetts to Puget Sound and have come to symbolize the frontier, particularly the American West.

Edgewood Log Structures, Ltd. in Idaho is keeping the symbol alive, but comparing its buildings with the cabins of the frontier is like comparing a Saturn IV with a bottle rocket. The resemblance is purely theoretical. The iron ax has been replaced by dramatically more advanced tools.

When Brian Schafer began his log home company in 1984, his mantra was "never leave a job until you're satisfied with it." His desire was not just to build log homes, rather to build the best. Edgewood has been built upon his desire, constructing hundreds of unique homes and commercial projects in the United States, Japan and Europe. By the beginning of the new century Edgewood log structures had evolved from the barebones, pre-designed log kit many log home companies provide customers to a finely designed, handcrafted

building envelope that includes customized, client-driven plans, engineering and an in-place structure ready for finishing.

Edgewood began performing in the international arena in 1987, when a representative of the Port of Portland, Oregon, offered to help Schafer find a way to export his product. Soon, Edgewood brochures were in American Consulates around the Pacific Rim, and two years later, the first Edgewood home was exported to Japan.

Success in Japan came because Edgewood was organized, qualified and the best at what it did. Entry into the Japanese market became of utmost importance to Edgewood, for it changed how Schafer saw his company and how Edgewood put its buildings together. Inspired by a request from one of his Japanese customers, Schafer began providing clients with a total package he calls the "handcrafted environment" which includes everything for the main structure including roof, windows, doors and custom wood accents.

If the handcrafted environment was a good idea, Schafer took the concept one step farther when he made a decision in the early 90s to follow his passion for unique design and focus on superior log construction that included professional, creative and original design services.

The Edgewood package has come to include not only drawings with the signature of a structural engineer, but also plans a client can "walk" into, thanks to ArchiCAD software from the Hungarian company Graphisoft. The program does much more

Following the Historic National Park Theme

than produce technical drawings, providing clients with an interactive CD that can be used to "visit" a building inside and out before it is built. A tour via QuickTime video, including elevations and several perspectives, lets clients explore the design of the home, visiting the great room, kitchen and viewing other features before a single course of log is handcrafted. Changes that might otherwise be impossible or expensive can be made in the virtual world.

An Edgewood-designed home has recently won *Log Home Living's* award for Best Log Home Design in America over 2,500 square feet. The same home won every category it was eligible for in the North Idaho Building Contractor's Parade of Homes, including Best Overall Architectural Design. And Edgewood products have gone far beyond private homes. Schafer's most ambitious project thus far is the Snake River Lodge in Jackson Hole, a 60,000-square-foot Edgewood project.

Edgewood uses modern methods to construct buildings that have the look of fine 19th-century craftsmanship. For walls, hand-selected spruce, white pine and lodgepole pine logs are air dried, lathed to remove the sapwood, then finished by hand with a drawknife. Roof trusses, posts and floor joists are of Western larch, known for its tensile strength and robust beauty. Corner notches and truss joints are hand-scribed, roughed with a chainsaw and finished with hand tools to ensure a perfect fit.

Each course of log in the walls is attached with lag bolts torqued to 400-foot-pounds, pre-compressing the logs and eliminating shrinkage that plagues all other log structures.

Exterior doors and windows are of Douglas fir, interior doors of alder, and all are hand built. Accents, including atrium walls called the "Glass Forest," are done in Western red cedar. The Glass Forests, the name of which Edgewood has trademarked, are spectacular: free-standing cedar trees separating massive floor-to-ceiling panes of frameless glass, bringing the expansive outdoors practically

Edgewood's unique "Glass Forest™" window wall

indoors, giving the impression that the forest actually begins inside the house.

Edgewood does not cut live trees for logs, but construction of an Edgewood structure does begin in the forest. Edgewood buildings are constructed of logs cut from trees that have died naturally in the woods, either from disease, insects or old age. In fact, Schafer was instrumental during the 1990s in getting the state of Idaho to allow selective salvage logging on its trust lands, and these sales directly benefit Idaho schools. The logging is done by independent loggers with guidance on log quality and technique from an Edgewood forester.

Edgewood structures are built twice — once at Edgewood's 88-acre showplace 15 miles north of Coeur d'Alene, Idaho, on Highway 95 and again at the actual construction site. The package is produced and put together at the Idaho yard, where each component is fitted exactly, then marked and indexed for reconstruction. The building is then disassembled, carefully packaged and shipped to the construction site.

Early in the new century, Edgewood began exporting to Europe, beginning in the midst of quality-conscious Austria and expanding into Germany, where it is thought log construction originated over 4,000 years ago. To assure that each structure is properly reconstructed, Edgewood trains Japanese and European craftsmen to assemble their buildings on site.

The log structure has come a long way in 4,000 years, from Europe all the way to America and back, via Japan, thanks to Edgewood Log Structures, Ltd.

Washington Trust Bank

When 28-year-old E. H. Stanton moved his family to Washington in 1890, he had no idea he would set the stage for his descendants to lead the largest independently owned full-service commercial bank in the region — Washington Trust Bank — into the 21st century. Today, Peter Stanton, the fourth-generation Stanton to serve as chairman of Washington Trust Bank, guides the financial institution with the same vision expressed by his great-grandfather: "Our efforts will be to make the Washington Trust Company second to none in the Inland Empire."

With 26 offices, branches from Seattle to Boise and total assets of almost $2 billion in 2001, Spokane-headquartered Washington Trust continues to excel and grow by providing customers what they want in a timely fashion. In addition, its commercial customers have direct access to decision-makers who know their business and react quickly. That's the local advantage Washington Trust maintains over rival national banks.

Originally named Washington Trust Company, the institution was established in 1902 by three Spokane businessmen who saw the need for a full-service bank.

In less than 10 years, the new bank outgrew its Mill Street (now Wall Street) location and moved to Post and Riverside.

Meanwhile E. H. Stanton had organized the Spokane Meat Company, applying his knowledge of the meat packing trade, which he had practiced successfully in his New Hampshire hometown. He bought out his partners over time and renamed the firm the Stanton Packing Company. Eventually Stanton sold his interest in the business to Armour and Company, which enabled him to purchase controlling stock in Washington Trust Company in 1919.

Stanton became a member of the board and his son, Fred, returned from California, where he had been seeking business opportunities, to join the bank. A graduate of Stanford University and former Army officer, Fred Stanton began the family tradition of learning the banking business from the ground up by starting as an assistant messenger at Washington Trust. Over two decades, he progressed through the ranks to become president in 1941 at the age of 54 — the youngest bank president ever in Spokane. By 1951 he was elected chairman.

Meanwhile Fred's son, Philip Stanton, continued the family tradition by working through various positions at the bank while earning his law degree from Gonzaga University. Improving upon his father's record, Philip was elected president of the bank — at age 31 — in 1961, and chairman in 1978.

Philip's son, Peter Stanton, took the notion of first-hand banking education one step further by working for a Seattle bank before joining Washington Trust.

(Below right) First location of the Washington Trust Company on Mill Street (now Wall Street)

E.H. Stanton family: (left to right) E.H. Stanton, Fred Stanton, Cora Stanton

In 1990, at age 34, Peter was elected president and CEO, carrying the family's tradition of youthful leadership into its fourth generation.

Thanks to the Stantons' guidance, Washington Trust's story is one of steady and strong growth. By 1943 it ranked among the top 600 banks in the nation. During World War II the bank demonstrated the Stantons' philosophy of exemplary customer service by accommodating thousands of defense workers and soldiers unable to make large deposits. It introduced Checkmaster, an innovative service that allowed customers to open checking accounts in person or by mail with as little as a $1 deposit and no minimum balance.

Throughout the years, Washington Trust continued to enhance its reputation as a leader in new customer-service ideas. In 1950 at 2nd and Wall in Spokane, it opened the first drive-in branch in the entire Pacific Northwest. The following year it installed a fully automated computer complex in the bank's Operations Center to speed handling of paperwork and expand customer services. The data processing system was one of the first installed in a bank this size in the country.

To accommodate its growth, Washington Trust's main office, which had moved to Sprague Avenue, was expanded and additional property acquired. The institution's name changed officially to Washington Trust Bank, and several branches were opened across the city. By 1960 the bank had grown to nearly $54 million in assets with four branch locations.

Washington Trust acquired more downtown property during the 1960s, leading to the announcement in 1972 of plans for a new 16-story office tower and bank headquarters to fill the entire block bounded by Sprague Avenue, Post Street, First Avenue and Wall Street. Opened in 1974 and continually updated, the Washington Trust Financial Center houses the bank's main offices today.

By 1978 the bank reached into the city's north side and Spokane Valley with 14 branches. It grew by expansion and acquisitions through the mid-1980s to serve customers in Deer Park, Wenatchee, the Columbia Basin and north Idaho, exemplifying the Stantons' deep commitment to the region.

By 1986 Washington Trust Bank was the second-largest state-chartered bank and seventh-largest commercial bank in Washington, and the only state-chartered bank still calling Spokane home. As the decade closed, Washington Trust acquired additional branches in Spokane and opened its new Operations Center at 2nd and Post.

Washington Trust experienced tremendous growth in assets, services and innovations, including online banking, throughout the 1990s. It kicked off the new millennium, with Peter Stanton as chairman, by opening offices in Boise, southeastern Washington and the Seattle area.

Above all, the Stanton family's focus on long-term stability instead of short-term gain has helped Washington Trust maintain its unique position in the market through good times and bad. Most notably, when the stock market crashed in 1929, Washington Trust stood strong while businesses and banks across the country failed. Throughout the Depression, the bank met every request for withdrawal of funds on demand and never closed, even for state bank moratoriums. At one point, Washington Trust was the only bank in Spokane open for business. That steadfast philosophy has sustained the financial institution through regional recessions and, most recently, through a surge of competitors' consolidations.

Today, celebrating a century of continuous service to the Northwest, Washington Trust remains true to its original mission of providing extraordinary customer service that is second to none in the communities it serves.

(Above left)
Pete and Philip Stanton, fourth- and third-generation Washington Trust Bank leaders

Current headquarters of Washington Trust Bank on Sprague Avenue

Northwest Farm Credit Services

As part of the nationwide Farm Credit System, Northwest Farm Credit Services is proud to support the men and women who have dedicated their lives to feeding the world. Their hard work and ingenuity have made a positive difference as American agriculture has evolved to meet the needs of a changing world. In Washington State, which boasts the highest yield of wheat per acre in America, production has increased from an average of 19.8 bushels per acre in 1900 to more than 68 bushels per acre 100 years later — an increase of more than 300 percent!

The Inland Northwest's soil and climate make it one of the most fertile areas for the production of soft white wheat and a variety of other crops. As a result, the region became one of the world's breadbaskets in the early 1900s, and has played a crucial role in agriculture ever since. Spokane's growth as a center for banking, commerce, and service came about in large part because of the region's agriculture and natural resources.

As a growing world population steadily increased the need for food, Americans turned to the wheat industry for their daily bread. Wheat farmers prospered as demand increased, but when the price of wheat failed to keep up with production costs, farms grew larger in order to survive — horses gave way to tractors, wagons gave way to trucks. The labor that once required 20 men using horses is now performed more efficiently by three people, a combine, a tractor, and a truck. Operations are larger, more productive, and supply a higher volume of food to both the American people and the rest of the world's population. In 1960 the average farmer fed 25.8 people. By 2001 the average farmer fed five times as many.

A century ago it was common to either live on a farm, or have a close relative directly engaged in production agriculture. Today many people are removed from agriculture by several generations, with less than two percent of the population engaged in its production. Its role, however, has not diminished. The enhancement of production agriculture has afforded the redeployment of the United States workforce to manufacturing, research, medicine, education, and technology, resulting in immeasurable benefits to society. Although many small farms evolved into larger operations, the land is still cared for with knowledge and passion as today's farmers prepare to pass it on to the next generation. The tradition of careful stewardship that comes from being close to the land has not been lost.

As a partner with these vital stewards in rural communities throughout Washington, Oregon, Montana, Idaho and Alaska, the 45 locations of Northwest Farm Credit Services provide approximately $4 billion in loans to the region's agricultural producers. A cooperatively owned company headquartered in Spokane, it is dedicated to Northwest farmers, ranchers, commercial fishermen and rural homeowners. The company also respects its customers' commitment to agriculture. It is a commitment Northwest Farm Credit Services shares.

Soft white winter wheat ripens in Eastern Washington. *Wheat Life Magazine*

Paul Stolp, c. 1920 in Sprague, WA. Continuing its family farm legacy, Stolp Farms continues operation today in land and livestock under the second and third generations.

Spokane Regional Chamber of Commerce

The Spokane Regional Chamber of Commerce has focused on regional issues for all of its 100-plus-year history.

Just as businesses must constantly refocus their programs to be competitive, so must the Chamber. The organization constantly monitors local, regional, national and international business, politics and trends to maintain its focus on the region's economic growth. And as a leadership organization, it calls people and businesses together for timely discussion and action.

The Chamber's goal is to help drive Spokane as a robust regional economic center. Four specific areas — business growth, public policy, work force development and regional image — have been targeted to meet that goal. Each of these areas includes specific strategies to direct the Chamber in meeting its mission, which is to provide leadership in creating an environment in which its members, businesses and community can succeed.

In the area of business growth, the Chamber works with a variety of large and small organizations and businesses on programs designed to promote the region. The Chamber partners with the Economic Development Council to create an integrated, comprehensive plan for economic development. Small businesses are promoted through seminars and roundtables, minority business development and partnership with the Spokane Area Business Information Center.

The Chamber links industry and higher education through the Higher Education Leadership Group, student recruitment and internships. Small- and medium-sized businesses are prepared for the global marketplace through Chamber programs. International advertising and cooperation with Chamber affiliate, the International Trade Alliance, support these efforts.

Public education programs increase awareness of value-added products in agriculture and natural resources. The Chamber supports capital improvements at Fairchild Air Force Base and works to strengthen relationships between the business community and the armed services.

In the area of public policy, the Chamber is an advocate for business at all levels of government on issues of business climate, economic development, work force, infrastructure, capital projects and government efficiency.

The Chamber also works to unite Washington state's 36 counties with members, businesses and chambers on regional environmental, energy and transportation issues.

Work force development is enhanced by the Chamber's support of employer needs through the Inland Northwest Technology Education Center, expansion of the On-Job-College program, participation in Job Shadow and other K-12 programs and the Spokane Youth Job Program.

The Chamber works with the Spokane Area Economic Development Council, Spokane Regional Convention and Visitors Bureau, International Trade Alliance and regional chambers on regional image programs that expand awareness of the region's business and quality-of-life assets.

Regional cultural diversity is recognized and promoted through partnership with AHANA Business and Professional Association. Businesses and individuals are commended through awards and recognition ceremonies such as the AGORA Awards, Community Service and Business Hall of Fame, and government employee awards.

The Chamber's membership is regional and so is its work. It is recognized as a leadership organization that is in touch with the constantly evolving regional workplace and the needs of large, small and emerging businesses, citizens, government, education, military and neighboring counties.

Downtown Spokane

4 Seasons Coffee Company

There's a serious chess match unfolding at a patio table within earshot of the espresso machine. The players are regulars at Spokane's 4 Seasons Coffee Company, and they're on their second round of double tall lattes.

Inside the restored brick building with its high ceilings, merchandise-laden antique furniture and cheerfully mismatched tables, three shoppers are fully engaged in ordering brewed, frothed, flavored and flourished coffee drinks to enjoy at a corner table that invites confidence sharing.

The coffeehouse culture, valued by Europeans for more than a century, is thriving in Spokane, according to 4 Seasons owner Leslie Hutchinson. Enjoying a cup of fine coffee seems to bring people together and sparks conversation, she says. And she should know. Business is regularly transacted over cups of Americano and any one of several made-to-order coffee drinks at 4 Seasons, and the shop has been the scene of at least one marriage proposal.

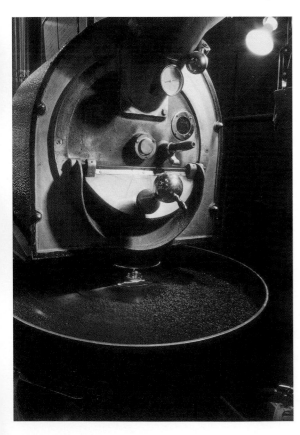

But the region's love affair with the coffee culture wasn't always so firmly entrenched. In fact, it was just beginning to brew in the mid-70s when Hutchinson and her husband, Tom, decided to move to Spokane from the San Francisco Bay area to roast their own beans and open a coffee bar in the city's bustling downtown.

The business wasn't new to the couple — Tom had worked with a green coffee brokerage firm for four years — and the Inland Northwest, with its varied climate and range of outdoor recreation opportunities, was appealing. The Hutchinsons arrived in 1976 and later that year, 4 Seasons Coffee Company opened its doors with 800 square feet of space, a coffee roaster, one table and the distinction of being one of the first coffee bars in the community.

Launching the new business proved to be a challenge. Coffee was still largely relegated to the breakfast table, the diner counter and thermos bottles. "Coffee was definitely not in capital letters," says Leslie. "Premium bean prices were at an all-time high and demand for coffee drinks built slowly."

But the Hutchinsons persevered and within two years they bought their first espresso machine. Set in a spot visible from the street, the intricate brewing process and the aroma of freshly roasted beans brought people into the shop, and 4 Seasons' regular clientele began to grow.

As the roasting and retail operation expanded, 4 Seasons outgrew its original site and moved to its present location on Howard Street in 1981. Less than a block from Spokane's signature Riverfront Park, the brick building was once a hotel, and the area that houses 4 Seasons Coffee Company was an elegant ballroom. During Prohibition, Dutch Jake's Speakeasy operated in the basement and its walls still boast murals from that era.

Today, the historic building echoes with mellow tunes from a CD player instead of an orchestra and patrons sip their drinks from pottery mugs and to-go paper cups instead of crystal glasses. Coffee beans from the darkest, heartiest French roast to lighter blends fill glass-front cases topped by an assortment of teas, pastry items and snacks. And today 4 Seasons' great coffee is fueling the company's rapidly growing wholesale roasting business.

Quality of product and consistency of process is 4 Season's formula for success, according to Leslie, who points out the company's philosophy inscribed on a hand-painted sign behind the counter — "A continuum in quality from bean to cup."

"We roast the finest beans we can find," she says. "It makes good coffee and good sense to begin with only the best."

Not unlike fine wines, exceptional coffees reflect the climate, terrain and soil in which they're grown, and 4 Seasons purchases its beans from more than a dozen countries. The Hutchinsons have walked the fields of many plantations that grow beans destined for their roasters to monitor quality and production standards from ground level. Their passion for fine beans is combined with an awareness of the environmental and social issues particular to the coffee growing business, including preference for farmers who practice environmentally sound agricultural methods and adequately compensate workers. The couple also favors organic coffees grown without pesticides and fertilizers and shade-grown beans from plants that thrive under the natural forest canopy.

While a fine cup of coffee begins with premium beans, the real character of the brew emerges in the roasting process. Once sacks of green coffee beans reach 4 Seasons, the roaster's touch takes over. The degree of heat applied to fully develop the beans' potential defines 4 Seasons coffee and each step of the process is carefully monitored. When the trade journal *Northwest Hospitality News* reviewed regional coffee roasters, 4 Seasons was one of four in Washington State and the only Inland Northwest roaster to be recognized for excellence.

Today, with a growing reputation for excellence, the company is focused on increasing the wholesale side of the business. When customers began asking for large volumes of coffee for their restaurants, businesses and espresso stands, the Hutchinsons knew they could meet the demand by expanding. In April 2001, 4 Seasons moved the roasting operation to a new warehouse just outside the city center where it expects to more than triple the 18,000 to 20,000 pounds of beans currently being roasted a month at the downtown facility.

Just as coffee has become a part of the American culture, 4 Seasons Coffee Company has become a Spokane fixture. The couple has turned down offers to open branch coffee bars in area shopping malls, preferring their downtown location and staying close to their customers.

Over the years, most members of the Hutchinson family have bagged and sold beans or worked the espresso machine. Leslie's mother retired from her barista position at 94, but she's still stopped on the street by customers who remember her energy, enthusiasm and warmth.

A family's desire to live where the climate is in perpetual motion prompted the name of 4 Seasons Coffee Company, but its logo is another story. A vintage biplane streaks across business cards and labels, its jaunty pilot holds a steaming mug of coffee aloft. Is it Tom in search of the world's best beans? Or does it simply reflect the Hutchinsons' philosophy that life is an adventure to be lived well and enjoyed with 4 Seasons coffee?

Olympic Foods

The gleaming silver tanker truck pulls into the unloading dock at Olympic Foods and begins pumping its golden cargo into holding tanks. However, this "gold" isn't oil or some other typically precious commodity and these bulk tank trucks aren't covered in grease and grime. The trucks are immaculate inside and out. And the gold is orange juice.

Weeks ago, fresh oranges were picked in groves as close as California or as far away as Florida, Mexico and Brazil. Their juice was extracted and the product was transported to this manufacturing plant in the Inland Northwest. By the time the product leaves Spokane's Olympic Foods, it will pass through rigorous testing and quality control in a state-of-the art facility that processes up to 400,000 gallons of refrigerated orange or apple juice a week. Olympic Foods produces 100-percent juice products for private label brands and for its own branded products distributed throughout the western region. Its own branded products are Citrus Sunshine, Tree Top Grower's Best, Washington Natural and Sunkist Pure refrigerated juices.

Olympic Foods didn't start out as a refrigerated juice processor. In 1964 the Spokane company produced corn dogs under the brand name Frank Fritter Corn Dogs. In the mid-60s the Early Bird Juice Company was formed as part of Olympic Foods and began producing "Chirps," a drink product.

By the 1970s Olympic Foods had developed a first-rate corn dog manufacturing facility, sold juice to dairies and began producing private label sales of both corn dogs and juice. The first private label juice, Western Family, was soon followed by Safeway Lucerne.

In 1985 Olympic Foods purchased Buckaroo Bagels. That venture was sold three years later. By the late 80s the juice business was taking off, the Western Family Seattle business was added, Citrus Sunshine Orange Juice was created and apple juice was introduced as Fresh Pressed. In 1995 the corn dog business was sold.

In just over 20 years, Olympic Foods has grown from a small specialty drink processor to a major western region producer known for high-quality products and an innovative approach to making juice and running a company. The American Institute of Industrial Baking has repeatedly given Olympic Foods superior ratings for compliance, good manufacturing practices, process controls and cleanliness.

Olympic Foods credits its success to a combination of art, science and people. The company slogan, the "Art of Juice," makes its way from state-of-the-art technology to fresh-picked good taste. The highly specialized systems and controls that go into preserving, blending, packing and delivering juice from the field to the consumer make the difference.

A quality assurance technician meets arriving product tankers to sample and test the raw product, and taste testers are on the final end of the process as well. In between, juice is pasteurized and cold filled, a process that preserves fresh juice characteristics.

Olympic Foods' blow mold system creates user-friendly plastic juice containers, from the single-serving size that fits perfectly into the palm of a hand to gallon jugs with convenient handles. Olympic Foods creates unique bottle designs in response to customer needs.

The Olympic Foods facility in Spokane, Washington

State-of-the-art pasteurization system

Processed juice fills the blow mold bottles and they are sealed without ever being touched by human hands.

But the art of juice and the science of juice are only two of the components that have led to Olympic Foods' success and its reputation for being a leader in the marketplace. The third ingredient is the company's employees.

One-hundred and twenty people make up the team at Olympic Foods. The company's team-based philosophy and accessible management contribute to low employee turnover, high loyalty and involved employees.

Plant production crews are cross-trained and can handle a variety of tasks in addition to their primary function. This ensures that all systems will run regardless of unforeseen absences, but equally important, it means that employees understand each other's jobs and the importance of each person's role.

Sales and marketing personnel are headquartered in Spokane with direct sales teams located across the west in key markets.

Communication isn't just a two-way street at Olympic Foods; management believes it goes up, down and sideways. Managers' offices and the human resources department are located close to the plant,

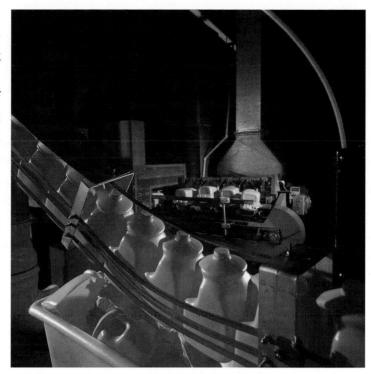

not so far away as to be inconvenient or intimidating. Management provides a safe, clean, communicative environment for its employees, and they in turn provide suggestions on how to improve systems or working conditions.

Outside the walls of the Olympic Foods plant, the company donates juice products to schools, athletic teams, charities and worthy causes in the Spokane area with little fanfare. This is not viewed as a marketing or public relations strategy, rather it is a way Olympic Foods management and employees can give back to the community they call home.

In December 1998 Olympic Foods helped establish the Positive Image Center in Spokane, an organization that helps men, women and children deal with physical changes that result from medical injury or illness. Hair loss and skin care challenges are addressed in a variety of ways to help bolster patients' self-esteem. The Spokane Positive Image Center is one of only two in the United States and operates under the City of Hope National Medical Center, a cancer, diabetes and AIDS research and treatment organization in Southern California.

Olympic Foods is firmly rooted in the Inland Northwest and committed to bringing top-quality juice to customers.

■ User-friendly stylized plastic containers

■ Juice-filling operation

Pearson Packaging Systems

An innovative machine invented by an entrepreneur in a garage on Spokane's South Hill in the early 1950s launched one of today's most well-respected companies in the international packaging industry — Pearson Packaging Systems.

This machinery manufacturer got its start when bottle shop superintendent R. A. "Lefty" Pearson asked his employer, Bohemian Brewery, for permission to work on an idea he had for a machine that would automatically erect cardboard carriers to hold six bottles of beer. After successfully inventing the first automatic carrier erector, Pearson gave the prototype to his employer and hired a machinist to work in his basement garage while he continued to work at Bohemian. Despite being diagnosed with terminal cancer, Pearson and his partner, Benny Weremiczyk, began to build machines for other northwest breweries and soft-drink bottlers.

Pearson's next invention was an automatic case erector and then an automatic sealer to securely close the case. The business that was founded in 1955 soon outgrew his home and moved into an old railroad building on South Division in the early 1960s, when Pearson left his old job and dedicated a full-time effort to the company. The next move was into a larger facility on East 2nd Avenue in the late 1960s and once again in 1978 to a newly constructed facility on the Sunset Highway.

The 40,000-square-foot assembly area at Pearson Packaging Systems has a wide variety of machines under construction at any one time.

Today, the company's machines are found in 30 countries and in nearly half of the Fortune 500 companies in the United States. While Pearson still serves the beverage industry, it has expanded to help automate glass and plastic bottle manufacturers, meat and poultry producers, as well as the personal care, home products, bulk packaging, pharmaceutical and packaged food industries.

Pearson machinery sets up, packs and seals "secondary packaging" — the corrugated cases into which, for example, multiple bottles of laundry detergent or boxes of cereal are shipped to grocery stores. Its product line of more than 65 standard machines includes case erector/bottom sealers, case packers, plastic bottle packers, top sealers, partition inserters, trayformers, multipackers, carrier erectors, plastic bag inserters and uncuffers, and hopper feeders. Additionally, the company is known for its ability to customize standard machinery or build special engineer-to-order equipment.

In 1970 as he was dying, Lefty hired Robert H. Graham from Coors Brewing Company to manage the business for him. In addition after Lefty's death in 1971, his wife, Alma, represented the family in the business for many years and still serves as chairman of the board of directors. Graham's involvement continued until 1983, when Ray Bly became vice president and general manager. Today, Lefty and Alma's daughter, Pamela Senske, and grandson, Michael Senske, manage Pearson Packaging Systems, along with General Manager Randy Stewart and a cadre of additional talented, dedicated people.

Pam Senske joined the family's manufacturing enterprise in 1986 to assess the company's strengths and weaknesses, direction and future potential. As a result, she became the catalyst for change the company needed. The company implemented MRP (Material Requirements

(Far left)
Pearson case erectors set up and glue the bottom of corrugated cases at speeds up to 75 cases per minute.

(Center)
Pearson trayformers have become an industry standard for the rigorous production environment of the meat industry.

The little machine that started it all, the updated carrier erector still has a major presence in the brewing industry.

Planning/Manufacturing Resource Planning) in 1986, which gave it the philosophical change and the tools to grow profitably. Senske became president in 1992 with Bill Parks as general manager. By 1994 the firm needed to expand its manufacturing facility and added an additional 40,000 square feet for a total of 110,000 square feet. Senske served as general manager from 1998 until Randy Stewart became general manager in 2001. Senske, along with her two brothers, Jack Pearson and Don Pearson, own 80 percent of the company stock.

Director of New Business Development Michael Senske's third-generation involvement in Pearson Packaging Systems began in 1997, signifying the Pearson family's commitment to the continued growth and long-term future of the privately held company. Michael came to Pearson from Microsoft, where he gained invaluable experience in product support services. With that background, he is focusing not only on helping the company to find new business opportunities but also to do things better internally.

As the new century began, Pearson Packaging Systems was making positive investments in its people and its infrastructure in order to be able to grow profitably in the future. As Michael noted, the environment in which Pearson operates today is much more competitive than it was when Lefty invented his first machine. Competition is worldwide. Much more new product development is required of Pearson today as well, because consumer products are constantly changing.

To meet these challenges, Pearson has committed itself to be customer focused, team based, process oriented and flexible. The company implemented Product & Industry teams to coordinate the efforts of sales, engineering, manufacturing, assembly and service required for a particular product line or for an entire industry. The purpose of the teams is to focus on customers' needs and on the markets the company serves, and to create "experts" in each of those areas. In addition, the company has put all of its computer systems on one platform and recently implemented a new companywide ERP system to replace its former MRP system. It has also implemented a 3-D CAD system to replace the old 2-D CAD. Currently the company is working toward aligning all of its employees around a common vision and goals for the future.

Pearson carries its commitment to its customers beyond design and delivery of machines into quality service after the sale. Technical support professionals are available worldwide 24 hours a day, seven days a week. The Pearson Service Parts department delivers high-quality spare and replacement parts, machinery upgrade kits and custom component parts every day to customers all over the world. It is capable of providing same-day service on a wide range of stocked parts. So no matter what a customer needs, Pearson is ready to respond quickly.

From an innovative idea that started in a garage on Spokane's South Hill, Pearson Packaging Systems has grown into one of the premier secondary packaging machinery manufacturers in the world today. With a talented, capable work force and a strong family commitment to success, it appears the company will continue to adapt and grow for generations to come.

Systems Roofers Supply, Inc.

Having a roof over their heads is something people take for granted — until it leaks or is blown off in a storm. At that point, it becomes a critical concern. A sturdy, durable roof offers security to homeowners not only by providing shelter and safety but also by adding to the overall value of the home. Throughout the state of Washington, Western Montana and the Idaho Panhandle, many homeowners and businesses enjoy the security of a high-quality roof because of Systems Roofers Supply, Inc. (SRS), one of the Northwest's premier roofing supply distributors.

SRS was founded in 1988 when Ted and Judy Anderson acquired the roofing products division of Savage Wholesale Building Materials. Since that time, the Andersons have expanded the business from a small enterprise with antiquated delivery trucks into a thriving company with a fleet of the newest delivery vehicles available. SRS also expanded beyond its original E. Broadway site in Spokane by adding two new locations: a satellite roofing yard that opened in the early 1990s on N. Government Way in Hayden, Idaho, and one that opened on Western Street NW in Auburn, Washington, in 1999. That same year the employees of SRS made the ultimate statement of faith in the company and its future by acquiring SRS through an employee stock option program. Ted Anderson now serves as CEO.

Systems Roofers Supply is a complete stocking distributor for the professional roofer, supplying the best and newest roofing materials and tools on the market. With a fleet of five boom trucks, five conveyor trucks and two semis, SRS delivers materials to retail lumberyards and offers rooftop or ground drop deliveries at contractor work sites. Some of the notable projects for which they have supplied roofing materials include the historic renovation of the Davenport Hotel in Spokane; the Selkirk Lodge in Sandpoint, Idaho; and the Montana homes of television celebrity David Letterman and investment magnate Charles Schwab.

The company is a wholesaler for Elk, Iko, Owens Corning and Certainteed consumer roofing products and Johns Manville, Genflex, Henry's and Fields commercial roofing products. SRS carries a full line of high-quality products, including asphalt shingles, single-ply membrane systems, CDX and OSB sheathing, cedar shakes and shingles, metal roofing and roof tile. It distributes coatings, drains, felt underlayments, insulation, cold process equipment, and ice and water shields. The company's array of products also includes walk pads, bur, wood fiber, metal flashing, gypsum, asphalt and a complete assortment of roofing tools.

In a relatively short time, SRS has established itself as the roofing supply wholesaler of choice in Eastern Washington and the surrounding areas. By offering a full inventory of products — and armed with the newest equipment and a knowledgeable and service-oriented staff with a vested interest in the company's success — Systems Roofers Supply is not only uniquely capable but sincerely committed to providing the security of a high-quality, lasting roof.

The facilities of Systems Roofers Supply, Inc., one of the Northwest's premier distributors of high-quality roofing supplies

Dollar Rent A Car

The wall behind the counter of Spokane-based Dollar Rent A Car is covered with plaques, certificates, awards, letters of appreciation and commendations. Rick Manfred, the owner and manager of the Spokane-Coeur d'Alene operation, calls it the wall of fame.

But a closer look at the mementos mounted on the wall reveals not just accomplishments but also a strong commitment to Spokane and Coeur d'Alene. Vehicles, financial contributions and employee time have all been part of the ways Dollar Rent A Car gives back to the communities that have supported it for the past 12 years.

Amateur athletics are the dominant theme. Dollar Rent A Car backs the athletic programs at Eastern Washington University and Gonzaga University, and supports Skyhawks Sports Academy, the Schweitzer Mountain Youth Racing Team, Spokane Raceway Park and Amateur Athletic Union basketball. Dollar recently added sponsorship of the USA Triathlon National Age Group Championship, which was held in Coeur d'Alene, Idaho, for the first time this year.

Sprinkled among the go-team symbols are indicators of additional community involvement. Dollar has been a member of the Spokane Area Convention and Visitors Bureau since 1990, has supported the city's annual Lilac Festival, has contributed time and money to the Diabetic Association and more. Members of Dollar's management team serve on committees and sit on the board of directors of several organizations.

Dollar is particularly proud of its involvement in S.T.R.I.V.E. a Spokane school district program that is dedicated to developing special education training and vocational resources for at-risk teens.

Dollar Rent A Car's Inland Northwest roots and philosophy of business go to back to the 1940s. At that time, entrepreneur Jerry Camp Sr. opened an automobile dealership in Spokane and built a family business based on the twin tenants of excellent customer service and high ethical standards.

Camp Chevrolet survived and prospered despite the area's economic ups and downs. For many years its showrooms were not located on major thoroughfares, usually a must for auto sales; but high customer loyalty, word-of-mouth advertising and excellent customer

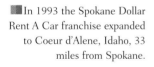
In 1993 the Spokane Dollar Rent A Car franchise expanded to Coeur d'Alene, Idaho, 33 miles from Spokane.

service ensured that shoppers would find Camp Chevrolet regardless of its location.

In 1989 Camp Chevrolet acquired the Dollar Rent A Car franchise and launched the rental company under the corporate umbrella name Cougar Investments. The cougar moniker comes from the Camp family's strong ties to Washington State University and its cougar mascot. It's a sentiment that's common in this part of the country.

Dollar's operation was modest at first — a fleet of 26 cars and a desk at the Spokane International Airport.

In 1993 the Spokane Dollar Rent A Car franchise expanded to Coeur d'Alene, Idaho. Just 33 miles from Spokane, the lake town was coming into its own as a golf and water sports mecca.

Dollar's management found a fitting location for their new facility — an old gas station that Dollar leased and transformed into a rental office. The location, directly across the street from the well-known Coeur d'Alene Resort, proved critical. The luxury lakeside hotel and golf course transformed the sleepy town into a bustling tourist destination.

When Coeur d'Alene Resort management agreed to use Dollar exclusively for their auto rental needs, a strong customer base was established and financial stability and success followed for Dollar's Inland Northwest operation.

The next five years saw tremendous growth for Dollar Rent A Car in Spokane and Coeur d' Alene. Several factors contributed to Dollar's success, including a 30-percent increase in passenger traffic at the Spokane International Airport. Local ownership and consistency of management were also big plusses. At this point, competition in the auto rental and leasing arena was fierce, but Dollar not only managed to hold its market share but to emerge as an industry leader.

In 1997, when it moved into the City Ramp garage, Dollar became the only car rental franchise in downtown Spokane. Management shake ups followed when Camp Automotive was sold to the western giant of vehicle sales and rentals, Lithia Automotive Group. The Camp family, however, maintained their control over Cougar Investments and the Dollar Rent A Car

franchise. With a handshake agreement, Camp passed management of the corporation to the current team.

Cougar Investments branched out and the company began purchasing properties in Spokane and Coeur d'Alene. The Dollar Rent A Car operation moved out of the remodeled gas station in Coeur d'Alene into a new facility on Northwest Boulevard, the main thoroughfare leading into town, tripling the size of the facility.

Today, Dollar Rent A Car has four rental locations, two sales facilities and a leasing division. The company that began 12 years ago with 26 cars at an airport facility now has 400 rental vehicles, 150 vehicles for lease and approximately 150 cars for sale. This rapid

> *Today*, Dollar Rent A Car has four rental locations, two sales facilities and a leasing division.

growth has occurred in spite of a regional economy that has risen about 1 to 2 percent in the past decade.

A team of 40 staffs the rental, sales and leasing facilities. Dollar Rent A Car has transferred its community care ethic to its employee relations and offers a variety of programs designed to provide something more than a paycheck to its personnel.

A 50-percent college tuition reimbursement is available to employees who maintain a 3.0 grade point average. Flex-time is built into Dollar's shifts and the company works hard to provide an environment that is responsive to change. Dollar hopes to launch telecommuting within the next year.

Dollar Rent A Car's corporate headquarters is well aware of the gem they have in the Inland Northwest franchise operation. In the past, the Spokane-Coeur d'Alene franchise has received the President's Cup Award and was ranked fourth in the nation in its category for top customer service.

Hotel Lusso

Walking into the lobby of Spokane's Hotel Lusso is like walking into a San Francisco boutique hotel. Maybe it's the smiling bell man who opened the door with a flourish. Or perhaps it's the warm shades of the plush carpet, the leather furniture and the

hand-painted ceiling mural. More likely, it's the lobby's centerpiece, a Mediterranean-style fountain surrounded by lush plants. There is nothing quite like Hotel Lusso from Seattle to Denver.

Dozens of large and small touches in the hotel's public areas speak of luxury and tranquility, and those promises are fulfilled in Hotel Lusso's 48 elegant guest rooms. Twelve-foot high ceilings, light-spilling arched windows and extra-high baseboards in the larger-than-average rooms contribute to the feeling of spaciousness. Cherry wood crown molding, custom furniture, oversized bathrooms with marble surrounds and tumbled marble floors all say relax, breathe deeply and be pampered. Even the individual room thermostats ensure quiet, comfort and serenity.

All of these details and more make it clear that Hotel Lusso is the sort of lodging establishment that takes the work out of business travel. It's also the sort of place that draws couples from around the Inland Northwest for a romantic getaway.

Husband and wife team Joe and Mary Dinnison are credited with the dream, the investment and the sweat equity that has become Hotel Lusso. He's a Spokane native and she has lived in Spokane most of her life. They have been buying and developing downtown real estate for years with a keen eye for old buildings and a commitment to historic preservation.

Before opening the doors of Hotel Lusso, the closest the Dinnisons had come to operating lodging establishments was staying in them. That was hardly a deterrent. They knew exactly what they liked — intimate, boutique hotels that were big on service, cleanliness and amenities. And they believed that Spokane could support a small, high-end hotel. Conveniently, they owned the historic Miller and Whitten buildings on the corner of Post Street and Sprague Avenue, as well as the upscale Fugazzi Restaurant on the ground floor.

By the time Hotel Lusso welcomed its first guests in January 1998, the Dinnisons' dream had become a $6.5 million investment. It is aptly named; Lusso means luxury in Italian and Ferrari fans may recognize it as one of the auto maker's early 1960s models.

Hotel Lusso's Cavallino Lounge, located on the Post Street side of the hotel, maintains the elegant theme. Cavallino means prancing horse in Italian and is also the Ferrari symbol. The cozy, sophisticated lounge is a favorite place to meet for after-work cocktails and has been voted the best spot to sip martinis by local newspaper reader polls.

Add Hotel Lusso's Fugazzi Dining Room to the mix, also winner of best polls, and the result is a memorable hotel stay in the heart of the Inland Northwest's largest city.

When Hotel Lusso opened its doors in January 1998, some heralded the Dinnisons as gutsy visionaries.

Others doubted that Spokane had business travelers with expense accounts that could handle Hotel Lusso's nightly price tag and they expected the hotel would stand elegantly empty. The skeptics lost that bet, and Hotel Lusso has seen its overnight occupancy rate climb to an average of 70 percent, a fair accomplishment in an industry that often runs at a 50 to 60 percent occupancy level.

Hotel Lusso's success can be attributed to a mix of developing and maintaining a specific niche, savvy marketing, consistently high service and excellent timing.

The Dinnisons and Hotel Lusso's management team believe that being on the road has its challenges and that where and how you sleep shouldn't be one of them. National trends indicate that a growing segment of corporate travelers look for first-class accommodations and will not hesitate to pay top dollar for an oasis of calm and comfort at the end of the day. Hotel Lusso has met that niche market and its business clientele returns time and time again.

A dedicated staff is the underpinning of Hotel Lusso's top-notch customer service. The little things add up: the front desk clerk remembers a client from a previous stay and actually greets them by name at check in. The bell man gives directions by walking the guest to the corner to make sure they find their way. The housekeeping staff brings the extra blanket within minutes of receiving the request. The room is immaculate, comfortable and quiet.

With a firm handle on business customers' needs, Hotel Lusso was filling rooms during the week, but weekends were a little too quiet. In order to attract Inland Northwest residents to the hotel for weekend stays, the marketing team devised a dinner-movie-museum-overnight package. In no time, folks from Spokane, Eastern Washington and North Idaho were leaving the kids at home and escaping for some downtown fun and relaxation.

And in the past three years, downtown Spokane has become downright lively. Not so long ago, entertainment venues like Metropolitan Performing Arts, Interplayers

Ensemble and the Opera House anchored city nightlife. Spokane was often deserted after businesses closed. Now a combination of new construction and historic renovation projects has brought a vibrant nightlife back to the city.

New projects like Riverpark Square with its shops, restaurants and multiplex theater attract people from around the region. Television station KHQ-TV moved its headquarters downtown into a new building and brought over 100 employees with it.

Historic buildings are being renovated at a surprisingly rapid pace. Within walking distance of Hotel Lusso, the Steam Plant Square, a former 1916 heating plant, was beautifully restored and houses a restaurant, lounge, shops and offices. The Spokane Symphony is in the midst of renovating the lovely art deco Fox Theater. Snazzy Far West Billiards opened last year in the rehabilitated Montvale Building and an arts, entertainment and residential district is taking shape in the neighborhood.

Spokane's largest historic renovation project, the Davenport Hotel, is located across the street from Hotel Lusso. Once one of the nation's grandest hotels, it sat vacant and decaying for years until a local developer purchased the property for $6.5 million. After an additional $15 million was invested, the hotel reopened in 2002.

As Spokane rediscovers its roots and its vibrancy, Hotel Lusso appears to be at the right place at the right time with just the right strategy to be in the center of activity.

Latah Creek Wine Cellars

One of the few family-owned-and-operated wineries in Washington, Latah Creek Wine Cellars has been at the forefront of the winemaking industry's development in the state. Owners Mike Conway and his wife, Ellena, brought the California style of winemaking to Spokane in 1980.

Mike started his career in the wine industry eight years earlier in the microbiology laboratory of E&J Gallo, the largest winery in the United States, and later worked as the microbiologist at Franzia Brothers Winery. In 1977 he became an assistant winemaker at the Parducci Winery in Northern California, where he was trained by John Parducci.

As a result of his experience, Mike was offered a full charge winemaking job with the responsibility of starting up and operating a new winery, Worden's, in Spokane. His speedy success there generated a joint venture with grape grower Mike Hogue. In 1982 two new wineries — Latah Creek and The Hogue Cellars — were started. Mike Conway was winemaker for both.

After two years, the operations were separated, allowing Mike and Ellena to devote their complete attention to their own winery, Latah Creek Wine Cellars. Mike handles management, winemaking and vineyard duties, while Ellena manages the winery's financials, accounting and its tasting room. In addition to themselves, there are only one full-time and a few part-time employees at the winery, which might seem surprising for an operation that produces 11,000 cases of wine each year.

Unlike other small wineries, Latah Creek was built specifically to be a winery. Consequently, the entire winemaking process takes place under one roof. The grapes Mike uses to create award-winning wines come from vineyards, including the Hogue vineyards, 150 miles to the south and west of Spokane on the Wahluke Slope and the Yakima Valley, a region known for its excellent grape-growing conditions.

Mike stays in tune with the unique regional market Latah Creek serves, responding to the changing tastes of consumers who are increasingly sophisticated about wine. Roughly 35 percent of Latah Creek's production consists of red wines. Another 35 percent is devoted exclusively to Chardonnay, and the remaining 30 percent is composed of smaller lots of Johannisberg Riesling, Muscat Canelli and proprietary blends of Moscato d'Latah, Maywine, Huckleberry Riesling and Spokane Blush.

Strong supporters of local business and the community, Mike and Ellena have donated their wines to events sponsored by organizations such as the Foster Parents Association, Spokane Symphony and Spokane AIDS Network.

Mike also served as president of the state's wine association at a time when the industry was floundering. He applied his small-business perspective to the situation, increasing membership more than 60 percent. In addition, he helped the local Spokane Winery Association come together to create two annual events to promote the industry.

Above all, Mike and Ellena intend to maintain Latah Creek's small size and concentrate on quality. Their goal is to continue to produce exceptional bottles of wine at a good price to ensure the region's everyday customers can afford to enjoy great wine.

Suki Yaki Inn

Customers rave that the Suki Yaki Inn's sushi is every bit as good as one would find in Seattle. It's no wonder generations of Spokane families have frequented this Japanese restaurant, which still stands on the same downtown site where it was first established in 1948 by Van Omine.

Originally from Okinawa, Japan, Omine moved from Honolulu to Spokane where he built his business serving authentic Japanese cuisine. Omine personally oversaw the daily preparations for almost 40 years. Throughout those years, he waited and watched for an individual who he could trust to carry on the tradition he had established. That special person was Emiko Collett.

As the wife of an American serviceman, Emiko moved from Sasebo city in Nagasaki prefecture, Japan, to Des Moines, Iowa, where she went to school. She followed her husband to Spokane, but later was divorced.

Emiko began work as a dishwasher and waitress at the Suki Yaki Inn in the late 1970s. As a self-described workaholic, she also sold cosmetics at The Bon Marche and taught Japanese at Sunrise Elementary and University High School — all while she was working full time at the inn. During her years at the restaurant, Emiko learned to make sushi, tend bar and eventually manage all the daily operations.

By 1995 Omine was in his 80s and certain he had found in Emiko the person he could trust with the business he had worked so hard to build. As a result, he allowed her to buy the restaurant from him.

Under Emiko's ownership, business at the restaurant and its popular bar quickly tripled. Little by little, she has remodeled the interior, which contains a sushi bar, large banquet room, private tatami rooms and lounge.

Open seven days a week, the Suki Yaki Inn is so popular reservations are a must on the weekends. Emiko takes particular pride in hearing customers say their grandparents had their first date at the Suki Yaki Inn and in serving family gatherings of three or four generations who return time and again. Many former customers whose lives have taken them away from Spokane make it a point to dine at the restaurant on return trips.

Japanese dishes customers may choose among include yosenabe, a variety of seafood steamed with napa cabbage and white onion served with lemon sauce; torikatsu, breaded and deep fried boneless chicken served with plum sauce; batayaki, cubed tenderloin steak sautéed with green onions, sliced mushrooms, ginger, garlic, sake and soy sauce; and, of course, suki yaki, thinly sliced beef with a variety of vegetables, tofu and bean noodles simmered in soy sake and sugar. For her sushi and sashimi, Emiko has fresh fish flown in from San Francisco if she is unable to find it locally.

One thing is certain — as long as Emiko owns it, she will be visible personally making sushi, waiting on her customers, and tending bar at the Suki Yaki Inn in downtown Spokane.

Avista Corp.

Not all companies capture the character of a place. Many operate, quite successfully, apart from their surroundings.

But another kind of company reflects the very community in which it does business. It enriches and is enriched by the people and the landscape, never losing sight of its connection to a story that extends far beyond itself.

Avista Corp. is such a company. Indeed, it was founded in direct response to local needs. Faced with increasing demand for electricity in the booming young city of Spokane Falls (as it was then called), trustees of the Edison Electric Illuminating Company sought funding from their backers in New York to build a power station on the Spokane River. Their request was denied because, they were told, water power held little or no value. Not so easily dissuaded, 10 stockholders opted to found The Washington Water Power Company — today known as Avista Corp. — and proceed with the project themselves. The year was 1889.

That decision began a long tradition of company and community joining forces to support the economy, care for the natural resources and promote the appealing quality of life of the Inland Northwest.

Among the employees of the newly formed Washington Water Power (WWP) was engineer Henry Herrick, who oversaw construction of the Monroe Street power station. Despite the devastating fire that raged through downtown in August 1889, destroying more than 30 city blocks, Herrick accomplished his task, bringing the hydroelectric project on line on November 12, 1890.

And while the company's interests naturally gravitate toward the local economy, Washington Water Power — which became Avista Corp. in 1999 — has a long tradition of commitment to education and to corporate philanthropy.

The completion of Monroe Street was the beginning of the end for the Edison Electric Illuminating Company. By 1891 WWP had acquired controlling interest in the organization, whose lack of vision had spawned WWP's own formation.

Lack of vision was never a problem for Washington Water Power, however. Early company officials saw tremendous potential in streetcar systems, both as users of the company's product and as a means to encourage growth in the city's residential

Spokane Falls, 1880

areas. WWP acquired the Spokane Street Railway Company and, in order to give passengers some place fun to go, it incorporated Natatorium Park in 1895. Both proved successful; at its peak, the streetcar system served nearly 25 million passengers a year, and Natatorium Park — at the west end of Boone Avenue — took its place as one of the region's most popular diversions for anyone who loved swimming, dancing, music, roller coasters, animals or baseball. Nat Park's long run ended in 1968, years after WWP had sold its interest and buses had replaced streetcars as Spokane's preferred mode of public transportation.

Both Spokane and Washington Water Power thrived as they entered a new century. The city of nearly 20,000 — host of the Northwest Industrial Exposition in 1900 — rapidly established itself as the region's financial and transportation center. WWP kept pace, building a 117-mile transmission line in 1903 to serve mines in northern Idaho's Silver Valley; at the time, it was the longest high-voltage line in the world.

The company extended its service almost continually from then until the early 1930s, constructing more than 1,500 miles of transmission lines to bring electricity to many of the region's rural towns. That same period saw increased investment in generation assets, yielding the Post Falls, Nine Mile, Post Street, Little Falls, Long Lake, Upper Falls and Chelan hydroelectric facilities. The company still operates every one of those plants today, with the exception of Chelan; that plant was condemned by the Chelan County PUD in 1955.

Such projects were huge undertakings. Long Lake, for instance, included 170-foot spillways — the highest in the world at the time — and the largest turbines then in operation. The construction camp built for workers at the site boasted a general store, post office, cement laboratory, office building, steam laundry, hotel, barber, cookhouse, a 250-person-capacity dining room, and a clubhouse featuring movies and vaudeville acts.

To tide the region over while hydroelectric projects were under construction, WWP built one steam plant and bought another.

The latter building stands as a particularly fine example of the company's commitment to use its resources to best serve the community. Eighty years later, after much renovation, Steam Plant Square opened its doors, offering unique and technologically advanced office and retail space to area businesses.

The company also devotes considerable resources to environmental matters.

Moving as fast as it could to respond to the public's growing appetite for electricity, Washington Water Power also turned to other providers. Between 1910 and 1936, WWP acquired 40 separate operating units or electrical systems, including a Colfax-based distribution system, the Okanogan Valley Power Company; the Inland Power and Light Company near Lewiston; and the Stevens County Power and Light Company. And in 1923 WWP connected with the systems of the Puget Sound Power and Light Company to the west and the Montana Power Company to the east, creating a 910-mile interconnection that allowed each utility to lend temporary assistance to the other in case of emergency. That arrangement, along with an earlier one formed with the Pacific Power and Light Company in Lind, Washington, served as a model for the Northwest Power Pool, an

■ Natatorium Park, 1916

electric interchange established in 1941 to link all electric utilities in five Western states and British Columbia.

With America's entry into World War II on December 7, 1941, Washington Water Power had the opportunity to serve more than the region, and the company rose to the occasion. More than 250 employees enlisted in the armed forces; those who stayed back home organized scrap drives and war bond sales. All told, WWP donated more than 2 million pounds of iron, lead and zinc to the war effort and bought the maximum amount of war bonds allowed. With materials and manpower so diverted, almost all normal activities — including construction and expansion — came to a halt.

When the war ended in 1945, the economy rebounded quickly and Washington Water Power again focused its attention on customers. The postwar boom taxed the Northwest's power supply, spurring voluntary conservation measures in 1948. Moving to resolve the supply problem in 1950, WWP applied for a license from the Federal Power Commission to build a dam at Cabinet Gorge on Montana's Clark Fork River. The application was approved just two months later in one of the speediest such decisions ever rendered.

The company set an ambitious construction schedule. Crews worked 24 hours a day, driving two 1,000-foot diversion tunnels and erecting the coffer dams a mere eight months after the license was approved. The dam itself — 208 feet high and 600 feet long — was finished on time. Total project time amounted to an unprecedented 21 months.

WWP had its next project already underway, and the first three units of Noxon Rapids — 22 miles upstream from Cabinet Gorge — came on line in 1959. It is the company's largest power producing facility.

The intense activity on the Clark Fork led some to raise concerns about environmental matters. True to form, Washington Water Power became the first utility in the country to hire a full-time fisheries biologist.

At about the same time WWP was developing Noxon Rapids, the last major hydroelectric project built in the Northwest by a private utility, the company began considering ways to incorporate natural gas into its energy mix. In 1958, a scant three years after natural gas was first delivered to the Pacific Northwest, Washington Water Power acquired the Spokane Natural Gas Company.

That line of business integrated quite naturally with the company's other operations. and its success influenced Washington Water Power's involvement in the Jackson Prairie Underground Gas Storage Project in western Washington. An innovative concept in 1970 when it was developed, Jackson Prairie stores 12.8 billion cubic feet of gas for use by the project's partners, WWP, El Paso Natural Gas and Washington Natural Gas.

Two years after WWP entered the natural gas business, the company extended its activities into yet another arena and acquired another asset, the Spokane Industrial Park. The owners

■■Cabinet Gorge hydroelectric facility

of the former Velox Naval Supply Depot, struggling to make improvements and attract tenants, believed WWP's expertise and stability could make a difference. Always ready to support the local economy, Washington Water Power consented — and to good effect. Today, the facility houses dozens of businesses employing thousands.

Washington Water Power has given a leg up to many other companies, as well. In 1977 WWP founded the now-independent Itron, a meter reading technology company. In more recent times, Avista Labs, Avista Energy and Avista Advantage were launched as corporate subsidiaries, creating hundreds of family wage jobs in the Spokane area.

And while the company's interests naturally gravitate toward the local economy, Washington Water Power — which became Avista Corp. in 1999 — has a long tradition of commitment to education and to corporate philanthropy. To demonstrate this commitment and to ensure a legacy of support to the communities served by Avista, the company formed the Avista Foundation in 2002.

The company also devotes considerable resources to environmental matters. Both Noxon Rapids and Cabinet Gorge operate under federally issued 40- or 50-year licenses. In 1999 Avista submitted its relicensing application as the final step in the largest relicensing effort in U.S. history. The company's collaborative approach — involving Native American tribes, conservation associations, property owners, non-governmental organizations and local, state and federal agencies — was so unusual that it generated a trademarked process called a "Living License." That year, Avista won a Hydro Achievement Award for Stewarding Water Resources from the National Hydropower Association.

Avista corporate headquarters, Spokane, Washington

That process stands as a testament to Avista's belief that it is a part of a greater whole. Indeed, many of the company's choices throughout its history — for the local economy, for the community's quality of life, for the region's spectacular natural resources — demonstrate that same belief. Avista is a company that knows where it is from.

Company founders:

H. Bolster
J. W. Chapman
Cyrus R. Burnes
D. C. Corbin
F. Rockwood Moore
W. S. Norman
William Pettet
J. Prickett
J. P. M. Richards
J. D. Sherwood

Completion dates of key hydroelectric facilities:

1890 Monroe Street Power Station
1906 Post Falls Hydroelectric Project
1908 Nine Mile Hydroelectric Project
1909 Post Street Substation
1910 Little Falls Hydroelectric Project
1916 Long Lake Hydroelectric Project
1922 Upper Falls Hydroelectric Project
1951 Cabinet Gorge Hydroelectric Project
1959 Noxon Rapids Hydroelectric Project

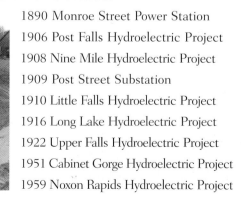

Avista linemen taking a break, 1906

Bernardo-Wills Architects

Every creation has its origin as an idea that must be translated into a physical reality. The homes we live in, the schools and houses of worship we attend, and the places where we work and shop were all created in the minds of professional architects who translated the concepts into a technical design. Bernardo-Wills Architects (BWA) of Spokane goes one step further, creating buildings that are not only functional but designed with aesthetics and the future in mind.

Robert Wills and Gary Bernardo founded Bernardo-Wills Architects in 1991 after a successful 12-year relationship with another Spokane architectural firm. Early in the partnership, they decided to strike a balance between private- and public-sector work, with Gary Bernardo as principal-in-charge for retail and commercial projects, and Robert Wills overseeing higher education, government and other public works business. As a result, the firm prospered, embarking on a path of continual growth in the number of staff, clients and complexity of its projects. A turning point came in 1992, when the firm participated with Mooney & Pugh Contractors in a design-build competition for Fairchild Air Force Base's Child Development Center. BWA not only won the contract, but the completed project went on to win an Air Mobility Command Design Award in 1996.

The firm's exemplary work on the Child Development Center marked the advent of a successful design-build partnership with Mooney & Pugh and led to more governmental projects. BWA next designed the Education Center/Library at Fairchild AFB – for which it won the 2002 Air Force Design Award – and three other projects for the U.S. Army Corps of Engineers Northwest District. The firm also designed the Child Development Center at Schriever AFB in Colorado and yet another project at Fairchild AFB, the Flightline Support Facility.

Bernardo-Wills Architects' best-known public works project, and an excellent example of the firm's commitment to providing long-term solutions, is the Concourse "C" expansion at Spokane International Airport. Rather than design a building that might be obsolete in a few years, BWA encouraged the Airport Board to look to the future and plan a building that would not only be functional in the present but an asset to future operations. The firm also designed the master plan for the Spokane International Airport Business Park in 2001.

In the private sector, BWA has focused on commercial work in Washington, Idaho and Montana. Projects have ranged in size from small, specialized shops to major retail centers, including buildings that house such well-known companies as Safeway Stores, Best Buy, Starbucks, Office Depot and T.J. Maxx. The firm won two major awards for the design of the Administration Building of Modern Electric Water Company in Spokane in 2000. In 2001 BWA designed the Spokane Valley Mall Plaza, Sundance Center, three branches of the Wheatland Bank and Nez Perce Plaza in Lewiston.

Founded on a commitment of creative excellence by wide-ranging contributions to community events and charitable causes, Bernardo-Wills Architects has quickly become an integral contributor to Spokane's quality of life. Like the designs of the firm's projects in the tri-state region, the legacy being built by BWA is one of excellence and continuing vision.

Bernardo-Wills Architects has designed many well-known projects, including the Concourse "C" expansion at Spokane International Airport. *Photo by Bob Rowan, Progressive Image.*

Hamilton Photography and Film Company

When Don Hamilton moved his commercial photography business from Southern California to Spokane more than 20 years ago, he brought more than just equipment and expertise. He came armed with a unique vision.

He was determined to establish a place where the fusion of art and commerce, the highest standard of customer service and superior technological prowess would all converge to communicate his client's message in the most effective and creative way possible.

The Hamilton Photography and Film Company is the manifestation of that vision.

In order to make his idea a reality Hamilton surrounds himself with talented people — directors, producers, still photographers, cinematographers, editors, graphic artists, set designers, grips, gaffers, make-up artists and food stylists — who use skill and imagination to do truly exceptional work.

Hamilton's production team works on large and small projects all over the world but they consider the Hamilton Studio in Spokane home. The Hamilton Studio has the largest soundstage in the Inland Northwest and is used for everything from executive portraits to feature-length motion pictures.

Along with the soundstage, the Hamilton Studio is outfitted with the latest production and post-production equipment for all manner of still photography, video and film projects. The Hamilton Studio has an extensive

inventory of camera, lighting, sound and grip packages. And the production team offers a variety of services including casting, location scouting, set design and construction, cinematography, sound recording and editing.

As an added bonus, the Hamilton Studio is also home to Chris White's award-winning House of Sound, a complete original score, sound design and audio post-production resource featuring a voice-over booth and cutting-edge audio equipment.

> ## Our mission:
> To help our clients communicate creatively and effectively through the arts and science of still photography and motion picture production.

For location shooting, the Hamilton Photography and Film Company has a three-ton grip truck equipped so thoroughly that it is essentially a soundstage on wheels.

Given how comprehensive the services are and how gifted and capable the production team is, it is no wonder that the Hamilton Photography and Film Company has earned a reputation for world-class work. The company's photography, film and video projects regularly win regional and national awards. That kind of consistent excellence has served the Hamilton Studio's clients well and elevated the standard of local advertising arts, which is what Don Hamilton had in mind all along.

Sharman Communications

After 10 years as director of public and community relations at Whitworth College, Linda Sharman started Sharman Communications in 1990.

Sharman Communications began on a tiny computer in the corner of Linda's kitchen. But because she was well known from her days at Whitworth and her work there had won many national awards, it wasn't long before her little business was quite the going concern.

Through Linda's high standards and enterprise, Sharman Communications quickly amassed a list of impressive clients and outstanding work, becoming a first-rate public relations, corporate communications and marketing company.

Five years later, Christianne Sharman, Linda's daughter, joined the business. Besides a solid background of her own in public relations and corporate communications, Christianne also brought skill and experience in producing films to the company. Because of Christianne's expertise Sharman Communications increased its services to include corporate film and video production.

In 1997 Linda began having health problems; eventually she was diagnosed with cancer. During her illness Linda tried to continue working but it often proved to be too difficult. It became clear that despite her best efforts, Christianne couldn't do the work of two people by herself, so Graham Sharman III, Linda's son, joined the company that year after returning from working overseas.

■Linda Sharman

> *Through* Linda's high standards and enterprise, Sharman Communications quickly amassed a list of impressive clients and outstanding work, becoming a first-rate public relations, corporate communications and marketing company.

Two years later, in July, Linda died at her home surrounded with the love of her family and friends. Linda's children mourned her passing along with so many other people whose lives she had touched. Even though Linda was gone, Christianne and Graham knew that she would want Sharman Communications to continue. They carry on the work Linda started — a living legacy to the woman who taught them so much about doing good work and serving clients well.

Excelsior Youth Center

Background and History

Excelsior Youth Center had its foundation with the Sisters of Good Shepherd. In 1907 the Sisters of Good Shepherd, a religious order, opened a program in Spokane as well as several other locations to provide a safe and nurturing place for wayward girls. The program continued in the old building until the early 1960s when they constructed a new campus in the northwest Spokane.

In 1982 the Sisters of Good Shepherd decided to use their resources in other serving endeavors and they turned the operation of their program over to Excelsior Youth Center. They chose Excelsior since it had a similar program in Aurora, Colorado. Subsequently, the Spokane location separated from the Colorado branch and incorporated in Washington. Both Excelsior Youth Centers still exist, sharing the same name and goals, but as independent entities.

Since 1982, Excelsior has been providing innovative programs that meet the needs of children and families in the Spokane area as well as the Pacific Northwest.

Services

Excelsior Youth Center has grown and diversified since it began. It has become a coed program that offers a broad spectrum of services to meet the current needs of children and families. The Services currently offered are Residential Treatment, on campus Education at the Junior and Senior High School levels, Therapeutic Foster Care, Family Preservation Services, Chemical Dependency Assessment, Diagnostic and Assessment for Emotionally Disturbed Adolescents, Out-patient Chemical Dependency, and a Recovery Program for adolescents who have completed an in-patient chemical dependency treatment program to assist in their treatment gains and successful reintegration in the community. Excelsior was also granted a contract to provide in-patient chemical dependency treatment.

Excelsior is fully accredited by the Council of Accreditation and continues to develop effective outcome-based programs for children and families. Excelsior is the only residential treatment program in Eastern Washington that takes both boys and girls and provides a full academic educational program on campus.

Community Presence

Excelsior Youth Center plays an active role in the local community. It employs over 120 people as therapists, counselors, group staff, maintenance and grounds keepers, kitchen and clerical staff. Its volunteer board of directors has a diverse background. Excelsior is an active member of the United Way of Spokane County, the Combined Federal Campaign and the Washington State Combined Fund Drive. It also is a member of Cars For Charity, the Spokane Chamber of Commerce, Washington State Children's Alliance, the Alliance for Children and Families, the Western Pacific Round Table for Quality Improvement and the Washington Association of Family Based Treatment Services.

Over the years Excelsior has received numerous citations and awards from various local organizations as well as state and national associations citing innovative programs.

The Future

Excelsior Youth Center plans to continue its efforts to involve the community in the lives of the children entrusted in its care. It is actively involved with several other social service agencies in order to provide the most cost-effective care possible. It plans further improvements to continue providing a safe, secure and comfortable treatment program. Its programs will continue to diversify to meet emerging needs and financial possibilities, but its goal will remain "To Connect Youth to Their Future."

AAA
Inland Automobile Association

"Spokane has developed too many motor-maniacs. Every time an accident occurs the entire automobile fraternity is placed under a cloud. It will be the aim of this association to work with the authorities to bring about better observance of the laws and of the rules of the streets and roads," said Frank W. Guilbert, president of the newly formed AAA Inland Automobile Association, in an article appearing in *The Spokesman-Review* on Sunday, July 28, 1912.

The association's beginnings took root in the spring of 1912 when D.E. Crowley circulated a petition for the organization of a local motor club to protect the use of the automobile by bringing respect to it and defeating a movement to outlaw motorized vehicles. About 100 automobile enthusiasts quickly organized, electing Frank W. Guilbert president, George M. Colburn vice-president, Herbert Witherspoon secretary-treasurer and Thaddeus S. Lane, Thomas H. Brewer, Dr. E.D. Olmstead, E.J. Cannon, Dr. T.M. Alquist and Joseph A. Borden members of the board of directors. A constitution and bylaws were in place on July 22.

To serve the public, a committee began to plan placement of signs along the roads of the Inland Empire. Actual road signing operations started July 13, 1913, from Spokane to Hayden Lake via the old Trent road and the old Sunset Boulevard to Medical Lake.

Throughout the rest of the decade, Inland AAA worked to limit speed-baiting by the sheriff's department, crack down on auto theft, map the region, lobby the legislature for a sound road program, promote a jay-walking ordinance, and secure federal funding for highways. By June 1920 membership stood at 350.

In December 1924 the club was incorporated as a non-stock, not-for-profit corporation, converting it from a small civic group to a modern cooperative organization capable of providing members money-saving personal services. With membership at 782, emergency road service began in 1925. And by 1927 a system of contracted emergency road service garages was in place.

In 1928 the club fought for a readjustment in the Hoover Road Budget, which originally gave the west side of Washington most of the state's road money and participated in the Idaho North and South highway effort. School patrols were formed, equipped and instructed by the club to promote safety, emulating a program introduced in 1922 by national AAA in Chicago. In its first eight years of operation, the Inland AAA grade school safety education program reduced the number of Spokane

Installing highway markers was an early project of Auto Club members.

Frank W. Guilbert driving a state highway near Almira, Washington, in 1918

children injured or killed in automobile accidents from 127 to 53.

By spring 1929 Inland AAA started a drive for planning Spokane streets to accommodate future traffic demands. Its annual report noted tourist services taxed the Club Touring Bureau to capacity, resulting in the distribution of 75,000 maps and 30,000 pieces of literature.

During the 1930s, the club joined A.L. White in his work to ensure the beautification of the new approach into Spokane from the city limits to the "Y" by persuading sign companies to agree to refrain from erecting signs on this section of road. In addition, it opened a branch Touring Bureau in Wallace, Idaho, and proposed reducing Washington's passenger car license fee to $3.

Inland headquarters moved from the Jones building, which it had occupied since 1918, into the Civic Building (Chamber of Commerce) on Riverside, and the club began regaining members who had dropped out because of the Depression. By 1937 there were 1,714 members.

Legislative successes included passage of Uniform driver's license laws in Washington and Idaho, which provided for the examination of drivers and mandatory suspension or revocation of licenses for serious violations, and adoption of the federal Uniform Anti-Theft Law (certificate of title) to protect buyers and sellers against stolen cars. The club also led the effort to secure enactment of the Safety-Responsibility law (insurance) to protect motorists from irresponsible drivers who caused accidents and made no effort to pay for the damages.

Libby Junior High and West Valley High were the first Inland Empire schools to adopt the club's "Sportsmanlike Driving" course, designed to teach driving and traffic safety — an effort that continues today. The club worked to have the course adopted by the Idaho and Washington State departments of education.

Thanks to Inland AAA's national publicity campaign promoting northern routes to the Pacific Northwest, news releases with maps and trip data appeared in hundreds of papers throughout the country, resulting in an increase in travel to the region.

However, World War II dramatically changed the AAA Inland Automobile Association's activities. In the club's 1942 Annual Report, Managing Secretary F.L. Crowe wrote, "...Travel by automobile which all A.A.A. clubs promoted to the utmost prior to the war had to be curtailed and necessitated our travel department changing to wartime footing instead of routing vacationists all over the American continent as in the past. Our travel bureau together with those of the other A.A.A. clubs are now engaged in rendering travel aid to the military authorities and to workers in defense plants who must move from one locality to another...

■ Frank W. Guilbert, first President of the Inland Automobile Association

■ AAA founded the School Safety Patrol program in 1922.

"...National headquarters kept the club fully advised promptly and accurately as to rationing regulations and its effect on the motoring public... Very often your club had information on these regulations several days in advance of the local rationing boards... "

By 1944 Inland AAA Manager David C. Guilbert — son of Frank W. Guilbert, the club's first general manager — was able to resume active direction of the club following a two-year leave of absence to assist in the local war transportation effort. Upon his return, Guilbert served as manager of the campaign in Washington State for House Joint Resolution No. 4, the constitutional amendment limiting the use of gasoline taxes and auto license fees to streets and highways. Voters approved the amendment, which according to club President Will H. Murgittroyd was "one of the most important victories for motorists in the history of this organization."

 (Far right) Traffic safety education for young drivers, begun in 1934, continues today.

Providing emergency road service to AAA members dates to the beginning of the AAA movement.

An upsurge of motor travel followed the end of World War II, creating growth in the demand for Inland AAA's touring and car trouble services. Membership, which had declined during the war, underwent a huge growth spurt as well, increasing from 2,337 in 1945 to 9,359 by the end of 1948.

The 1950s and 1960s were decades of continued growth for Inland AAA. In the early 1950s the club expanded its service area in Washington by opening branch offices in Walla Walla and Ephrata. Served by a staff of 46, membership grew to 16,304 across eastern Washington and northern Idaho.

The club helped secure financing for the Maple Street Bridge, co-supported an Inland Empire anti-litterbug campaign with the *Spokane Daily Chronicle*, continued to enroll increasing numbers of high school students in its drivers' training program, and added new money-saving services.

In 1962 Inland AAA moved into its newly constructed headquarters on 4th Avenue, from which member services continues to operate today. Dale F. Stedman became secretary and general manager, succeeding David Guilbert, in 1967. Under Stedman's leadership, membership climbed to 31,539 by the end of 1969.

By the mid-1970s, another branch office opened in Lewiston, Idaho. As the decade progressed, emphasis in the club's newsletter to members shifted from naming communities who had received AAA pedestrian safety awards to gas conservation and rationing caused by the oil crisis. Inflation-fighting services, such as a

Daily Hospital Benefit Insurance Plan offering protection against rising medical costs, were offered. Membership passed the 50,000 mark in June 1977.

Continuing its legacy of pro-active legislative work, Inland AAA supported a yes vote on the North-South Freeway Ballot Issue and opposed 105-foot-long triple-bottom trucks being allowed on the state's highways. It updated its bylaws in April 1979, changing the titles of several leadership positions, including that of Stedman to president.

New offices opened in the Spokane Valley on Sprague Avenue and at the North Spokane Financial Center on Division in the 1980s. By spring 1989 membership reached 75,000.

In 1993 retiring President Dale Stedman handed the reins to incoming President Stanley E. Miller, who had been an Inland AAA employee since 1974. Continuing to enhance member services, the club opened its new AAA Communications Center in Spokane in August 1994 to handle emergency calls from all Inland members, all members of AAA Idaho and all AAA Washington members living in the 509 area code. A new service center opened in Coeur d'Alene, Idaho, the following year, and by spring 1996 Inland AAA was accessible to members through the Internet.

As Inland AAA entered the new millennium, it further expanded services to include financial products. Miller expects the association, which is approaching its 100th anniversary, to continue to set the standard for travel and emergency road services, accommodation and repair shop ratings, driver education and legislation favorable to motorists, highways and transportation. On November 1, 2002, the Inland Automobile Association consolidated its operations with AAA Washington of Bellevue, Washington, to become AAA Washington/Inland with a combined membership of 825,000.

Fox Theater

Like the intersection of two seemingly separate but interdependent worlds, Spokane's cultural past and cultural future meet in the city's fabulous Fox Theater. Because the Fox was built with an attitude that "the show begins on the sidewalk," the theater was designed to be an integral part of the total entertainment experience. With the restoration begun, that legacy will be recaptured and the city's famous downtown landmark rejuvenated, providing a spectacular new home for the Spokane Symphony and local and regional performance groups.

One of the last large movie theaters constructed in the United States, the Fox was built by Fox West Coast Theaters in 1931 with a vow that "no expense (would) be spared in equipment or decorations." From its earliest days the theater has been one of the most distinctive buildings in Spokane. Designed by Robert C. Reamer, the Fox's Art Deco style was daring for the times, with a sleek simplicity of flat surfaces and minimal structural ornamentation. More than 50,000 people jammed the corner of Sprague and Monroe to witness the spectacle of the theater's grand opening.

The Fox was in constant operation as a movie theater for nearly 70 years. From 1968 until 1974, it was also the home of the Spokane Symphony. When the Symphony moved to the Spokane Opera House in 1974, the Fox was converted into a three-screen cinema. It continued as a movie theater for almost 25 years, until it fell on hard times and plans were made for its demolition in 2001. Galvanized by the prospect of losing the city's precious landmark, the Spokane Symphony and the citizens of Spokane joined forces to save the Fox. Within a remarkably short time, $1.1 million was raised to purchase the theater. In 2001 a major campaign was launched to revitalize, modernize and expand the Fox into a multi-purpose performing arts theater and a permanent home for the symphony.

The Fox Theater starburst light and Art Deco proscenium retain their 1931 elegance.

The result will be a new creation that preserves and restores the theater's original glamour while adding major structural, acoustic and aesthetic improvements. Plans call for the restoration of classic chandeliers, the addition of new lighting, refurbishing the ceiling's famous starburst and meticulously reproducing the famous "Under the Sea" mural. The theater's back wall will be moved to accommodate a full 80-member symphony and a chorus of 150, and the orchestra pit will gain a hydraulic lift and new acoustical shell. The elegant lobby will also be refurbished and expanded to provide enough space for an audience of 1,600 to mingle during intermissions.

Coming full circle from its origins as one of Spokane's crown jewels, the Fox will once again be a beloved symbol of the city's cultural vitality. One of the best preserved original theaters in the United States, the new Fox will also be an aesthetically invigorating hall with superior acoustics. And by providing a home not only to the symphony but to local and regional performance groups, and opening its facilities to schools, businesses and civic organizations, the Fox Theater will be in the position to make an even greater civic contribution than ever before.

Community Colleges of Spokane

The strong roots of Community Colleges of Spokane (CCS) stretch back to 1907. That year a Civil War veteran who homesteaded in Spokane in 1879, Col. David P. Jenkins, endowed the Jenkins Institute. Operated by the YMCA as the area's first vocational education project, the institute enrolled boys who could not afford to attend regular high school classes.

By 1916 vocational education found its way into public school with the establishment of a print shop class at North Central High. It was the first program of its kind to qualify for federal matching funds under the Smith-Hughes Act, inspired by World War I demands for skilled workers in agriculture and industry. Later a machine shop was added.

A forerunner to liberal arts education in today's community colleges began as Spokane Valley Junior College in 1933. Gustav H. Schlauch, who later became head of the Whitworth College sociology department and a sociology instructor at Spokane Community College (SCC), organized the junior college, which was one of only six in the state. It offered two-year programs in liberal arts and sciences and was accredited by the University of Washington, which accepted transfers of credits earned.

In 1937 North Central High created the position of director of vocational education. Apprenticeships in baking and plumbing were added by 1939. To relieve overcrowding, a committee of citizens and educators facilitated the approval of state funding to remodel the former Hawthorne Elementary School. Built in 1898 on Fourth Avenue between Wall and Post streets, the school had been used during the Depression as a Works Progress Administration vocational training center. In 1940 it opened as Spokane Trade School.

During World War II, Spokane Trade School became a primary Eastern Washington training center for aircraft fabricators, shipyard workers, radio and electronics technicians, machinists, electricians, welders and aircraft maintenance personnel. Special programs for military personnel were conducted at Geiger Field and Fort George Wright. Classes were in session 24 hours a day. From 1941 through May 8, 1945 (V-E Day), 44,000 men and women were trained in one or more skills.

When the school returned to civilian status on June 1, 1945, its popularity continued. By 1947 overcrowding at the Hawthorne site was a serious problem. Alternate sites were explored, but residents resisted establishment of a trade school in their neighborhoods.

Renamed the Spokane Technical and Vocational School in 1953, the institution acquired four blocks of property adjacent to Mission in 1954. Architects George Rasque and Jack Sackville-West drew plans for a 38-room school to house industrial classes, such as diesel, automotive, aircraft, welding and machine shop. The Hawthorne location was retained for clerical, stenographic, commercial, practical nursing and electronics subjects until a second school unit was completed in 1959. At that time the Hawthorne building — which had become known as the Lewis and Clark Annex because the high school occupied some of its previously vacated classrooms — was demolished to make way for Interstate 90.

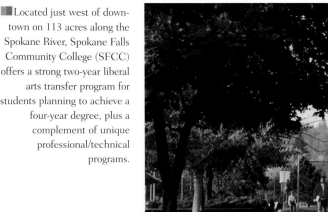

Located just west of downtown on 113 acres along the Spokane River, Spokane Falls Community College (SFCC) offers a strong two-year liberal arts transfer program for students planning to achieve a four-year degree, plus a complement of unique professional/technical programs.

In 1961 the State Board of Education denied a proposal to make the school a community college. Under Chamber of Commerce sponsorship, educators and citizens continued to advocate for consolidation of vocational education with academic subjects. In July 1963 the State Board for Community and Technical Colleges authorized a Spokane community college program with college credit transferal provisions.

On September 16, 1963, Spokane Technical and Vocation School became Spokane Community College, with an enrollment of 1,298. By the next year enrollment had risen to 2,065. In 1965 voters approved a bond issue supporting construction of a second facility on 118 acres of government surplus property at Fort George Wright.

Construction began early in 1966, and the second campus was occupied in the fall of 1967. Meanwhile, the Washington State Legislature created a statewide system of 22 community college districts, including Washington State Community College District 17 to serve Spokane, Ferry, Pend Oreille, Stevens, Whitman and part of Lincoln counties. By 1968 enrollment on both campuses totaled 4,846, plus 15,000 more enrolled in evening and extension programs at 32 locations throughout the District.

In 1970 the board of trustees gave each college the right to develop "unique and individual personalities... to minimize duplication and enhance economic efficiencies." Spokane Community College and the Fort Wright campus, renamed Spokane Falls Community College (SFCC), became separate entities, functioning independently but cooperatively.

Enrollment grew steadily, reaching 26,729 in 1979. Even though the community colleges were serving more students than ever before, they faced a financial crisis in 1980. Declining state revenues reduced funding to the district, which meant CCS served 2,000 more students than the state would fund.

State budget cuts threatened programs and instructional equipment, too. So the Community

Colleges of Spokane Foundation stepped into the forefront finding ways to raise funds to meet the needs.

In 1983 the Board adopted Community Colleges of Spokane as the new designation for the system. The colleges reached out to the six rural counties in Eastern Washington through the Institute for Extended Learning (IEL) and telecommunications system links. As interest in liberal arts broadened, so did course offerings at SCC. Today, the District's three entities offer students approximately 150 program areas — ranging from aviation to saddle making, commercial baking to commercial truck driving, and accounting to zoology.

During the 1990s the Foundation aggressively acquired numerous properties to lease to CCS at favorable rates to ease the negative effects of continuous budget reductions by the state. By 2000 the Foundation acquired the Riverpoint One Building at the Spokane Higher Education Park, making it possible for CCS's administrative offices to move from the SCC campus to the heart of Spokane's downtown where educational and business synergy abounds.

Measured by enrollment, which reached 53,000 in 2001, Community Colleges of Spokane is one of the largest districts in the state. It will continue to be a major player in economic development efforts in the Inland Northwest. Services such as customized corporate training, Head Start childcare, distance education and worker retraining for individuals in transition supplement traditional technical and liberal arts programs. As a result, the future for Community Colleges of Spokane is brighter than ever.

Situated on 103 acres along the Spokane River east of downtown, Spokane Community College (SCC) offers more than 100 professional/technical programs ranging from traditional trades, business, office and computer technology to allied health sciences, all of which are complemented by a full range of liberal arts courses.

Hidden Lakes Golf Resort

Once upon a time, men took up sticks and chased small balls through the wilds of Scotland. From that beginning grew golf, an endeavor in which both men and women still take sticks and chase small balls through the wilds, wherever they happen to be.

One of the most beautiful places to do the chasing is the delta of Idaho's Pack River, seven miles west of Sandpoint on Idaho State Highway 200, where the 18 holes of Hidden Lakes Golf Resort wander through oxbow lakes and fingers of deep forest under the blue-green crest of the Cabinet Mountains.

After centuries of sculpting by the river, with no visitors other than wildlife and migrating Native Americans, the land on which the course is built saw many changes after the arrival of the railroads in the late 19th century. It was logged in 1900, leaving huge stumps that still stand along the fairways. In 1910 it became a dairy farm and in 1924 a cattle ranch.

Hidden Lakes began taking shape in the mind of the original developer, Jim Berry, nearly 20 years before the first round was played. Berry acquired the ranch in 1968, but not until 1983 did clearing to build the course begin.

When the course opened in 1986, it was good but raw and wild. Designed by Jim Krause, it took advantage of the river's work, winding through the abandoned meanders and cutbanks of the delta, an 18-hole, par-71 layout that featured water on 17 holes. It improved each year as groundskeeping incorporated natural features to enhance the golf experience. By the mid-90s, it teetered on the edge of greatness, but financial struggles made slow going.

It was then that Villelli Enterprises acquired the course, and the Resort began a move into a new era. By the turn of the 21st century, the course had matured into one of the most challenging in the Northwestern United States, with the potential to be the centerpiece of one of the finest golf resorts in the country.

Villelli Enterprises began real estate development in 1952 in La Habra, California where Anthony Villelli succeeded by finding what his buyers wanted, rather that just trying to sell what he had. The company credo came to be "putting client, community, family and environment ahead of pure economic results." His sons, Dick and Tom, followed in his footsteps, and Villelli Enterprises gained holdings in Washington, Colorado and Idaho. Dick Villelli made Idaho his home in 1986 and became involved with Hidden Lakes in 1990, finally acquiring the property outright in 1994.

Looking far beyond the original vision of Hidden Lakes, Villelli began a master plan that included an in-course development of 171 lots and realignment of the rest of the course to accommodate a spectacular 17,000-square-foot log clubhouse on the banks of the Pack River and a grouping of condominiums around the clubhouse.

Villelli also acquired Idaho Country Resort at Trestle Creek on the north shore of Lake Pend Oreille, three miles east of Hidden Lakes on Highway 200; and a large tract of land just across Highway 200 on Moose Mountain, named for the largest of the ever-present wildlife that make the course their home.

Hidden Lakes sits in an ecologically sensitive place. The beautiful waterways and forests that draw humans to the delta also makes for fine wildlife habitat. Birds, from siskins to Canada geese and eagles; as well as moose, deer, elk, bear and many smaller mammals fill the resort. Because of this, the permitting process for the clubhouse, building lots, water, power and sewage systems, and improvements to the course itself took nearly four years.

In 2000, though, the concerns of the government agencies involved as well as the ideals of Villelli were finally fully addressed, and the clubhouse and four new holes were built, including new beginning and finishing holes. The clubhouse was runner-up in Golf, Inc.'s Best New Clubhouses in America survey. By good planning, the course became more manageable for the average golfer yet more challenging from the back tees, from which the course stretches 7,134 yards, with a slope rating of 139.

The changes made Hidden Lakes the No. 1 golf challenge in Idaho, Eastern Washington and Western Montana. *Maximum Golf* magazine rated Hidden Lakes as one of America's 100 Best Value Courses, while *Golf Digest* awarded it a four-star rating. *Golf Week* named it one of Idaho's three best courses.

Hidden Lakes became more than a place to chase the little white ball. Besides the residences being built within the course, the new lodge includes an 80-seat gourmet restaurant with facilities to accommodate up to 500 people for a summer wedding. In winter the lodge converts to a Nordic center for cross-country ski enthusiasts.

In Villelli's master plan the resort is the core of development at Moose Mountain, the property at Trestle Creek and The Highlands, a series of three-quarter- to seven-acre lots that overlook the course's west side.

At Trestle Creek, a waterfront community is planned with a 100-slip marina, a restaurant on the water and luxury hospitality accommodations. On Moose Mountain, another nine golf holes may be built, along with five-acre ranchettes and 20-acre estates, each with access to sewer, water, natural gas and power. Also envisioned is a 20,000-square-foot mountaintop Wellness Center.

Villelli's planning includes a building "envelope" on each lot, outside of which minimal change may be made under the covenants of ownership. This allows nature to "stay natural" within the developments with a goal of retaining 70 percent of the original forest canopy to ensure good habitat for birds and animals, as well as humans — especially humans who wish to take up sticks and chase small balls through the wilds. Compared to golf's 400-year history, Hidden Lakes Golf Resort has not been here long, but even St. Andrew's is not as beautiful a place as the Pack River delta of Idaho.

Higher Education in Spokane

COMMUNITY COLLEGES OF SPOKANE

- Public, multi-college district, two-year degrees/certificates
- Year founded: 1963
- Enrollment: 18,572 in degree/certificate programs; 31,444 in non-credit programs
- Faculty/student ratio: Spokane CC 1:18; Spokane Falls CC 1:21

Community Colleges of Spokane is the second-largest community college system in Washington state, serving some 50,000 students annually, including 18,572 enrolled in 145 degree and certificate programs

and thousands more taking continuing education classes. The six-county district — composed of Spokane Community College, Spokane Falls Community College and the sprawling Institute for Extended Learning — is the state's largest provider of work force training, on campus and onsite. With an annual budget of $62.5 million, the district operates one of the country's largest allied health sciences programs and is the region's largest provider of computer training.

EASTERN WASHINGTON UNIVERSITY

- Public, comprehensive, undergraduate, graduate
- Year founded: 1882
- Enrollment: 9,000
- Faculty/student ratio: 1:19

Eastern Washington University offers bachelor's degrees in 128 majors, 10 master's degrees, four graduate certificates and 80 master's programs. The 300-acre campus is located 17 miles southwest of Spokane, where offerings include the only undergraduate program in biotechnology in the state and a variety of technology and computer science programs. In Spokane, Eastern offers upper-division and graduate programs in business, public administration, physical and occupational therapy, dental hygiene and communication disorders. Eastern was listed in *The Best 201 Colleges for the Real World* on the basis of cost, convenience and quality.

GONZAGA UNIVERSITY

- Private, comprehensive, undergraduate and graduate
- Year founded: 1887
- Enrollment: 5,128
- Faculty/student ratio: 1:11

Gonzaga University is a Catholic, Jesuit university, offering 92 fields of undergraduate study, 23 fields of master's study, a doctoral program in leadership studies and a juris doctor program through the Law School. In addition to the College of Arts and Sciences, Gonzaga offers professional programs in the schools of Business Administration, Education, Engineering and Professional Studies. Over the past 15 years, Gonzaga

consistently has been ranked among the best comprehensive colleges and universities in the West by *U.S. News and World Report, The Princeton Guide* and others.

WASHINGTON STATE UNIVERSITY SPOKANE

WSU Spokane is the urban, advanced studies and research campus of Washington State University, a public doctoral/research extensive institution.

- Year founded: WSU Spokane, 1989; WSU 1890
- Enrollment: WSU Spokane: 556; WSU: 18,600
- Faculty/student ratio: 1:9

Washington State University Spokane's teaching, research and service focus on learning in an interdisciplinary environment and on the application of outcome-oriented research engaging urban issues in the community. Located in new facilities at the Riverpoint Higher Education Park, programs concentrate in the health sciences, design disciplines, engineering, educational leadership, criminal justice

and business. WSU is one of just two Northwest universities ranked among the Top 50 Public Universities in America by *U.S. News & World Report* and was called a "public ivy" by *Money Magazine*.

WHITWORTH COLLEGE

- Private college of the liberal arts and sciences
- Year founded: 1890
- Enrollment: 2,046
- Faculty/Student Ratio: 1:12

Founded in 1890, Whitworth is a private liberal arts college affiliated with the Presbyterian Church (USA). Serving 2,000 students in 50 undergraduate and graduate programs, Whitworth is committed to its mission of providing "an education of mind and heart" through rigorous intellectual inquiry guided by dedicated Christian scholars. The college's 200-acre campus offers a beautiful, inviting and secure learning environment. Whitworth is ranked by *U.S. News & World Report* among the top 10 regional universities and best values in the West.

(Far left)
The Gonzaga Institute for Action Against Hate sponsors forums and research on the seeds of oppressive actions, and ways to stem hateful behavior.

WSU Spokane's advanced studies and research programs have brought more than $45 million in outside funding into the Spokane community since the campus's founding, most of it for research in the health sciences. With over 145,000 gross square feet of research labs, clinics, classrooms, and offices, the new Health Sciences Building (shown here) provides a vital piece of Spokane's biomedical research and development infrastructure.

Whitworth's successful, 18-team varsity athletics program scores points in competition and in the classroom. Both the women's track and field team and the women's basketball team posted the highest combined GPA of any NCAA Division III team in their respective sports in 2000.

Mead School District

In the late 1800s and early 1900s, small school-houses served the children living in the outlying areas north of Spokane. Students came by foot, horse-back and wagon to classrooms at Half Moon Prairie, Wildrose Prairie, Beaver Creek, Monfort, Green Bluff, Dragoon Creek, Mount Carlton and other small schools dotting the prairies and forested land.

In July 1887 James Berridge had moved with his family to north Spokane County to farm 160 acres of land. A Civil War veteran, Berridge laid out a township and named it in honor of the Union Army Brigadier General George Gordon Meade, victor at the Battle of Gettysburg. Early records dropped the "e" from Meade and the name change continued through the years. Under the direction of Berridge, the first school in Mead was opened in 1911, with Union High School opening 16 years later. In 1942 Mead and the surrounding districts were consolidated to form the Mead School District #354. Since then its boundaries have changed little, and the original high school still stands, currently serving as Mead Middle School.

The actual township of Mead is easy for visitors to miss — its center consists of one street of small retail establishments and a post office. As a result, when Spokane County residents hear the name Mead, they usually think of the school district, which covers approximately 180 square miles that include densely populated suburban housing, prairie farmland and fruit orchards. Bordered on the south by the

(Bottom photo)
Mt. Spokane High School

Union High School

city of Spokane, the district stretches across the wide-open spaces of the Little Spokane River valley and the rugged terrain of Mount Spokane State Park, offering residents the benefits of both city and country living.

The Mead School District experienced considerable growth as Spokane County's population pushed north. By 2002 the district had seven elementary schools (grades K-6), two middle schools (grades 7-8), two high schools (grades 9-12) and an alternative high school program (9-12). Elementary school enrollment totals more than 4,000 among the Brentwood, Colbert, Evergreen, Farwell, Meadow Ridge, Midway and Shiloh Hills schools. The two middle schools — Mead and Northwood — serve more than 1,300 students, and the two 4A high schools — Mead and Mt. Spokane — have a combined enrollment of more than 2,600. M.E.A.D., an alternative program for grades 9-12, enrolls 131 students.

Because the district enjoys strong school bond and levy support, its schools are well equipped to foster student learning and activities. Mead has a highly professional staff that understands children, works collaboratively for the continuous success of students and is excited about the future of teaching. Of the 530 certified staff, an impressive 75 percent hold advanced degrees. Their efforts are supplemented by a support staff of 400 that keeps the district running smoothly. Curriculum development is ongoing and coordinated among schools and between grade levels. Services are available to special-needs students beginning with preschool and continuing through high school; the district also provides program support for gifted students. Community Learning Centers at six school sites offer after-hours tutorial assistance, recreation activities and career preparation classes for all ages in the community. Because Mead's strong academic standards prepare students for rigorous academics, many of its high school graduates continue their education at top national universities. A recent Washington State Superintendent of Public Instruction review praised the district for its inviting learning environment and collaboratively developed vision for the future of education.

As an integral part of its philosophy, the Mead School District fosters a culture of participation by actively seeking input from residents, staff members, business leaders and students of the district. Volunteers are welcomed at all grade levels, and parents are recognized as important partners in a student's education. Citizen-staff study committees and community forums are routinely part of the decision-making process on important issues. Such collaborative efforts have defined the district's three guiding principles: 1) Focus on students and their learning; 2) Create democratic structures for participation; and 3) Increase the connections between parents, business, community and schools. These guidelines have helped the Mead School District continue to move forward and to measure its progress and success.

The culture of participation and inclusion extends to student activities as well. Mead's programs could be truly called a "wrap around" approach to learning. Extra-curricular and co-curricular activities are designed to keep students fully engaged. Each grade level, for example, has a music specialist teaching theory, skills and music appreciation in vocal and instrumental music. Both high schools have state-of-the-art performing theaters used for K-12 performances and community productions. In addition to extensive music and performance opportunities, district students enjoy debate, fine art and academic interest clubs that successfully compete at state and national levels. A recently developed technology plan is guiding the instructional use of technology in all learning environments.

The district also has a strong athletic tradition of 4A competition. Mead maintains a no-cut athletic policy at the elementary and middle school levels, and the high schools field more than 100 teams in 13 sports. As a result, between 50 and 60 percent of all students at Mt. Spokane and Mead High Schools take part in competitive team sports during the year. Varsity teams compete as members of the Greater Spokane League and frequently claim top spots in league, regional and state play. More importantly, Mead teams have historically been recognized by the Washington Interscholastic Activities Association for developing scholar athletes and maintaining a high team grade point average.

From its earliest days, the Mead School District has been built on a strong and enduring sense of community, a cooperative effort to help children and residents achieve their life's goals. The district's logo, unveiled in 2001, symbolically captures core constituents holding hands in a show of support and acceptance. For Mead, the logo is more than a mere symbol; it is a daily practice.

Athletes from Mead High School and Mt. Spokane High School compete in the 4A Greater Spokane League.

Northern Quest Casino

When a craps player at Northern Quest Casino throws the dice, he has a better likelihood of rolling double sixes than the casino did of opening. When it did in December 2000, in Airway Heights, 10 miles west of Spokane, it seemed heaven, earth and the U.S. government had been moved.

The casino, with 625 video slots; 30 live table games; keno; a poker room; a gourmet version of the traditional, inexpensive, well-laden buffet; and over 500 employees, is owned by a small Native American tribe living on a tiny reservation. In 2001 the Kalispels had 333 members, 5,000 acres near Usk on the Pend Oreille River northeast of Spokane and a casino in Airway Heights.

The story of the Kalispels is the story of many native tribes. In antiquity they lived on the Pend Oreille, claiming 3.5 million acres and 200 miles of river, but growth of the United States confined them to a few thousand acres. As their culture began to die, so did the people. A population of 1,600 at the turn of the 19th century, decimated by alcohol, disease and prejudice, fell to 100 in 1911. The reservation was established in 1914, but by 1965 only two houses had running water, and one telephone served the whole tribe.

In the 1970s two young native men, Glen Nenema and David Bonga, drove around in the hills above Usk, always talking about the same thing. What could be done to improve the lot of the Kalispel? In 1985, when David returned from Washington State University, Glen had become an influential member of the Kalispel Tribal Council. The conversations lost some of their "what if" quality.

The Kalispels are People of the Pend Oreille. One of their staples was camas, a tall, delicate lavender-blue wildflower that still grows along their river. It sprouts from a bulb gathered by women with baskets and digging sticks in summer to be roasted in pits or dried and stored against winter.

Bonga, Nenema and others now envisioned The Camas Center, named for the plant that sustained their ancestors. It was to be a counseling center for families of native people undergoing treatment for drug and alcohol abuse. But after federal funding for treatment dried up, the question became, how could The Camas Center be paid for?

The Tribe acquired land in Airway Heights with the idea that they would build a trade center to help fund The Camas Center. The trade center didn't materialize, but reservation gambling was expanding under the Indian Gaming Regulatory Act (IRGA). It was suggested they put a casino on the property.

The first answer was, "We don't want to." The Kalispels had already been forced to close a couple of businesses due to inexperience, and nobody on the council had any gaming experience. The regulatory hoops they would have to jump through would be monumental.

In 1996 after a long legal process, the land in Airway Heights was designated part of the reservation. Still, Reservation status alone did not allow for gaming at the site. Since the land was acquired after the passage of the IGRA in 1988, the Kalispels had to comply with the act, which included getting approval from the Department of Interior and the state Governor.

In the end, the tribe became only the second Indian tribe in the nation to obtain approval for a casino away from the main reservation. And the Tribal Council finally agreed to a casino upon the condition of finding a squeaky clean, experienced partner with deep pockets willing to support the original idea, now called The Camas Institute.

The first prospective partner was Merv Griffin's Players International. When that didn't work out, Carnival Cruise Lines stepped up, and financing to build the casino became available.

As the casino was being designed, the relationship between Carnival and the Kalispels deteriorated. The cruise line wanted too much of the bottom line, exceeding limits set by IGRA, and was unable to obtain approval from the National Indian Gaming Com-mission. Carnival bowed out. The Kalispels began to cast around for other managers.

After a tentative agreement with another Northwest Tribe fell through, they had to admit they would soon have a casino but no management agreement with anyone.

The tribe then made a key decision and put together a management team of local people with experience working in Indian country and people from outside the area with gaming experience. The casino

opened and the question almost immediately became, not if the tribe could run their casino, but how to best spend the money.

Visitors to Northern Quest are greeted at the entrance and graciously ushered in by people in colorful uniforms. They find themselves standing on an undulating blue walkway of terrazzo tile under a school of fish and a stylized canoe with a distinctive Kalispel sturgeon-nose design. The carpet on both sides of the tile "river" emulates field patterns of North Central Washington and white fabric clouds sail above the gaming areas. The land of the Kalispel is represented beautifully, and symbols of abundance — the river, fish, sky and earth — all signal success.

Northern Quest Casino employs 550 people, donates over $500,000 a year to the city of Airway Heights and local charities, and sponsors charitable events. First priority, though, after a $1 million-a-month pay-roll, is The Camas Institute, which has become a source of training, education, treatment and employment.

The Institute provides a learning center on the reservation; tutoring, youth and parent development programs; healthy lifestyle education; financial aid for college and continuing education; cultural arts work-shops; and a mentoring program. Thanks to Northern Quest Casino, The Camas Institute has become what it was envisioned to be — a source of help and sustenance for the Kalispels, People of the Pend Oreille.

Sacred Heart Medical Center

If healing always involves a touch of the divine, then Sacred Heart Medical Center is truly a sacred place. One of the largest hospitals in the Northwest, Sacred Heart is a nonprofit, Catholic medical facility sponsored by Providence Services. It not only offers a broad spectrum of health care, but also does so by blending the best of faith and science in the healing of the whole person.

A Mission of Fulfilling Unmet Needs

In 1886 Spokane Falls was a growing frontier town of 3,000 without adequate medical care. The Sisters of Providence, a French Canadian Roman Catholic order dedicated to meeting unmet needs and serving the poor, sent Mother Joseph and a small band of Sisters to rectify the situation. By January of the next year, they had built Sacred Heart Hospital, a 31-bed, wood-framed structure. In 1888 the Sisters added a

The original Sacred Heart Hospital at Trent and Browne streets. Photo is c. 1905 and shows 1889 and 1902 additions.

wing and doubled the number of beds. Ten years later, when the number of patients had grown too large for the Sisters to care for them personally, the hospital opened the School of Nursing to train lay nurses.

By 1910 — with Spokane's population exceeding 100,000 — Sacred Heart had outgrown its original location. A new hospital was opened on its current site, with 240 beds, a maternity ward and a charity dining hall. Medical internships for training new doctors began in 1931, and the facility continued to expand in size, services and reputation. In 1971 the aging hospital was replaced with a new $35 million Sacred Heart Medical Center, which featured a nine-story patient tower. The first free clinic for Spokane's homeless opened downtown five years later, followed by the addition of major new health care services and facilities over the next 25 years.

The Mission Continues through Faith and Science

Today, Sacred Heart Medical Center has more than 600 beds and employs more than 4,000 health care professionals and support staff, including more than 900 specialists and primary care doctors. Each year the hospital admits approximately 24,000 patients and provides emergency treatment for more than 42,000 people. Continuing its tradition as a vital part of the Inland Northwest, the hospital provides exemplary inpatient and outpatient services, including a Level II trauma center in partnership with Deaconess Medical Center, and programs which are usually found only in university settings.

Perhaps chief among these is Cardiac Services. For more than 50 years, Sacred Heart has been known as a leader in the treatment of heart disease. Not surprisingly, Cardiac Services has attracted outstanding physicians, nurses and technicians who provide a wide range of the latest treatments and procedures, including a heart and lung transplant program that achieved the highest survival rate — 93 percent — in the country in 1997.

With more than 2,000 births recorded each year, Women's and Children's Services have long been one of the cornerstones of Sacred Heart's ministry. The Birth Place offers the best in family-centered maternity care, including a specialized Newborn Intensive Care Unit and an antepartum unit for women who experience complications. Committed to meeting the needs of all pregnant women, Sacred Heart operates the Maternity Clinic, where women without the means to pay can receive the same superior prenatal care. Caring for children's medical needs is another cornerstone, and the hospital also provides a Pediatric Unit, a Pediatric Intensive Care Unit and a number of clinics.

In 2001 two additional Sacred Heart specialties took huge strides forward with new technological advancements. Radiology, already known for the latest in diagnostic and treatment services — introduced positron emission tomography (PET), a powerful new tool for early diagnosis of cancer, coronary artery disease and brain disorders. The hospital also opened a new Wound Care Center, offering greater hope for patients whose natural healing abilities are hampered by poor circulation, diabetes or other problems. The center provides comprehensive therapy for chronic sores, from inpatient treatment to educating patients on caring for their conditions after leaving the program.

Sacred Heart also employs state-of-the-art technology and advanced treatment options in a broad range of other programs, including Radiation Oncology, Kidney Dialysis and Transplant Services, Neurology/Stroke, the Sleep Disorder Center and Psychiatry.

And because the hospital knows that a healthy soul is crucial to physical well-being, Sacred Heart tends to spiritual needs through a variety of services, including the innovative music therapy program "Sounds for the Soul" and Providence Center for Faith and Healing, a former convent that offers a peaceful healing setting. In 2000 the Sisters of Providence opened Emilie Court, a spacious assisted living facility with 60 studio apartments and 24-hour resident care.

Caring for All

Sacred Heart was founded on the Christian principles of providing care with respect for the dignity of each person, especially the poor and needy. From its earliest days, the hospital has refused to turn away

anyone who could not pay for care. This commitment is not just to providing basic medical care, but also to providing a full spectrum of services through many channels, including the Maternity Clinic, Internal Medicine Clinics and a walk-in facility at Spokane Catholic Diocese's House of Charity. In 2000 alone, Sacred Heart provided more than $5 million in community programs and $1.6 million in charity care.

Much has changed since the Sisters of Providence arrived in Spokane. And change in the form of expansion, construction and new technology will continue as the hallmark of Sacred Heart's future. Beginning in 2002 the hospital will embark on an ambitious three-year construction program that will add 11 new surgery suites and create a Women's Health Center and Children's Hospital. The Madison Inn, a four-story, 61-unit hotel offering comfortable and affordable accommodations for patients and families, will become a reality. And the new Inland Neuroscience and Spine Center will centralize services for patients dealing with brain, spine and nervous system disorders.

As always, Sacred Heart Medical Center will keep pace with the community, adapting and growing to meet changing needs. The only constant is the hospital's founding commitment: to provide the best possible health care with love and respect, regardless of social status. That is a mission that is just as valid — and just as vital — as it was when Sacred Heart Medical Center began.

Spokane Regional Health District

Few people are aware of the vital role played by local governments in safeguarding the public's health. Many of the things people take for granted — the purity of the water they drink, the safety of the food they eat in restaurants and protection from outbreaks of communicable diseases — are provided by public health agencies that work largely in anonymity to ensure these things are there when needed. Taking that role to an even higher level, the Spokane Regional Health District (SRHD) not only protects the public's basic health but also strives to enhance it through vigilant and progressive programs and services.

SRHD was originally established as the Spokane County Health District in January 1970, when the city of Spokane and Spokane County merged their health departments into one agency. With a staff of 45 and an initial budget of $1.1 million, the Health District provided basic public health services that included environmental evaluation and monitoring, a diagnostic laboratory and a public health clinic. After moving into its new home seven years later, the agency continued to evolve and expand. In 1994 the Health District's official name was changed to the Spokane Regional Health District to reflect the increased scope of services and geographic coverage.

The mission of SRHD is to serve as the region's public health leader and partner, promoting and protecting the public's health. The agency is part of a much larger network that includes the federal Centers for Disease Control and Prevention, the Washington State Department of Health, 33 other public health jurisdictions in the state, and a wide variety of local and regional partnerships and collaborations. Under the direction of Dr. Kim Thorburn, who was named Health Officer in 1997, SRHD now has approximately 270 employees at five different sites and serves a population of more than 400,000 in Spokane County. It would be virtually impossible to find anyone in the region whose health is not protected by the agency, whose programs serve such populations as children of all ages, pregnant women, families, senior citizens, child care providers, school districts, businesses, health care providers, Native American tribes and several rural counties beyond Spokane County.

The Spokane Regional Health District employs a broad spectrum of services to create a safer and healthier community. Some of the most visible programs are provided by the Community and Family Services division (CFS), which addresses the preventive and secondary health needs of Spokane County high-risk families and children. For infants, children and expectant mothers, CFS focuses on prevention and early health care intervention, providing public health nursing outreach, assessment of children with special health care needs and partnering with child care providers. Health screenings are made available for at-risk children, and CFS provides 17,000 Medicaid-eligible children with access to dental services.

Under the auspices of Community Health Intervention and Prevention Services (CHIPS), the Health District strives to decrease substance abuse through community outreach and treatment services and stem the spread of communicable diseases through public health clinics. CHIPS offers evaluation, treatment and case management for alcohol and drug

Public Health Nurses educate parents and assess the growth, development, health and safety of hundreds of at-risk children in their homes each year, including children with special health care needs.

addiction, as well as outreach and assessment of individuals who are eligible for temporary aid to families and in need due to HIV/AIDS or addiction problems. The division provides immunizations, testing, contact tracking and treatment for tuberculosis and sexually transmitted diseases, and operates one of the only methadone treatment programs in Eastern Washington.

The Environmental Health division serves and protects the greatest number of people in the community through permits and inspections of food establishments and water systems. SRHD inspects and monitors more than 2,100 food service operations, provides training and permits for nearly 13,000 food and beverage workers in the county each year, and inspects and monitors the area's drinking water in cooperation with the State Department of Health and the State Department of Ecology. Environmental Health is responsible for inspecting solid and liquid waste facilities, performs site hazard assessments and inspects public schools and pools for safety. The division also investigates animal bites to help prevent the transmission of disease.

Knowing that education provides the best foundation for prevention, SRHD's Health Promotion programs offer people knowledge to help them make informed choices for healthier lives. Educational programs include efforts focused on senior wellness and nutrition, injury prevention and chronic disease, HIV/AIDS outreach and reproductive health. Much of the work of the Health Promotion division is carried out through community coalitions, such as SAFE KIDS, which works to prevent injuries to children from birth through age 14; Tobacco Free Spokane; and the Community Asthma Coalition. One of the most effective HIV/AIDS outreach tools, syringe exchange, has been operating at SRHD since 1990. The division's programs also include Senior Nutrition, which provides up to 1,000 meals per day in 16 sites and through home delivery, and the Women, Infant and Children nutrition program (WIC), which serves more than 10,000 clients per year with food and nutrition education. The division also offers free breast and cervical health screenings, referrals and treatment to eligible women in nine Eastern Washington counties.

The Health District's public health infrastructure is supported by the Laboratory/Vital Records division, the Office of Assessment and Epidemiology and administration services. The SRHD Public Health Laboratory is the largest in Eastern Washington. It ensures clean, safe water through environmental testing. The clinical laboratory carries out microbiologic tests for tuberculosis and sexually transmitted diseases and supports diagnostic clinical screening functions in CHIPS and Health Promotion. Vital Records registers Spokane County's birth and death statistics. The Office of Assessment and Epidemiology carries out the core public health function of understanding the community's health through performing various assessments, disease surveillance and outbreak monitoring. Administrative services provides support to all agency programs, including the vital function of public information.

The Spokane Regional Health District permits and inspects over 2,100 food service establishments each year to ensure food is safely prepared, stored and served.

Protecting and enhancing the public's health is a multifaceted challenge. The Spokane Regional Health District knows this requires vigilance, expertise, compassion and a commitment to excellence that expresses itself through meaningful educational outreach and community partnerships. SRHD also knows that more is needed: the courage to stand for public health values and the vision to meet the rapidly changing needs of an ever-changing community. By following this vision, the Spokane Regional Health District strives to make its vision of a healthy and safe community a reality for all.

The Heart Institute of Spokane

Applying what is known through high-quality cardiac care, sharing what is known through educational programs, and advancing beyond what is known through clinical and basic research — this is the three-fold mission of The Heart Institute of Spokane, a nonprofit organization that harnesses the talents of four hospitals and dozens of cardiologists and cardiac surgeons to provide leading-edge cardiac care in the Inland Northwest region.

The Heart Institute opened its doors in 1991 following decades of groundbreaking work in cardiac medicine that took place in Spokane.

In the 1950s, for example, Spokane physicians performed the first open-heart surgery in the region, becoming just the seventh open-heart surgery center in the nation and the first outside of a major university medical center.

In the 1970s local cardiologists and cardiac surgeons determined that early surgical intervention dramatically improved outcomes for heart-attack patients and established systems to ensure that such surgery would occur, although it was contrary to conventional practice at the time.

In 1980 a group of Spokane health-care professionals published a landmark study in the *New*

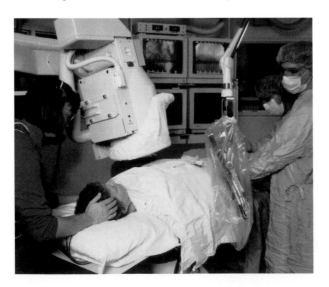

England Journal of Medicine that concluded the vast majority of heart-attack victims have a blood clot in one of the arteries surrounding their heart. The study revolutionized the world's understanding of coronary events and as a result drew international attention to the Inland Northwest as a cardiac-care center.

The 1980s saw the arrival of greater numbers of cardiologists and cardiac surgeons in the region, prompting discussions about the need for a specialty-care facility to bring those talents together under one roof. Such a building would create a dynamic center for education and research and provide space to perform state-of-the-art diagnostic procedures. In addition, it would act as a magnet for heart patients from around the region, ensuring that health-care dollars would stay in the Inland Northwest and bolster what already was one of the most important aspects of the regional economy. Construction of the $14 million Heart Institute building began in 1989.

Since it opened, The Heart Institute of Spokane has continued the region's tradition of providing world-class cardiac care. In recent years, that has meant expanding the Institute's scope to include studying and caring for overall vascular health in recognition of the role that blood vessels play in cardiac health. The Heart Institute's outlook, which is shared by an increasing number of progressive medical organizations, is one of treating health as a system of interrelated parts rather than treating each part separately.

In its decade in existence, The Heart Institute has made an impact on the community, the region and on medical knowledge through its three primary mission activities — cardiac care, education and research.

Cardiac Care: The Heart Institute offers diagnostic services to patients, such as exercise testing, X-rays and blood tests and has 14 patient beds for use before and after procedures. It also has two laboratories that perform cardiac catheterization, a diagnostic test that reveals how well a patient's heart muscles are working as well as whether there are obstructions in the arteries around the heart. Revenue from these services helps support the Institute's research and education initiatives.

The Heart Institute on W. 7th Avenue also houses the offices of about 50 cardiology and cardiac-surgery physicians. Currently, the building is full, and The Heart Institute is considering ways to either free up space or add more square footage so that it can expand the number of procedure beds and diagnostic laboratory services it offers. In keeping with its expanded focus, the organization also hopes to draw physician members in non-cardiac specialties, such as vascular surgeons, to care for patients at the Institute.

Education: Since its inception, The Heart Institute has offered an annual forum to enable health-care professionals from throughout the Inland Northwest to learn about the latest developments in cardiac and vascular medicine. Called Cardiovascular Update, these symposia bring in experts from around the world and typically draw an audience of 400 health-care professionals. For those who can't attend Cardiovascular Update, the Heart Institute recently began publishing a semi-annual magazine that recaps topics discussed in the seminar, plus other issues in heart and vascular medicine.

For the community, The Heart Institute and its nine health care partners produce a major heart month media campaign and free annual distribution of 80,000 copies of The Heart Institute Food Plan. The booklet covers heart-healthy nutrition and diet, plus a newsletter that contains general-interest topics about heart and vascular health. The Institute also does weekly radio and television spots, special events and extensive work in partnership with area restaurants to provide healthy menu choices.

Research: The Heart Institute takes part in both basic and clinical research projects. Some of the original studies that have taken place under the auspices of The Heart Institute include one that gave physicians a powerful new screening tool for coronary artery disease as well as one that showed that using stents along with angioplasty helped patients who had severe plaque

build-up in their renal arteries. Currently, The Heart Institute is studying recent heart attack patients to compare the effect of eating a traditional "Mediterranean diet" versus the American Heart Association Phase 2.

What's more, The Heart Institute acts as the coordinator for many of the clinical trials that take place in Spokane hospitals every year, including: evaluating a surgical technique and medical devices to alleviate negative heart events, testing the effectiveness of various medications on people who have suffered a heart attack and evaluating the use of pacemakers in cardiac patients.

In recent years, The Heart Institute has embarked on an effort to undertake more basic science research in order to further the understanding of the processes that cause disease. Some topics it has tackled include research into processes that injure the kidneys in diabetes and the use of gene therapy to combat hardening of the arteries. The Heart Institute funds its basic-science research through grants, internal funds and contributions.

Now a decade old, The Heart Institute is undergoing something of a transition that includes its expanded focus on heart and vascular care and efforts to increase the amount of space it devotes to that care. In addition, its physician board of directors has become more diverse with the addition of three new community members.

The next decade promises to be an exciting time of even more significant discovery and contribution to the community.

Washington State University

The national recognition, distinguished alumni, top-caliber faculty and diverse student body at Washington State University (WSU) are impressive. They tell an important part of the WSU story, but they only hint at the spirit and importance of this Inland Northwest institution.

It was the little school that could — the little school that did. From humble beginnings as an agricultural college in the late 1800s, Washington State University has become a well-respected research institution and one of the top public universities in the nation.

In 1890 the Washington State Legislature provided the two federal land grants that established the Washington Agricultural College and School of Science in Pullman, 76 miles southeast of Spokane. Two years later the college opened its doors with a faculty of five, 29 students and 63 preparatory students. In 1905, under the leadership of President Enoch A. Bryan, the institution became Washington State College, committed to the liberal arts as well as fields such as engineering and veterinary medicine. In 1959 the college's name was changed to Washington State University, recognizing its status as a doctoral-degree-granting institution.

Cougar Pride wasn't far behind. The buff-colored cat is synonymous with the university, and its half-snarling, half-smiling profile has been part of the distinctive crimson Washington State University logo since 1936. Cougar pride isn't limited to students — it extends to alumni and countless fans across the region. It's not uncommon to see soccer moms and business executives driving cars with Washington State license plate frames.

The good-natured rivalry between Washington State and the University of Washington Huskies is legendary, and each year fans trek across the mountains to one campus or the other to cheer on their teams in the spirited competition for the Apple Cup. On game day, Inland Northwest elementary school youngsters have been known to wear Cougar crimson while the outnumbered Husky fans bravely don UW purple.

It is no surprise that the Pullman campus is rooted in agriculture. The area was settled in the 1870s by hard-working homesteaders who cut patchwork plots in the rich soil and began growing wheat, lentils and peas.

No other university in the United States has a setting quite like Washington State's. The rolling hills of the Palouse look like a giant piece of silk billowing in the wind, turning green, gold or white with the seasons. Turn-of-the century barns and picturesque farm houses punctuate the landscape, and in some spots, the ghostly remnants of pioneer farms still stand.

This combination of natural beauty, pioneer grit, 21st-century technology and visionary leadership have grown Washington State into what *U.S. News and World Report* called one of "America's Best Colleges" three years in a row. In 2000 Washington State was ranked as one of the top 50 public universities in the United States.

"Washington State University is a world-class research university that is committed to students," says President V. Lane Rawlins. Rawlins is past president of

Washington State University provides students with opportunities to work side by side with world-class faculty who care about their success. The university's location in the beautiful Palouse area of southeastern Washington enables students to participate in a wealth of outdoor-oriented learning and recreational activities throughout the year.

the University of Memphis and a former WSU faculty member in economics who returned to Washington State in June 2000 to assume the presidency. "We all have deep roots with this place because of the true commitment this community has to advancing knowledge and empowering students to lead productive lives."

Washington State's catalog lists 4,300 courses in 150 major fields of study. Bachelor's degrees are available in all major areas, and master's and doctoral degrees are available in most. Statewide enrollment at the Pullman campus and three branch campuses (Spokane, Tri-Cities and Vancouver) reached a record high in 2001 at 21,794 students. The University is home to the largest contingent of plant scientists in the country in the renowned Institute of Biological Chemistry; it has the fastest-growing management information systems program in the Northwest; and has one of the top communication schools in the country, the Edward R. Murrow School of Communications, named for the esteemed graduate. The Institute for Shock Physics and the Thomas S. Foley Institute for Public Policy and Public Service are also among the highly respected programs.

Washington State's colleges include agriculture and home economics, business and economics, education, engineering and architecture, liberal arts, nursing, pharmacy, sciences, veterinary medicine, a nationally recognized university honors college and a graduate school. In 1999 *Yahoo Internet Life Magazine* named Washington State the most wired public university in America. In 2002 the new Center for Undergraduate Education opened with the latest teaching technologies in every classroom and a cybercafe for students. Distance learning allows students throughout North America and in more than 15 countries around the world to study for six bachelor's degree programs over the Internet.

Admission to Washington State University is becoming increasingly competitive. With the new Regents Scholars program and other initiatives to attract a diverse, competitive student population, the number of students with a 3.6 GPA or higher is expected to reach an all time high in the 2002-2003 academic year.

Another point of pride for Washington State is its ability to provide quality education in a caring, personalized academic environment. Dubbed "World Class. Face to Face," the commitment is supported by small classes (75 percent have fewer than 30 students) and a stated goal of offering the best possible undergraduate experience in a research university as well as a world-class environment for graduate education, research, scholarship and the arts.

Cougar alumni, the lifelong beneficiaries of this commitment, are legendary for their devotion to the school and give to the university at a rate that is among the highest in the nation. This loyalty is fueled by PAC-10 conference athletics, which finds Cougars rooting for and playing in 17 varsity sports. The new $41 million student recreation center, ranked by numerous publications as one of the finest university fitness facilities in the nation, encourages and provides facilities for active and healthy lifestyles as part of campus life.

Over 100 years have passed since the Washington Agricultural College and School of Sciences opened its doors on the rolling Palouse. The first administration building, Thompson Hall, was built from bricks made of the clay on the campus grounds. The building still stands and is now on the National Register of Historic Places. It is a fitting testament to the endurance of Washington State University.

The university's College of Business and Economics prepares students for success in today's global economy by combining one-on-one classroom learning opportunities with real-world experience gained through internships, study-abroad programs and guest lectures by top CEOs and executives. These experiences provide outstanding career opportunities for the college's graduates.

Inland Imaging

Radiology, the science that helps doctors to diagnose illness and injury by viewing the innermost reaches of the human body through the use of X-ray, CT, ultrasound, MRI and more, is one of the most rapidly advancing technologies in the health care industry. The Spokane-based company — Inland Imaging — is at the forefront of these state-of-the-art advancements, which can be the first step in saving lives.

Services provided by Inland Imaging include MRI and MRA (magnetic resonance imaging and angiography), CT (computed tomography), mammography, stereotactic breast biopsy, bone densitometry, ultrasound, nuclear medicine, vascular and interventional radiology, general X-ray and fluoroscopy.

As the largest provider of medical imaging services in the Inland Northwest, Inland Imaging is known for the sub-specialization of its radiologists. This sub-specialization ensures that patients receive the best expertise in women's health, pediatrics, musculoskeletal, neuroradiology (brain and spine), vascular (vein and heart) and interventional radiology.

Over the past 70 years Inland Imaging has extended its services to patients across eastern Washington, northern Idaho and western Montana. Today, Inland Imaging operates seven imaging centers in Spokane, an outpatient center in Moses Lake and maintains affiliations with 13 hospitals in the region. Its 36 radiologists interpret over 500,000 patient studies each year.

Inland Imaging is on the leading-edge of medical technologies. The ImageChecker, teleradiology, and GE LightSpeed Plus CT Scanners are only a few examples of innovative technologies Inland Imaging recently introduced to the region.

The ImageChecker is a computer-aided detection system that works as a second review in mammography and has been found to increase detection of breast cancer by nearly 20 percent. When breast cancer is detected early, it is one of the most treatable forms of cancer. With the ImageChecker, Inland Imaging ensures that Inland Northwest women have the most advanced detection services available.

Teleradiology is an innovative Web-based data transfer and patient information system (known as Imaging Suite) that virtually eliminates radiology films. With the click of a computer mouse, radiographic images and diagnostic reports speed their way to referring physicians throughout the region within minutes rather than hours, carrying vital patient diagnostic information.

Inland Imaging's new GE Lightspeed Plus CT Scanners allow doctors to capture enhanced quality images of a patient's anatomy in 3-D, giving radiologists the ability to use CT scanning in completely new applications such as screening for coronary artery calcification (blocked arteries) and lung cancer.

Inland Imaging is also a leader in the use of Interventional Radiology — less-invasive, lower-risk, reduced-cost procedures that allow radiologists to perform life-saving operations with incisions as small as the point of a pencil.

With a commitment to remain in the forefront of quality patient care and technology advancements, Inland Imaging keeps its eye on the future and extraordinary new models for radiology, such as molecular radiology. While conventional 20th-century medicine treats the effects of disease, molecular medicine will treat its causes before the patient is aware of any symptoms.

As a leader in the field of medical imaging, Inland Imaging continues to strive to provide high technology with compassion to patients throughout the region.

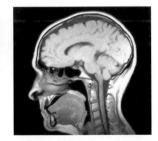

Specialized radiologists and state-of-the-art technology ensure quality medical imaging services to patients throughout the region.

Northwest Museum of Arts & Culture

The silhouette of the massive arching wood roof on the Northwest Museum of Arts & Culture's (Eastern Washington State Historical Society) new Exhibit & Education Center joins other notable Spokane architectural landmarks as a symbol of the region's history, growth and potential. This "must see" cultural treasure was first established in 1916 and reopened to the public in December 2001 after a two-year, $30 million expansion project that more than doubled the size of the facility in Spokane's historic Browne's Addition neighborhood.

The Museum campus is located on West First Avenue. It includes the Exhibition & Education Center where a bank of windows spans the entire length of the building and offers visitors sweeping and dramatic views of the Spokane River valley from all public levels. The new building features an orientation gallery, Café MAC, five underground exhibition galleries, Museum store, Washington Trust Bank Education Center, Gilkey Community Room, Beschel Volunteer Room and the U.S. Bank Center for Plateau Cultural Studies.

The block-long campus also includes a three-level parking garage, outdoor amphitheater, as well as the existing 1898 Campbell House and fully renovated Cheney Cowles Building that houses the Joel E. Ferris Research Library & Archives, Eric A. Johnston Memorial Auditorium, Helen South Alexander Lobby & Gallery, and collection storage and administrative offices.

A striking feature of the new Museum is an innovative landscaping plan. The south view of the Museum is designed to harmonize with the historic Browne's Addition neighborhood. The landscape in the courtyard and the north side is characteristic of the aboriginal plateau and riparian landscape that provided regional American Indians with shelter, food, tools, medicines and implements that helped sustain their culture.

All exhibits and programs focus on the Museum's three major disciplines: American Indian and other cultures, regional history and visual art. Permanent collections include more than 2,000 fine art objects, 22,000 regional history artifacts, and more than 36,000 American Indian cultural items representing the Plateau, Plains, Northwest Coast, Arctic, Southwest, Eastern Woodlands, Southeast and other cultures. The Joel E. Ferris Research Library & Archives houses thousands of items including books, films, photographs, oral histories, manuscripts and an extensive American Indian photograph collection. Also included are diaries, ledgers, correspondence, scrapbooks, and records of prominent individuals as well as businesses, fraternal and other social organizations.

The historic Campbell House, built in 1898, is open to the public with a new interactive program that takes the form of a historical novel, complete with biographies and conflicts. Visitors are transformed by trained docents into a "character" associated with the Campbell family including a maid, politician and detective. A visit to Campbell House is included in the regular admission fee.

The Museum also operates the Art @ Work Gallery in downtown Spokane featuring the work of more than 100 leading regional artists representing all mediums. All work in this gallery is for sale or rent. This contemporary art gallery also hosts monthly artist presentations and participates in regular communitywide visual arts tours. The gallery is open free to the public.

Rockwood Clinic

The year was 1930. Across the nation, the Roaring 20s had come to an abrupt halt and the Stock Market Crash of 1929 had plunged America into the Great Depression. The Inland Northwest was struggling along with the rest of the country.

Into these unsteady financial times, a young doctor began building what was to become one of the Northwest's largest outpatient clinics and regional referral centers for multi-specialty care. Dr. William W. Robinson, a Spokane native and graduate of Rush Medical College in Chicago, returned to Spokane in 1930 to establish a medical practice. With a staff of four, Robinson opened Rockwood Clinic on Spokane's South Hill. Today, the young doctor's clinic is a recognized medical leader and an integral part of the health care services in the Inland Northwest.

Robinson promised, "The hospital will be giving a new type of service where a complete examination and necessary medical and surgical services will be available under one roof under the close personal supervision of the physician in charge."

Rockwood Clinic prospered until World War II when many of its physicians were drafted or enlisted, forcing the hospital to close. In 1945 Robinson returned to Spokane and began recruiting his colleagues to join him in a new style of medical practice. Individual doctor's offices were being replaced by group practices, similar to the Mayo Clinic model.

By 1957 Rockwood Clinic moved to a larger facility on Eighth Avenue in a rapidly growing area that was becoming the medical center of the Inland Northwest. Physicians were added to the staff, and in the 1980s planning began for a new facility. In the fall of 1987 a 103,000-square-foot clinic opened on East Fifth Avenue. It served as the hub of the Rockwood Clinic satellite system and offered multi-specialty, urgent care and primary care (family practice, pediatrics and obstetrics/gynecology).

Over the years, Rockwood Clinic physicians were some of the first in the Northwest to provide radiation therapy, pediatric intensive care and laparoscopic surgery. Additionally, Rockwood's physicians have received national recognition for advances in arthritis treatment using new drug therapies. In 1997 Dr. Rex T. Hoffmeister received the National Arthritis Foundation Virginia Engalitcheff Award for Impact on Quality of Life for his pivotal role in the use of methotrexate as a primary treatment in rheumatoid arthritis.

During the past decade Rockwood Clinic has established a research department and Medical Research Foundation to allow physicians to participate in research and development of new pharmaceutical diagnostic therapies.

Today, Rockwood Clinic serves a geographic area with a population of 1.5 million and provides care to over 120,000 patients annually. Over 120 providers and 600 staff members work in the main clinic and nine satellite facilities. Rockwood Clinic provides easy access to primary care physicians and the option of referrals to specialists for more extensive consultation, diagnosis and treatment. Over 26 separate specialty areas are represented by Rockwood Clinic's physicians.

The clinic continues to be owned and governed by its physicians, who believe that the group practice model emphasizes an integrated patient-focused approach to medicine and a commitment to working together.

Rockwood Clinic continues in the spirit of its founder, Dr. William Robinson, by providing compassionate, comprehensive, integrated care and the "tradition of caring" that has become Rockwood Clinic's hallmark for over 70 years.

The present Rockwood Clinic building at East 400 Fifth Avenue

Spokane Area Economic Development Council

Room to Grow

A diverse and impressive mix of new businesses relocated their corporate headquarters or opened satellite offices in the Spokane region thanks to the efforts of the Spokane Area Economic Development Council (EDC). An e-commerce service firm, a global business-to-business software services provider and a specialty advertising company are just a sampling of the businesses that recently decided to call Spokane home.

The community-based, nonprofit EDC is the region's business cheerleader and it provides the leadership and the legwork necessary to attract new industries to the area. In the past 15 years, the EDC has helped bring more than 10,000 jobs and 100 companies to the Spokane area, including such powerhouses as BF Goodrich, Safeco, Pitney Bowes and Boeing.

The EDC's comprehensive and personalized service helps expanding or relocating companies navigate rough spots that might occur in permitting, real estate, utilities and more.

Business recruitment successes are easy to spot. Less obvious but equally important are business growth and retention. The EDC leads an aggressive business growth and retention program that is designed to connect regional business resources with local business needs. The underlying goal is to ensure that local businesses don't change ZIP codes. The EDC partners with a group of 27 community organizations that can assist businesses in areas such as international trade, government regulations, work force training and education, financing and market development.

However, these successes wouldn't be possible if the EDC did not have a pretty special carrot to offer potential and existing businesses. That carrot is the quality of the labor force in the Inland Northwest.

Spokane's work force has been heralded as one of the most productive and well-educated in the nation. Twenty-one percent hold college degrees and 85 percent have high school diplomas, putting the community 10 percent above the national average in educational levels of workers.

Spokane's solid infrastructure includes major rail and interstate highway links, an international airport and an extensive telecommunication network.

The cost of doing business in the region is comparatively low. There is no personal income or corporate income tax, the permitting processes is fast, affordable business sites are readily available and energy costs are among the lowest in the nation.

If Spokane is a great place to do business, it's an even better place to live. Families find an award-winning K-12 education system and an abundance of higher education opportunities. As a regional health care center, Spokane provides critical services and peace of mind.

The EDC is more than happy to recite the Inland Northwest's resume of recreational and cultural attributes. Mountains, lakes, parks, golf courses and ski resorts are all within an easy drive. Over 80 arts organizations offer a constant stream of theater, music, museums, galleries and top-draw entertainment. Plus, Spokane is the Inland Northwest's retail hub.

With the winning combination of the EDC's efforts, the Inland Northwest's natural beauty and region's high quality of life, it's easy to see why Spokane's job growth ranks among the top 25 percent of U.S. metropolitan areas.

The Spokane Area Economic Development Council strives to attract, create and retain quality jobs for residents of the region.

Spokane Regional Convention and Visitors Bureau

The Spokane Regional Convention and Visitors Bureau (CVB) has been promoting Spokane and the region as a great place to meet and vacation since 1976. Thanks to the work of the Spokane Regional CVB and its partners, tourism has become a $549 million annual business in Spokane County.

The 1974 World's Fair provided much of the impetus to create a convention and visitors bureau. Spokane was the smallest city ever to host "Expo," and as the event date loomed, city leaders began a massive downtown revitalization effort. The rail yards that dominated the center of town were replaced with what was to become the city's showcase, 100-acre Riverfront Park. A performing arts center, the Spokane

The Spokane Opera House and Convention Center overlook the Spokane River and Riverfront Park.

Opera House, was built to host the fair's world-class performers. Downtown shops and restaurants took on new life as they prepared to serve Expo's 5.6 million attendees.

Expo '74 brought more than visitors to Spokane. It brought a new understanding of the value of the tourism and hospitality industry. Meeting space, performance venues and new hotel rooms that had been built to accommodate the world's fair were now ready and waiting for more visitors. Community tourism and hospitality leaders recognized the need for an organization whose exclusive role would be to market Spokane and the region as a travel destination. The CVB was officially created in 1976.

Today, the CVB formally defines its mission as creating economic growth in Spokane County by effectively marketing Spokane and the region as a preferred convention and visitor destination.

The visitor industry has obvious and subtle impacts on Spokane and the Inland Northwest. Direct results are tax revenues and employment. In the year 2000, countywide room tax revenues equaled $1.4 million and nearly 6,000 people were directly employed in the industry. The indirect benefits of the visitor industry are increased recreational opportunities for local residents and an enhanced quality of life.

Spokane's visitor mix consists of convention delegates, leisure travelers and group tours. Annually, the CVB brings an average of 200 convention groups to Spokane, with an estimated economic impact of $55 million. These gatherings bring new dollars to the region and support the quality hotels, restaurants, retail stores and attractions that help make Spokane a vibrant community.

Spokane is an important destination for leisure travelers as well. Located in the heart of the Inland Northwest, Spokane's scenic beauty, unique cultural offerings, outdoor recreation and wide variety of shopping opportunities draw visitors from around the world. Through its Visitor Information Centers, Web sites and aggressive promotional efforts, the CVB publicizes the area and provides information and assistance to visitors once they arrive.

Tour groups arrive in Spokane by the busload, coming from across Washington, neighboring states and Canada to attend theater productions and concerts, shop, dine and visit museums and galleries.

The CVB's efforts bring a variety of visitors to the region, which in turn brings new dollars to the region and helps diversify the economy. Those visitors leave the Inland Northwest with fond memories of one of Washington's loveliest cities.

Bibliography

General: Washington

Alwin, John A. *Between the Mountains, A Portrait of Eastern Washington.* Bozeman, MT: Northwest Panorama Pub., 1984.

Anglin, Ron. *Forgotten Trails: Historical Sources of the Columbia Big Bend Country.* Pullman, WA: WSU Press, 1995.

Armitage, Susan and Elizabeth Jameson, eds. *The Women's West.* Norman: University of Oklahoma Press, 1987.

Ashton, Linda. "Ice Age Floods Left Their Mark." *Seattle Times* June 4 2000.

Barnes, Kim. *In the Wilderness - Coming of Age in Unknown Country.* New York, NY: Doubleday, 1996.

Bohm, Fred C. & Craig E. Hosslstine. *The People's History of Stevens County.* Colville, WA: The Stevens County Historical Society, 1983.

Brokenshire, Douglas. *Washington State Place names - From Alki to Yelm.* Caldwell, ID: Caxton Printers, 1993.

Brumfield, Kirby. *This Was Wheat Farming.* 1997. A Pictorial history of farms and farmers in the Northwest.

Bureau of Business Research. *Pacific Northwest Industry.* University of Washington, January 1948.

Derkey, Robert E. "The Metallic, Nonmetallic, Industrial Mineral Industry of Washington in 1995." *Washington Geology.* vol. 24, March 1996.

Dion, N.P. *Primer on Lakes in Washington.* Olympia, WA: State of Washington, Dept. of Ecology, 1978.

Dorpat, Paul and Genevieve McCoy. *Building Washington: A History of Washington State Public Works.* Seattle, WA: Tartu Publications, 1998.

Edwards, Thomas and Carlos Schwantes, eds. *Experiences in a Promised Land: Essays in Pacific Northwest history.* Seattle, WA: University of Washington Press, 1986.

Fahey, John. *The Flathead Indians.* Norman, OK: University of Oklahoma Press, 1974.

Fahey, John. Hecla: *A Century of Western Mining.* Seattle, WA: University of Washington Press, 1990.

Fahey, John. "Irrigation, Apples and Spokane County." *Pacific Northwest Quarterly*, January 1993, v.84, no.1, pp. 7-18.

Fahey, John. *Inland Empire Unfolding Years 1879 - 1929.* Seattle, WA: University of Washington Press, 1986.

Fahey, John. *The Kalispel Indians.* Norman: University of Oklahoma Press, 1986.

Ficken, Robert E. & Charles P LeWarne. *Washington, A Centennial History.* Seattle, WA: University of Washington Press, 1988.

Hamer, John. "An Industry in Transition." *Washington Industry Profile Forest Products Magazine,* 1988.

Heuterman, Thomas. *The Burning Horse - The Japanese-American Experience in the Yakima Valley 1920-1942.* Cheney: EWU Press, 1995.

Hitchman, Robert. *Place Names of Washington.* Tacoma, WA: Washington State Historical Society, 1985.

Kirk, Ruth and Carmela Alexander. *Exploring Washington's Past - A Road Guide to History.* Seattle, WA: University of Washington Press, 1990.

Kjack, Jeanne. *Window to the Palouse.* Rosalie, WA: J. Kjack, 1998.

Landers, Rich and Ida Row Dolphin. *100 Hikes in the Inland Northwest.* Seattle, WA: The Mountaineers, 1996.

Leitz, Glenn. *A History of Waverly & Pioneer Life Along This Part of Hangman Creek.* Glenn Leitz, 1999.

McGregor, Alex. "A Sense of the People and the Land." *Columbia,* Vol. 7, No. 1, Spring 1993.15-20.

McGregor, Alexander C. *Counting Sheep, From Open Range to Agribusiness on the Columbia Plateau.* Seattle, WA: University of Washington Press, 1982.

Miller, Thelma Kay. *Grass is Gold*. North Quincy, Mass.: The Christopher Publishing House, c.1969.

Morava, Lillian B. *Camper's Guide to Washington Parks, Lakes, Forests and Beaches: Where to Go and How to Get There*. Houston, TX: Gulf, 1995.

National Geographic Society. *America's Spectacular Northwest*. Washington D.C.: Special Publications Division, National Geographic Society, 1982.

Northwest Marine Trade Association. *Boating means Business in Washington*. Seattle: The Association, 1986.

Okanogan Highlands Alliance. *Buckhorn Bulletin*. No.23. Tonasket, WA, February 1999.

Okanogan Highlands Alliance. *Buckhorn Bulletin*. No.25. Tonasket, WA, August 1999.

Phillips, James W. *Washington State Place Names*. Seattle: University of Washington Press, 1971.

Reeder, Richard J. "Retiree-Attraction Policies for Rural Development." Food and Rural Economics Division, Economic Research Service, United States Department of Agriculture. *Agriculture Information Bulletin* No 741., 1998.

Scheuerman, Richard. *Palouse Country - A Land and its People*. College Place, WA : Color Press, 1994.

Schwantes, Carlos. *Hard Traveling: A Portrait of Work Life in the New Northwest*. Lincoln, NE: University of Nebraska Press, 1994.

Schwantes, Carlos. *In Mountain Shadows: A History of Idaho*. Lincoln, NE: University of Nebraska Press, 1991.

Schwantes, Carlos. *The Pacific Northwest*. Lincoln, NE: University of Nebraska, 1996.

Schwantes, Carlos. *The Pacific Northwest: An Interpretive History*. Lincoln, NE: University of Nebraska, 1989.

Schwantes, Carlos ed. *The Pacific Northwest in World War II*. Manhatten, KS: University Kansas Press, 1986.

U.S. Department of Agriculture, Forest Service. *Forest Industries of Eastern Washington*. Resource Bulletin PNW-17, Prepared by Brian R. Wall, Donald R. Gedney, Robert B. Forster. Portland, Oregon, 1966.

Walcott, Ernest E. *Lakes of Washington*. Olympia, WA: 1961-1964.

Walter, Edward M. and Susan Fleury. *Eureka Gulch; The Rush for Gold: A History of Republic Mining Camp 1896-1908*. Colville, WA: Don's Printery, 1985.

Washington State Dept. of Agriculture. *Washington's Centennial farms, Yesterday and Today*. Olympia, WA: Washington State Dept. of Agriculture, 1989.

Washington State Parks and Recreation Commission. *Dry Falls: A Washington State Parks Heritage Area*. P&R 45-66500-1. Olympia, WA, 1999.

Zeisler-Vralsted, Dorothy. *A History of the Kennewick Irrigation District, State of Washington, 1880-1987*. Ph.D. diss., Washington State University, 1987.

Community History: Washington

Bamonte, Tony and Suzanne Schaeffer Bamonte. *History of Newport Washington*. Spokane, WA: Tornado Creek Publications, 1998.

Bamonte, Tony and Suzanne Schaeffer Bamonte. *History of Pend Oreille County*. Spokane, WA: Tornado Creed Publishing, 1996.

Bohm, Fred C. and Craig E. Holestine. *The People's History of Stevens County*. Colville, WA: The Stevens County Historical Society, 1983.

Bond, Rowland, ed. *Sprague - Lamont - Edwall Washington 1881-1981 - Stories of Our People, Land and Times*. Fairfield, WA: Ye Galleon Press, 1982.

Briley, Ann. *The Great North Road and Other Stories*. Spokane, WA: A. Briley, 1995.

Caldwell, Bert. "Mine Firms Flock to Republic." *Spokane Spokesman Review*. 1985.

Community Development Study. *The Tekoa Story - From Bunchgrass to Grain*. 1962.

Fahey, John. *Selling the Watered West: Arcadia Orchards. Pacific Historical Review*. 1993, pp. 455-474.

Fahey, John. *Shaping Spokane, JP Graves and his Times*. Seattle, WA: University of Washington Press, 1994.

Helmstetter, Riley I. *And the Coyotes Howled - Family Adventures in Pleasant Valley*. Wilsonville, OR: Book Partners, Inc., 1997. This book is about everyday country life during the Great Depression in rural Eastern Washington, near Rice, Washington.

Higgins, Shaun O'L. *Measuring Spokane: A Numerical Look at a City and Its Region*. Spokane, WA: New Media Ventures Inc., 1998.

Kondo, Kara. Editor. *Profile: Yakima Valley Japanese Community, 1973*. Yakima, WA: Yakima Valley Japanese Community, June 1974.

Kuykendall, Elgin Victor. *History of Garfield County*. Fairfield, WA: Ye Galleon Press, 1984. This book is a history of the area around Pomeroy, WA.

Lage, Laura Tice. *Sagebrush Homesteads*. Pullman, WA: WSU Press, 1967.

Leitz, Glenn. *A History of Waverly & Pioneer Life Along This Part of Hangman Creek*. Glenn Leitz 1999. Fairfield, WA: Self-published, n.d.

Pitzer, Paul C. *Grand Coulee - Harnessing A Dream*. Pullman, WA: WSU Press, 1994.

Martin, George M., Paul Schafer, and William E. Scofield. *Yakima - A Centennial Reflection 1885-1985*. Yakima Centennial Commission, 1985.

Orchard, Vance. *Life on the Dry Side - A Nostalgic Journey Down the Backroads of the Inland Northwest*. Walla Walla, WA: Pioneer Press Books, 1984.

Schmeltzer, Michael. *Spokane, A City for Living*. Helena, MT: American & World Geographic Pub. & New Media Ventures, Inc., 1996.

Solberg, S.E. and Sid White, ed. *Peoples of Washington - Perspectives on Cultural Diversity*. Pullman, WA: Washington State University Press, 1989.

Stensrud, Mary. *Mount St. Helens Ash Potpourri-Yakima's Story*. Yakima, WA: Shields Bag & Printing Co., 1985.

Stratton, David H. *Spokane and the Inland Empire - An Interior Pacific Northwest Anthology*. Pullman, WA: Washington State University Press, 1991.

Wilson, Bruce A. *Late Frontier - A History of Okanogan County, Washington*. Okanogan, WA: Okanogan County Historical Society, 1990.

General: Idaho

Anderson, Nancy Mae. *Swede Homestead*, Caldwell, ID: Caxton Printers, 1942.

Bankson, Russell A. and Harrison, Lester S. *Beneath These Mountains*. New York: Bantage Press, 1966. This book is about mining in Idaho.

Boone, Lalia. *Idaho Place Names: A Geographical Dictionary*. Moscow, ID: The University of Idaho Press, 1988.

Conley, Cort. *Idaho for the Curious*. Cambridge, ID: Backeddy Books, 1982.

Crawford, Robert, S.L. Gardner, Jonathan Mozzochi and R.L. Taylor. *The Northwest Imperative: Documenting a Decade of Hate*. Portland, OR: Paragon Printing, 1994.

Derig, Betty. *Roadside History of Idaho*. Missoula, MT: Mountain Press Publishing Co., 1996.

Fahey, John. *The Ballyhoo Bonanza: Charles Sweeney and the Idaho Mine*. Seattle, WA: University of Washington Press, 1971.

Fahey, John. *The Days of the Hercules*. Moscow, ID: University of Idaho Press, 1978.

Farbo, Tom. *White Pine, Wobblies, and Wannigans - A History of Potlatch Logging Camps in North Central Idaho 1903-1986*. Lewiston, ID: Tom Farbo, 1996.

The Northwest Coalition for Human Dignity. *A Lasting Legacy: Aryan Nations Impact on the Inland Northwest*. Seattle, WA: Northwest Coalition for Human Dignity, 2000.

Russell, Bert, ed. *Rock Burst*. Moscow, ID: University of Idaho, 1998. Mining in Northern Idaho.

Tate, Stan. *Jumping Skyward - Wildfire and Wilderness; Men and God: Met in the Mountains of Idaho*. ID: Stan Tate, 1995.

Wuether, George. *North Idaho's Lake Country*. Helena, MT: American & World Geographic Pub., 1995.

Community History: Idaho

Elsensohm, Edith M. *Idaho Chinese Lore*. Cottonwood, ID: Idaho Corporation of Benedictine Sisters, 1970.

Moore, Bud. *The Lochsa Story - Land Ethics in the Bitterroot Mountains*. Missoula, MT: Mountain Press Publishing Co., 1996.

Peterson, Keith C. *Company Town - Potlatch Idaho, and the Potlatch Lumber Company*. Pullman, WA: Washington State University Press, 1987.

Russell, Bert, ed. *Hardships and Happy Times*. Harrison, ID: Lacon Publishing, 1978. This is a compilation of oral histories of people in Idaho's St. Joe Wilderness.

Russell, Bert, ed. *North Fork of the Coeur d'Alene River*. Harrison, ID: Lacon Publishers, 1984. Oral histories gathered from loggers in the region.

Shadduck, Louise. *At the Edge of the Ice - Where Lake Coeur d'Alene and its People Meet*. Boise, ID: Tamarack Books,1996.

Simpson, Claude and Catherine Claude. *North of the Narrows - Men and Women of the Upper Priest Lake Country, Idaho*. Sandpoint, ID: Keokee Co. Publishing, 1981.

Sonneman, Toby. *Fruit Fields in My Blood - Okie Migrants in the West*. Moscow, ID: University of Idaho Press, 1992.

Williamson, Darcy. *River Tales of Idaho*. Caldwell, ID: Caxton Printers, 1997.

Yahr, Warren. *Smoke Chaser*. Moscow, ID: University of Idaho Press, 1995. One man's account of fire fighting in Idaho's Clearwater forests during the 1940's.

Columbia and Snake Rivers

Allen, John Eliot, Marjorie Burns, and Sam C. Sargent. *Cataclysms on the Columbia*. Portland, OR: Timber Press, 1986.

Cone, Joseph. *A Common Fate. Endangered Salmon and the People of the Pacific Northwest*. New York: Henry Holt & Co., Inc., 1995.

Clark, Robert. *River of the West - Stories from the Columbia*. San Francisco, CA: Harper Collins West, 1995.

Dietrich, William. *Northwest Passage - The Great Columbia River*. Seattle, WA: University of Washington Press, 1995.

Dill, Clarence C. *Where the Water Falls*. Spokane, WA: Clarence C. Dill, c.1970. This book is about damming the Columbia River and the politics behind it.

Jordan, Grace. *Home Below Hell's Canyon*. New York, NY: Thomas Y Crowell Co., 1954. History of the Idaho Panhandle in the 1930s.

Lang, William L., ed. *A Columbia River Reader*. Washington Historical Society, Tacoma WA: Washington Historical Society, 1992.

Mighetto, Lisa and Wesley J Ebel. *Saving the Salmon: A History of the US Army Corps Engineers' Efforts to Protect Anadromous Fish on the Columbia and Snake Rivers*. Seattle, WA: Historical Research Associates, Inc., 1994.

Pezeshki, Charles. *Wild to the Last - Environmental Conflict in the Clearwater Country*. Pullman, WA: WSU Press, 1998

Pitzer Paul C. *Grand Coulee, Harnessing a Dream*. Pullman, WA: Washington State University Press, 1994.

Pitzer, Paul Curtis. *Visions, Plans, and Realities: A History of the Columbia Basin Project*. Ph.D. diss., University of Oregon, 1990.

Roberge, Earl. *Columbia, Great River of the West*. San Francisco, CA: Chronicle Books, 1985.

White, Richard. *The Organic Machine*. New York, NY: Hill & Wang, 1995.

Index

Index of Partners & Web Sites